HARRY S. TRUMAN

Harry S. Truman, Inaugural Address, Washington, D.C., January 20, 1949 (U.S. Army. Courtesy Harry S. Truman Library).

HARRY S. TRUMAN

Presidential Rhetoric

Halford R. Ryan

Great American Orators, Number 17

Bernard K. Duffy and Halford R. Ryan,
Series Advisers

Greenwood Press
Westport, Connecticut • London

Library of Congress Cataloging-in-Publication Data

Ryan, Halford Ross.
    Harry S. Truman : presidential rhetoric / Halford Ross Ryan.
      p.   cm.—(Great American orators, ISSN 0898-8277 ; 17)
    Includes bibliographical references and index.
    ISBN 0-313-27908-X (alk. paper)
    1. Truman, Harry S., 1884-1972—Oratory. 2. United States—
Politics and government—1945-1953. 3. Political oratory—United
States—History—20th century. I. Title. II. Series.
E814.R93 1993
973.918′092—dc20   92-18350

British Library Cataloguing in Publication Data is available.

Library of Congress Catalog Card Number: 92-18350
ISBN: 0-313-27908-X
ISSN: 0898-8277

First published in 1993

Greenwood Press, 88 Post Road West, Westport, CT 06881
An imprint of Greenwood Publishing Group, Inc.

Printed in the United States of America

The paper used in this book complies with the
Permanent Paper Standard issued by the National
Information Standards Organization (Z39.48-1984).

10 9 8 7 6 5 4 3 2 1

Copyright Acknowledgment

The author and publisher are grateful to the following for use of their material:

Halford R. Ryan, "Harry S. Truman: A Misdirected Defense for MacArthur's
Dismissal," *PSQ* 11 (1981). Permission granted by the Center for the Study
of the Presidency, publisher of *Presidential Studies Quarterly*.

Contents

vi   Contents

Series Foreword

The idea for a series of books on great American orators grew out of the recognition that there is a paucity of book-length studies on individual orators and their speeches. Apart from a few notable exceptions, the study of American public address has been pursued in scores of articles published in professional journals. As helpful as these studies have been, none has or can provide a complete analysis of a speaker's rhetoric. Book-length studies, such as those in this series, will help fill the void that has existed in the study of American public address and its related disciplines of politics and history, theology and sociology, communication and law. In books, the critic can explicate a broader range of a speaker's persuasive discourse than reasonably could be treated in articles. The comprehensive research and sustained reflection that books require will undoubtedly yield many original and enduring insights concerning the nation's most important voices.

Public address has been a fertile ground for scholarly investigation. No matter how insightful their intellectual forebears, each generation of scholars must reexamine its universe of discourse, while expanding the compass of its researches and redefining its purpose and methods. To avoid intellectual torpor new scholars cannot be content simply to see through the eyes of those who have come before them. We hope that this series of books will stimulate important new understandings of the nature of persuasive discourse and provide additional opportunities for scholarship in the history and criticism of American public address.

This series examines the role of rhetoric in the United States. American speakers shaped the destiny of the colonies, the young republic, and the mature nation. During each stage of the intellectual, political, and religious development of the United States, great orators, standing at the rostrum, on the stump, and in the pulpit, used words and gestures to influence their audiences. Usually striving for the noble, sometimes achieving the base, they urged their fellow citizens toward a more perfect Union. The books in this series chronicle and explain the accomplishments of representative American leaders as orators.

A series of book-length studies on American persuaders honors the role men and women have played in U.S. history. Previously, if one desired to assess the impact of a speaker or a speech upon history, the path was, at best, not well marked and, at worst, littered with obstacles. To be sure, one might turn to biographies and general histories to learn about an orator, but for the public address scholar these sources often prove unhelpful. Rhetorical topics, such as speech invention, style, delivery, organizational strategies, and persuasive effect, are often treated in passing, if mentioned at all. Authoritative speech texts are often difficult to locate and the problem of textual accuracy is frequently encountered. This is especially true for those figures who spoke one or two hundred years ago, or for those whose persuasive role, though significant, was secondary to other leading lights of the age.

Each book in this series is organized to meet the needs of scholars and students of the history and criticism of American public address. Part I is a critical analysis of the orator and his or her speeches. Within the format of a case study, one may expect considerable latitude. For instance, in a given chapter an author might explicate a single speech or a group of related speeches, or examine orations that comprise a genre of rhetoric such as forensic speaking. But the critic's focus remains on the rhetorical considerations of speaker, speech, occasion, and effect. Part II contains the texts of the important addresses that are discussed in the critical analysis that precedes it. To the extent possible, each author has endeavored to collect authoritative speech texts, which have often been found through original research in collections of primary source material. In a few instances, because of the extreme length of a speech, texts have been edited, but the authors have been careful to delete material that is least important to the speech, and these deletions have been held to a minimum.

In each book there is a chronology of major speeches that serves more purposes than may be apparent at first. Pragmatically, it lists all of the orator's known speeches and addresses. Places and dates of the speeches are also listed, although this is information that is sometimes difficult to determine precisely. But in a wider sense, the chronology attests to the scope of rhetoric in the United States. Certainly in quantity, if not always in quality, Americans are historically talkers and listeners.

Because of the disparate nature of the speakers examined in the series, there is some latitude in the nature of the bibliographical materials that have been included in each book. But in every instance, authors have carefully described original historical materials and collections and gathered critical studies, biographies and autobiographies, and a variety of secondary sources that bear on the speaker and the oratory. By combining in each book bibliographies, speech texts, and critical chapters, this series notes that text and research sources are interwoven in the act of rhetorical criticism.

May the books in this series serve to memorialize the nation's greatest orators.

Bernard K. Duffy
Halford R. Ryan

Foreword

The seeds of the Cold War were sown before the end of World War II at the conference table at Yalta where Roosevelt, Churchill, and Stalin divided up the real estate of the post-war world. Here the Big Three made the decisions that would lead to the assembling of the nations constituting the Soviet bloc and, on the other side of the iron curtain, those that would join NATO. Here, too, according to his Republican critics, did Roosevelt lose China to the Communists. The war had created the Soviet super-power and it had, furthermore, unleashed upon the world the atomic bomb, which in due course the Soviets would also possess. The Cold War was a war of nerves, of lines drawn in the dirt, of bluster and posturing, of pronouncements and doctrines, of brinkmanship diplomacy and frustratingly indecisive military conflicts, which, however, stopped short of world war. John F. Kennedy, in his inaugural address, lyrically expressed the essence of the Cold War: "Now the trumpet summons us again—not as a call to arms, though arms we need; not as a call to battle, though embattled we are, but a call to bear the burden of a long twilight struggle year in, and year out, 'rejoicing in hope, patient in tribulation.'" Rhetoric did not merely describe the Cold War, it animated it. Harry Truman's presidential rhetoric established the stance and national self-image of the United States in this long epoch of U.S. foreign policy. The United States became in the words of David Horowitz "the free world colossus," or, to use Dante Germino's equally apt expression, a "supernation," that took upon itself the responsibility of protecting and championing the cause of freedom against its Communist foe.

For forty years the nation fought in word and deed against the perceived threat of Communist world domination. In the first decades of the Cold War Communism was understood as a single enemy, centrally controlled from within the walls of the Kremlin. To stem the tide of Communism, the Truman administration embraced the principle of Communist containment that was originally authored by state department official George Kennan. In his Congressional address, the Truman Doctrine, Truman articulated a Manichaean vision of the world in which free nations were locked in a struggle against their Communist adversaries. The necessity of aid to Greece and Turkey, indeed to all nations so circumstanced, was expressed in terms of the global conflict between freedom and totalitarianism. That the successful monarchists in Greece and the dictatorship in Turkey that the administration wished to support were also totalitarian seemed not to matter to the president. In fact, as Horowitz points out, Truman had determined to articulate his doctrine at least a year and a half before the events in Greece and Turkey gave him what he believed was a persuasive illustration (*The Free World Colossus* 68). The Truman Doctrine threw down the gauntlet at the feet of the Soviet Union, which responded by further fulfilling Truman's pronouncement of a world divided by political doctrine. Making reality conform to the terminologies invented to describe it is, Kenneth Burke tells us, a product of human nature and of symbol "(mis)using" (*Language as Symbolic Action* 16, 19).

The Korean War was an illustration of how Truman's tough rhetoric, which spoke hopefully of the prospects of victory over Communism in Korea, was inconsistent with his administration's policy of limited war, which made victory in the traditional sense difficult to achieve. Truman was a political causality of the gap between his rhetoric and the reality of the so-called Korean conflict. MacArthur was a casualty of his own determination to win a decisive victory in Korea and to blame his military failures on the Truman administration's strictures against widening the war. Truman, Professor Ryan claims, did not successfully justify his dismissal of MacArthur in the terms Ryan believes his audience would have found acceptable: MacArthur's insubordination. Although in my own study of Truman's speech I have reached a different conclusion, I am pleased to see that Professor Ryan, who first published my study in his *Oratorical Encounters*, has carried the debate forward by offering a brief rejoinder to my position. Although this is not the place to respond, it should be said that which of us is correct in his interpretation is less important than the questions the interpretations attempt to answer.

This leads me to another observation about this book. While interesting to scholars, it is also accessible to new students of rhetoric and to the casual reader. Ryan writes both as a scholar and a teacher; his purpose is to instruct, not to mystify or impress. In his chapter on the Truman Doctrine speech, for example, he carefully applies the principles of rhetorical logic, concluding that Truman expected his audience to complete the premises in his enthymemes, while also hoping that they would be swayed by his oft committed fallacy of *petitio principii*, begging the question. Throughout the text Ryan points out the use of tropes and figures and explains their effectiveness. Following a unique critical method he has successfully developed in a variety of other analyses, he frequently approaches the task of rhetorical criticism by examining the interactions between Truman and his speech writers, carefully explaining the importance of decisions made during the process of rhetorical invention. We also discover that Truman, whom Samuel I. Rosenman, Franklin D. Roosevelt's and Truman's speech writer, said was less involved with his speeches than was Roosevelt, often exhibited rhetorical instincts that surpassed those of his speech writers. To illustrate, one of Truman's most successful speeches, Ryan points out, was his nomination acceptance speech, which he delivered extemporaneously. Beyond his examination of the speech writing process, another trademark of Ryan's critiques is his consideration of the correspondence that flowed into the White House after each presidential address. The letters and telegrams often contained telling observations and frank criticisms that exemplified the range of public reaction.

I am able to generalize about Professor Ryan's critical method because he has written voluminously on the subject of American oratory. This is his third book in the Great American orators series. The series itself is an outgrowth of our co-editorship of two books on American orators and of our friendship. For in addition to being a careful and prolific scholar, Professor Ryan is also a splendid colleague whose work I appreciate and admire. I trust those who read this book will respond to it with an enthusiasm equal to my own.

Bernard K. Duffy

Acknowledgments

The research for this book was conducted in the Harry S. Truman Library, Independence, Missouri. Without a Glen Grant from Washington and Lee University, I would have been unable to manage the research, which is the backbone of this book. I thank Dean John Elrod, who arranged subvention for the preparation of the speech texts in "Part II: Collected Speeches," and Karen Lyle, who expertly typed the texts. Washington and Lee University also accorded me an academic leave to write the book.

The staff at the Truman Library was very helpful. I thank especially Phil Lagerquist and Pauline Testerman, who extended a helping hand with archival sources and audiovisual materials.

I
HARRY S. TRUMAN

Introduction

This book treats Harry S. Truman's presidential oratory within the constraints of the Great American Orators series. As conceived, the series presents critical chapters that are keyed to addresses appended in "Part II: Collected Speeches." Thus, the series' formulation invites the commentator to make choices, of which there are two basic kinds: (1) the critic sciects one or more speeches and then matches these to a chapter or (2) the critic has a chapter in mind and then chooses the appropriate rhetorical artifacts. In selecting the speeches and chapters, I draw from both routes, for in either case there is a nexus between a speech and its intended exegesis.

The speeches and chapters, or the chapters and speeches, focus on two major, pivotal, persuasive themes in Truman's presidential rhetoric. If one were to play a word-association game, then surely "Truman" would connote the Truman Doctrine and certainly Korea. In fact, these topics had at their epicenter the anti-Communist rhetoric that was a staple of Truman's enduring responses to the Cold War. In addition, if one pictures Truman in the mind's eye, then there is a likelihood that one would recall with delight (if one is a Democrat) or with rankling (if one is a Republican) that famous 1948 photograph of Truman's holding aloft the *Chicago Daily Tribune*'s headline: "Dewey Defeats Truman."

Thus, with regards to Harry S. Truman as a subject for the Great American Orator series, the critic necessarily offers depth of focus at the expense of breadth of scope for selected Truman speeches. In truth, this caveat is uttered not without cause. Mindful of Robert Underhill's *The Truman Persuasions*, one would have to claim some compelling reason for portraying anew the broad canvas of HST's presidential speeches, for Underhill accomplished a masterful tome in his book-length study.[1] Still, something fresh may be offered in a close textual analysis of selected speeches.

As the thirty-third president of the United States, Harry S. Truman planted, nurtured, and reaped the political bounty of his Cold War rhetoric from the mid-1940s until 1953. Although he created the essence of anti-Communist rhetoric as a response to that era, the general tone of his oratory endured, practically unaltered, until the end of the Cold War in 1990. To be sure, later presidents embellished the theme, such as Ronald Reagan who manipulated, appropriately enough, a motion picture metaphor to typify the evil empire and advocated a Star Wars defense to counter the Soviets; but Truman's reply to communism remained a rhetorical constant in presidential persuasions for almost fifty years to real and perceived Soviet and Chinese threats. Thus, President Truman's invention and handling of Cold War discourse warrants close attention.

Chapter 1 is devoted to the Truman Doctrine speech, March 12, 1947. The speech was an archetype that subsequent presidents used to model their verbal attacks against communism. Truman's address to the Congress also crystallized the verbal chemistry that innervated rhetorical and military responses to the Red Menace.

Unfortunately, rhetoric has a way of coming full circle to birth its own reality, and this was especially the case when Cold War rhetoric justified combat in Korea. Although HST found that anti-communist rhetoric could persuade Americans to spend more on defense at home and abroad, and could even motivate an early acceptance of putting civilian words into military deeds in Korea, the rhetorical tiger eventually devoured its presidential rider. Hence, the next chapter is a logical and thematic application of Truman's Cold War rhetoric.

Chapter 2, The Korean Quagmire, discusses the rhetorical successes and failures that plagued President Truman until January 20, 1953. Although initially successful in rallying the country behind the Korean War, in the long run Truman was unable to explain convincingly to the American people why young men should die in the Far East merely to obtain the *status quo ante bellum*. Then, when initially favored in expanding the war to reunite the two Koreas, Truman was unable to adjust the American audience to military reality. The Korean War was a prototype of the undeclared, limited war that was new to the American experience. It was also suasory millstone around Truman's neck. In creating archetypal rhetorical responses to the Korean military situation, he committed some rhetorical mistakes. However successful George Kennan's containment policy was, and it is generally acknowledged to have succeeded in 1991 when Soviet communism failed, it did have an inherently difficult persuasive task. Indeed, as Presidents John Kennedy,

Lyndon Johnson, and Richard Nixon increasingly discovered, military adventures, which have as their stated or implied goals the return to things-as-they-were before Communist aggression, are difficult to sustain persuasively. And, although the specter of communism had little to do with the 1991 war with Iraq, President George Bush faced rumblings that his and the New World Order's nemesis was still ensconced in Baghdad. With such a short war and with such light Americans losses, Bush was spared what Truman was not: a longer war and unconscionable loss of lives.

As a denouement of the Korean quagmire, Chapter 3 treats the Truman-MacArthur controversy. The speech under investigation is HST's Far Eastern Policy, April 11, 1951, in which Truman announced his reasons for firing General Douglas MacArthur. Rather than frontally attacking MacArthur, Truman tried to justify U.S. involvement in Korea. This strategy played into MacArthur's hands because the general favored a traditional military victory, which the American people thought was a more reasonable war aim.

Chapter 4, "Doing Unto Dewey," is more uplifting, for it investigates the persuasive feat that Truman performed in his election to the presidency. Truman won the Miracle of '48 by scrappy campaigning, which practically amounted to pulling himself up by his own bootstraps. Sadly deficient regarding FDR's flair with language, but fortunately lacking Governor Thomas Dewey's complacent dullness in delivery, Truman wisely utilized his best weapon. He ran against the Do-Nothing Eightieth Congress. In unadorned, easily understood language, HST canvassed the country and hammered home on economic, social, and labor issues that appealed to the voter's everyday lives.

Doing Unto Dewey will treat two of Truman's major speeches in the 1948 presidential campaign. The first address is HST's acceptance speech at the Democratic National Convention, July 15, 1948. Delivered under the most disadvantageous conditions, Truman eventually roused the exhausted delegates to their feet at 2:00 A.M. with his frontal attacks on the Republican Congress. Some critics believe that the acceptance speech was one of Truman's most stirring addresses. The second speech, which foremost exemplifies the thrust of his 1948 campaign oratory, is his Doctor Dewey and the Republican Record, delivered in Pittsburgh, October 23, 1948. In a speech that combined humor with a devastating counterattack on Dewey's earlier speech in Pittsburgh, HST delivered one of his most spirited attacks on Republicanism, for he was doggedly determined to dominate Dewey at his own game. The campaign will also be discussed by quoting typical passages that warranted the major issues that Truman addressed in the campaign. Many of these illustrative quotations will be taken from short talks that he delivered during his whistle-stop campaign.

Free at last from the long shadow of Franklin D. Roosevelt, Harry S. Truman shaped in his inaugural address a term of office that he had won. Chapter 5, Point Four, treats Truman's famous points:

- To the United Nations, a concept that began under FDR's tenure, Truman pledged his own brand of support.
- Toward the Marshall Plan, of which Truman was a major architect, he promised more aid for world trade.
- For those countries facing communist conquest, Truman committed the U.S. to security pacts, the most important of which was the germination of the NATO alliance.
- To the world, Truman promised that the U.S. would make its scientific benefits available.

Moreover, Truman's inaugural is noteworthy because it altered an inaugural's traditional focus on domestic affairs by centering almost exclusively on foreign affairs, and because it veered from tenets of a genre theory for inaugural speeches.

The Conclusion considers Truman's valedictory, January 15, 1953. This speech functions well for summary purposes, for it was HST's personal statement of the triumphs and tragedies of his administration, and because it recapitulates the major themes of this book.

So far, the focus has been on the speaker and his speeches, Harry S. Truman and his presidential addresses. But I would mention the third party to a persuasive encounter, that is, the audience, to whom Truman delivered his speeches for some desired effect. To gauge something of his success, I employed the Truman Library's public reaction files that chronicled contemporary letters and telegrams to the president. Although anecdotal, I rely on these letters to reveal how Americans received Truman's rhetoric, for in many ways these typed or handwritten messages from ordinary citizens far better convey the essence of Truman's speeches than any other sources. I also seek insights from the other primary materials in the Truman Library (audiovisual sources, oral histories, and editorial files from national newspapers) as well as from traditional bibliographical sources, in order to gauge Truman's persuasive presidency.

THE RHETORICAL PRESIDENCY AND PRESIDENTIAL RHETORIC

The rhetorical presidency is now an accepted construct on which to base an investigation of Harry Truman's presidential speaking. Tersely stated, the theory holds that the president gives "programmatic speeches" to move the Congress to support the president, and to "'go over the heads' of Congress to the people at large in support of legislation or other initiatives." Indeed, as it will be demonstrated, Truman practiced his own version of a two-pronged Wilsonian concept of the rhetorical presidency: "First, the President should employ oratory to create an active public opinion that, if necessary, will pressure the Congress into accepting his program. . . . Second, in order to reach and move the public, the character of the rhetoric must tap the public's feelings and articulate its wishes. Rhetoric does not instill old and established principles as much as it seeks to infuse a sense of vision into the President's particular legislative program."[2]

All of the speeches anthologized in this book, except for the valedictory, functioned within the framework of the rhetorical presidency. HST delivered these addresses to actuate the Congress and the people to support his legislative programs, to support his executive decisions, and to elect him to the presidency. Although the valedictory did not seek legislative action from the Congress and the people, it did nevertheless serve to justify Truman's enduring personal ethos, for he sought to put a most favorable light on himself and his presidency for posterity.

Presidential rhetoric, on the other hand, refers to the speeches and addresses that the chief executive delivers to the Congress and people.[3] By affirmation and negation, Theodore Windt, a pioneer in presidential persuasions, established the parameters of presidential speaking: "Presidential rhetoric is a study of how Presidents gain, maintain, or lose support of the public. It is not a study of literary or rhetorical style. It is not an academic study of rhetorical techniques intended to refine rhetorical theory. It is a study of power, of the fundamental power in a democracy: public opinion and public support."[4]

To dismiss rhetoric as an opening gambit in a study of presidential rhetoric is a paradox of paramount proportions. For how could a president gain, maintain, or lose approbation except through the art of rhetoric, the craft of suasory discourse? From the time of the ancient Greeks and Romans to the present day, classical and contemporary rhetorical critics have held, as I do in this book and have elsewhere,[5] that persuasive technique does matter. In fact, the practice and criticism of rhetoric still owes today a debt to the five classical canons of rhetoric that were codified in the first century *B.C.* in the *Rhetorica ad Herennium* (author unknown). To argue that a speech's invention, *inventio*, which is the discovery of its arguments and reasoning, by the president and his speech staff is not of scholarly or rhetorical import is to ignore the rich resources that can illuminate the birthing of an address and the evidence that warrants the speech's claims. To advance that organizational or dispositional strategies, *dispositio*, have little or no impact on the audience's reception is to disregard the care with which the president and staff purposefully arrayed the address for persuasive effect. To assert that verbal choice, language, or style, *elocutio*, is of little consequence is to deny the regard with which presidential addresses are crafted with special attention given to the right word in the right place for the right effect. To assert that delivery, *actio*, plays a minor role, if any role at all, in convincing people is plainly erroneous: one has only to compare FDR's delivery with HST's to understand the handicap under which Truman operated. *Memoria*, the fifth canon, dealt with the orator's mastery over mnemonic devices to remember the speech. Admittedly, this canon is not practiced today, primarily because of the teleprompter; however, Harry Truman's habit of reading his speeches certainly detracted from his overall dynamism, and it often invited comparisons with his predecessor that invariably found HST wanting. Needless to say, this book not only warrants the efficacy of the classical canons of rhetoric in explicating persuasive speaking, but it also demonstrates that the president and his speech staff paid particular attention to the four important canons: invention, disposition, style, and delivery (whether they knew them by name is not at issue, and there is no evidence to suggest that they did).

PLAIN SPEAKING: TRUMAN ON THE ART OF PERSUASION

Harry S. Truman was not a Franklin D. Roosevelt. Truman knew it, his speech staff knew it, and the American people, if they did not already recognize it, quickly came to understand that fact.   Whereas Underhill determined that "Roosevelt enjoyed nuances of language and was ever alert for an appealing word or slogan. . . . Truman asked only that the speech be as brief as possible and that his statements be accurate." If FDR was eloquent, Truman was prosaic. Inasmuch as Roosevelt gave the nation "Four Freedoms," Truman was content with just numbers, to wit his "Twenty-One Point Message" in 1945 and his "Point Four" inaugural address in 1949.   Nor could Truman generally arouse an audience. Indeed, Clark Clifford, special counsel to the president and the head of Truman's speech staff, realized Truman's deficiencies with regard to his skills in delivery: "He generally read poorly from written texts, his head down, words coming forth in what the press liked to call a 'drone.' The contrast with the brilliant and compelling style of his predecessor made the problem all the more serious." Moreover, as Samuel Rosenman, who served as Roosevelt's principal writer and who served Truman until January 1946, remembered, Truman did not participate in the drafting of speeches to the extent that FDR did: "The President [FDR] wrote and dictated a great deal more than President Truman."[6]

Nonetheless, Truman achieved a symbiosis between his delivery and choice of language that worked well for him in confrontational situations. Truman's favorite gesture was a downward chop or slice of the hand, which was pejoratively characterized by pundits as the wood-chop-gesture. But, in conjunction with speeches against communism or Republicans, this otherwise hackneyed gesture communicated a man hewing to the line of right and letting the chips fall where they may. And at least there were chips, for HST usually hacked his opponents down to size. Truman also tended to press his points with quick, downward head motions. Again, HST's head and hand movements visually reinforced his meanings. Truman's "short, punchy style"[7] of speaking seemed more like a drill sergeant's or Captain Harry's than a president's. Yet Truman's unvarnished delivery and diction had a certain effectiveness. When yoked to Cold War rhetoric, Truman's *elocutio* and *actio* proclaimed a pugnacious dynamism, which was lacking in FDR's more suave pronouncements, that well suited the anti-Communist or anti-Republican tone and temper of Truman's addresses.

On the whole, Truman's speeches also lacked the verbal artistry of FDR's. Whereas FDR favored alliteration, anaphora (beginning parallelism in language), metaphor and simile, asyndeton (without a connective), epistrophe (ending parallelism in language) and rhythmical cadences,[8] Truman's speeches marched to the unadorned beat of subject, verb, object. Yet, his insistence on plain words in simple sentences had merit when discussing the Cold War or the Eightieth Congress. Blunt language conformed to the exigency, for one dealt with Communists and Republicans in the language they, Americans and Democrats, understood: frank talk.

If Truman was famous for his forthright language in public, he was infamous for the expletives that peppered his conversations in private. Underhill has catalogued the four-letter words that Truman usually favored in informal talk amongst political associates and aides, but Underhill noted that Truman rarely swore in public and not in the presence of women.[9] Truman's reputation for public profanity seems to stem primarily from the 1948 and 1952 whistle-stop campaigns.[10] Although one is hard pressed to point to a speech where the president actually swore as he blasted away at the Republicans, a certain Methodist minister wrote Truman in 1948 to scold him "for cussing in public"; Truman wrote back to the minister (the letter was never mailed) that "the only Congress I ever damned was one that needed more than that. . . . Public use of emphatic language, in certain cases, is a prerogative that the President will never forego."[11] To a degree, Truman's profanity was a red herring that detractors used to besmirch him, for "in hindsight, Americans now know that Truman was little better or worse than his predecessors or his successors in using profane language; they just hid it from view. That seems to be Truman's major mistake: he was not a hypocrite."[12]

Harry Truman was not an great orator, if by that term one has in mind a Daniel Webster, a Woodrow Wilson, or a Franklin Roosevelt. HST was a garden variety orator, or perhaps it would be more appropriate to term him a presidential persuader. If Truman was not a great orator, it may be traced to two factors: his lack of training and his mulish insistence on not improving his delivery skills. Over the former he had little control, but concerning the latter, he could have changed for the better.

In a 1953 interview with two speech professors, Eugene White and Clair Henderlider, private citizen Harry Truman commented upon a number of questions that focused on his speech giving. Truman admitted that whatever he learned about speaking he "learned the hard way," that he never took a course or read a book on speech making, and that no coach ever trained him on how to speak.[13] In fact, although Truman won his first judgeship in Jackson County, Missouri in 1922, even his close friends admitted his first speech in the campaign was a disaster: "Boy, it was about the poorest effort of a speech I ever heard in my life"; another compatriot thought Truman "was a very poor speaker but he developed."[14]

Most charitably, one could opine that Truman's speaking was always developing even while he was president. To be sure, he gained valuable experience when he campaigned vigorously for his Senate seat in 1934 and 1940. Throughout those canvasses, he gave numerous off-the-cuff speeches to assembled audiences around Missouri, and for radio addresses he read from a prepared text.[15] But it was being a New Deal Democrat, rather than an orator, that earned Truman a seat in the United States Senate in 1934 and 1940. By all accounts, though, Truman was much better as an off-the-cuff speaker than as one who read from a manuscript. Rosenman believed that "President Truman was always at his best when he spoke extemporaneously."[16] Extemporaneous speaking is usually defined as a speech that is delivered without a manuscript, but a speech that is nevertheless grounded in considerable reflection with attention given to the points to be addressed. Even as president, and this was especially the case in his Democratic acceptance speech and in the 1948 campaign, Truman persuaded optimally when he relied on minimal notes or when he spoke without notes:

Truman was not an effective manuscript speaker. What happens to most other manuscript speakers happened to him: his rate was too fast, his phrasing was poor, his pitch tended to be unvarying, he often slurred and mispronounced words, and his voice was faintly nasal. . . . On the other hand, he was effective as an extemporaneous campaign speaker or any other time he spoke without relying on a written text. In this area, he was probably FDR's superior. Freed from the obligation of saying words on paper, HST was able to be his greatest asset, himself, because he could communicate energetically, enthusiastically, and effectively with his live audiences   Freed from the constraints of a written manuscript style, Truman communicated in a direct conversational style.[17]

Unfortunately for his listeners, most of Truman's presidential rhetoric was delivered from a manuscript, except for his whistle-stop campaign speeches and his convention address, so his speech making was something to be endured.

Although Truman was admittedly not a polished speaker, neither was he at pains to improve significantly his manner of address. First, unlike FDR, Truman did not enjoy giving speeches. To him, an address was something to get through as painlessly and quickly as possible; part of this was doubtless because he realized he was not a gifted orator. Second, he refused to slow his rate of speaking, although aides tried unsuccessfully to pace him in a more conversational style. Whereas Franklin Roosevelt spoke at about 95 words-per-minute (wpm) before live audiences and about 120 wpm over the radio, Truman raced along at about 150 wpm, whether over the radio or before live audiences.[18]   Third, HST tended to be involved tangentially and rather late in the preparation of his addresses. Although FDR had speech writers, he preferred to work in tandem with them throughout the composition process. Thus, Roosevelt had a better grasp over a speech's content and how to deliver the words so that they achieved their maximal impact. Truman, on the other hand, came to the process late and therefore was not intimately acquainted with the nuances of language that had to be delivered orally. Roosevelt often practiced his speeches and timed them for length. By his own admission, Truman affirmed that before delivering an address, "I like to read it aloud a time or two,"[19] which is not enough to master the speech for vocal emphasis, pacing, rhetorical pauses, and the like. Consequently, Truman often misspoke words, stressed unimportant thoughts, and sometimes got lost in his train of thought as he turned the pages of his speech. And the last element, which in a sense hindered Truman's delivery, was his concept of oral style, to which we now turn.

For better or worse, Truman was committed to a plain style, or *elocutio*, that had a direct relationship to his undistinguished skills in *actio*. Even a polished orator would experience difficulty in delivering eloquently Truman's plain and simple words.

Yet, Truman did have a reasonable rationale for insisting on ordinary diction. Roosevelt preferred to address the American audience in a style that was elevated: Everyman could not employ language as the president did, but Everyman appreciated that Roosevelt spoke for them in such a fine manner and so eloquently. On the other hand, Truman selected language that ran closer to the ground. In doing so, he was, probably unknowingly, following the advice of Plato who counseled that "the simple soul must be presented with simple speeches"[20] (Plato also opined that complex souls needed elevated speeches, but Truman did not conceive the American audience in that fashion). Truman revealed that he purposefully cast his language in simplistic terms because of the nature of the audiences he addressed:

> People don't listen to a speaker just to admire his techniques or his manner; they go to learn. They want the meat of the speech—a direct statement of the facts and proof that the facts are correct—not oratorical trimmings. Of course, the political speaker must remember that the education of the average man is limited. Therefore, he must make his message as simple and clear as possible.[21]

Since the typical intelligence of the average American listener could not have diminished appreciably from FDR's era to Truman's, one can only guess that Truman's rhetorical theory, such as it was, disclosed his ordinary background whereas FDR's reflected his Groton and Harvard training. Said another way, it is the difference between Truman's 1948 acceptance speech that was characterized as the "Turnip Day" address versus FDR's famous 1936 acceptance speech in Philadelphia that resonated with the diction of "a rendezvous with destiny" and those infamous "economic royalists."

Truman possessed a rudimentary rhetorical theory that centered around the concept of plain speaking. In fine, Truman claimed to follow Cicero's advice to state your case and prove it. First, HST was cognizant of the basic structure of a speech, which includes an introduction, discussion, and conclusion. Although the organizing principle often varied from speech to speech, Truman stated that he liked to indicate the importance of the subject to the audience in his introduction, and that he used a summary to conclude his address because he preferred to let the facts speak for themselves. As for the body of his speech, he indicated that he tried to "present my arguments in what I believe is a logical sequence. I try to state them clearly and concisely, so that anyone can understand."[22]

Truman elected to organize his speeches in a deductive fashion. Following Cicero's advice, Truman would state his thesis and then warrant it with supporting arguments and evidence. Unlike Roosevelt, who used an inductive and circuitous route, Truman broached the thesis early and explicitly in the speech. In fact, no other speech better capsulized Truman's brand of rhetorical theory than the introduction for his 1948 acceptance speech. After the impromptu, subsidiary introductory remarks about accepting the nomination, Truman contended in candid, concise language that everyone could comprehend: "Senator Barkley and I will win this election and make those Republicans like it—don't you forget that! We will do that because they are wrong and we are right, and I will prove it to you in just a few minutes."[23] Although not eloquent, Truman's sentences had a juggernaut-like cadence that repeatedly buffeted the subject-verb-object sequence so that the thoughts sailed inexorably forward to engage the enemy.

The introduction for his acceptance address also reveals Truman's penchant for mental absolutes that runs throughout the major addresses studied in this book. As an aspect of the plain style, Truman was comfortable with dichotomies. The Republicans were wrong, the Democrats were right. Striking steel workers were wrong and Truman right. And communists were evil, and the United States was good. Thus, the plain style was an excellent vehicle for portraying absolutes because it did not address the bothersome grey areas that might give one pause for careful reflection. In fact, the plain style is a perfect bridge to the next section on Cold War rhetoric, for in Truman's handling of these two concepts, they mutually reinforced one another magnificently well.

CRISIS AND SUPERNATION RHETORIC: THE COLD WAR

Given that Chapters 1, 2, and a portion of 3 will treat President Truman's speeches with regard to two theoretical, rhetorical constructs, it is appropriate to discuss them here in some detail.

The first construct is presidential crisis rhetoric. Theodore Windt determined that the commander in chief uses a genre of speaking to gain support from the Congress and people by creating a rhetorical crisis that may or may not exist in reality. In a typical crisis speech, the president announces the New Facts over which he has command and about which only he knows. In a foreign crisis, particularly the case in Truman's time, the prime mover of the emergency is often traceable to Communists. The problem here is that the audience may not have the time nor ability to verify the veracity of the New Facts, so it must assume that the president knows best. The New Facts lead inexorably to the New Situation, which the president defines as a crisis, usually of a military nature, that confronts the United States of America. Hence, the issue is not so much *whether* the United States should respond but *how* it will react to this dangerous new circumstance. To respond to the grave situation, the president presents his policy, which is often announced as a fait accompli. The president then argues for acceptance of the course of action, or seeks to justify the policy if it has already been set in motion, by appealing to Americans' sense of patriotism and manliness. And throughout this rhetorical depiction of the New Facts, New Situation, and announcement of the policy, the president casts his language in devil/angel, good/bad, black/white dichotomies. Although Windt's germinal essay discussed how presidents John Kennedy and Richard Nixon utilized crisis rhetoric, the construct could just as profitably be applied to George Bush's use of crisis rhetoric in order to marshall support for the 1991 war on Iraq, and it will be employed in this book to explicate how Truman used it in the Truman Doctrine, the Korean War speeches, and tangentially so in his inaugural address.[24]

The second construct is supernation rhetoric. The public philosophy of the United States in the eighteenth and nineteenth centuries had been concerned with the freedom and safety of the American people, which was best realized by eschewing foreign alliances and foregoing meddling in the internal affairs of other countries. However, in the mid-to-late 1940s, according to Dante Germino, "there was a decisive break in the continuity of the American public philosophy, around the end of World War II, when America began to promise what it could not deliver." Thus, after World War II, one witnessed a rather abrupt shift in the tone and temper of public rhetoric, especially at the presidential level with regard to foreign affairs. This so-called Cold War rhetoric had two leitmotifs. On the one hand, Germino heard a "new note of the quasi-apocalyptic transformation of the world in a final battle with demonic communism." Thus, the critic would expect to find, and does find in Truman's rhetoric, Manichaean imagery that "contrasts the 'light' of the western democracies and the 'darkness' of Communism."[25] Manes, c. *A.D.* 300, a Persian philosopher and follower of Zoroastrianism, divided the world into the forces of darkness and light. Interestingly enough, the famous motion picture *Star Wars* pitted the hero against the Dark Force, and President

Ronald Reagan often referred to the Soviet Union as the "Evil Empire."

On the other hand, Cold War depictions tended to debase language and to distort actuality. In the rush to portray the world in Manichaean terms, presidents often fell prey to redefining, wrongly Germino insists, the traditional concepts of American freedom and democracy, and in doing so, they warped reality:

> The result has been the arbitrary division of the world into that of the "free" and the "enslaved," even though a majority of countries with whom the United States has made alliances can scarcely be called "free" in the American public philosophy's understanding of freedom. Instead of being defined in relation to that philosophy, freedom becomes defined as non-Communist. The non-Communist nations of the world are "free" ones in cold war presidential rhetoric. . . . With the expansion of Soviet power after World War II, however, a new theme is sounded. Regimes formerly seen as unfree in terms of the American public philosophy (military dictatorships and feudal autocracies) now became bastions of "liberty" if they appear to be threatened by Soviet expansion.[26]

The stance one takes regarding presidential crisis, supernation rhetoric in the historical period under investigation here pivots on whether one believes the Soviet-Chinese Communist threat was a clear and present danger during Truman's presidency. It is beyond the purview of this book to address in detail that issue or to decide it. Rather, the purpose is to show that Truman did use presidential crisis, supernation rhetoric, that he tended to overstate the case, and that public perceptions were manipulated thereby.

NOTES

1. Robert Underhill, *The Truman Persuasions* (Ames: The Iowa State University Press, 1981). My only criticism is Underhill's conceiving Truman as a debater, which he clearly was not; see my review in *Presidential Studies Quarterly* 12 (1982): 115-116.

2. James W. Ceaser, Glen E. Thurow, Jeffrey Tulis, and Joseph Bessette, "The Rise of the Rhetorical Presidency," *Presidential Studies Quarterly* 11 (1981): 159; Jeffrey K. Tulis, *The Rhetorical Presidency* (Princeton: Princeton University Press, 1987), p. 4; Ceaser et al., "The Rise of the Rhetorical Presidency," p. 163.

3. Halford R. Ryan, *Franklin D. Roosevelt's Rhetorical Presidency* (Westport, Conn.: Greenwood Press, 1988), pp. 3-5; Craig Allen Smith and Kathy B. Smith, *The President and the Public: Rhetoric and National Leadership* (Lanham: University Press of America, 1985), pp. xx-xxii.

4. Theodore Windt, *Presidential Rhetoric (1961-1980)* (Dubuque: Kendall/Hunt, 1983), p. 2.

5. See my *Franklin D. Roosevelt's Rhetorical Presidency*, p. 4, and my *Classical Communication for the Contemporary Communicator* (Mountain View: Mayfield, 1992), pp. 1-28.

6. Underhill, *The Truman Persuasions*, p. 165; Clark Clifford, *Counsel to the President* (New York: Random House, 1991), p. 199; Samuel I. Rosenman, oral history transcript, September 1969, p. 52, Harry S. Truman Library, Independence, Missouri. Hereafter given as HSTL.

7. Clifford, *Counsel to the President*, p. 74.

8. Ryan, *Franklin D. Roosevelt's Rhetorical Presidency*, pp. 162-164.

9. Underhill, *The Truman Persuasions*, pp. 328-332.

10. For a typical cartoon that portrays Truman as a train whistle shrieking "GIVE 'EM HELL!" see *The Harry S. Truman Encyclopedia*, edited by Richard S. Kirkendall (Boston: G. K. Hall, 1989), p. 27.

11. *Strictly Personal and Confidential: The Letters Harry Truman Never Mailed*, edited by Monte M. Poen (Boston: Little, Brown, 1982), pp. 63-64.

12. Halford R. Ryan, "Harry S Truman (1884-1972), Thirty-Third President of the United States," in *Methods of Rhetorical Criticism: A Twentieth-Century Perspective*, edited by Bernard L. Brock, Robert L. Scott, and James W. Chesebro (3d ed. Detroit: Wayne State University Press, 1989), p. 69.

13. Eugene E. White and Clair R. Henderlider, "What Harry S. Truman Told Us About His Speaking," *Quarterly Journal of Speech* 40 (1954): 38.

14. Quoted in Underhill, *The Truman Persuasions*, p. 64.

15. White and Henderlider, "What Harry S. Truman Told Us About His Speaking," p. 39.

16. Rosenman, oral history transcript, p. 83.

17. Halford R. Ryan, "Harry Truman," in *American Orators of the Twentieth Century: Critical Studies and Sources*, edited by Bernard K. Duffy and Halford R. Ryan (Westport, Conn.: Greenwood Press, 1987), p. 402.

18. Ryan, *Franklin D. Roosevelt's Rhetorical presidency*, pp. 19-20, Robert Underhill, "Speeches and Speech Writing," in *The Harry S. Truman Encyclopedia*, p. 336.

19. White and Henderlider, "What Harry S. Truman Told Us About His Speaking," p. 41.

20. Plato, *Phaedrus* (Indianapolis: Bobbs-Merrill, 1956), p. 72.

21. White and Henderlider, "What Harry S. Truman Told Us About His Speaking," p. 39.

22. White and Hinderlider, "What Harry S. Truman Told Us About His Speaking," pp. 39-41.

23. Acceptance speech, Democratic National Convention, Philadelphia, Pennsylvania, July 15, 1948, *Public Papers of the Presidents, Harry S. Truman: 1948* (Washington, D.C.: GPO, 1964), p. 406.

24. Theodore Windt, "The Presidency and Speeches on International Crises: Repeating the Rhetorical Past," in *Essays in Presidential Rhetoric*, edited by Theodore Windt, with Beth Ingold (Dubuque: Kendall/Hunt, 1983), pp. 61-70.

25. Dante Germino, *The Inaugural Addresses of American Presidents: The Public Philosophy and Rhetoric*, preface and foreword by Kenneth W. Thompson (Lanham: University Press of America, 1984), pp. 19, 21, 22.

26. Germino, *The Inaugural Addresses of American Presidents*, pp. 23, 24.

1
The Truman Doctrine

"In his address to a joint session on March 12, 1947," Lynn Hinds and
Theodore Windt wrote, "President Truman officially committed the United
States to an ideological cold war," and Robert Donovan appraised the
significance of the Truman Doctrine speech: "The collectively written
speech he delivered was certainly the most controversial of his presidency
and remains probably the most enduringly controversial speech that has
been made by a president in the twentieth century."[1] Indeed, the speech's
composition, rhetorical techniques, and reception by the body politic
contributed to its overall success.

THE EMERGING RHETORICAL SITUATION

On February 24, 1947, because their economy was near collapse,
especially owing to the ravages of World War II and the harsh winter of
1946-47, the British informed the United States that Great Britain would
no longer be able to send money and military aid to Greece and Turkey,
and that it would withdraw all of its troops by March 31, 1947. This was
a fortuitous boon to Truman, for with the Republican's having seized the
House and Senate in the 1946 elections, his presidency seemed superfluous.
Although this opportunity invited the president to lead in foreign affairs,
it would take some deft maneuvering, for the Republicans were pledged to
budget reductions, especially in foreign aid. Indeed, Truman told his
cabinet that his aid program was "the greatest selling job ever facing a
President," for he knew that "the situation was more precarious than it
would have been with a preponderantly Democratic Congress."[2]

On February 27, Truman, Secretary of State George C. Marshall, and Undersecretary of State Dean Acheson met with the congressional leadership in the White House. After Marshall failed to actuate his small audience, Acheson asked to speak, and narrated to the lawmakers the perils that faced Greece and Turkey if they should slip into the Soviet sphere. Then, Senator Arthur Vandenberg (R-Michigan) told Truman: "Mr. President, if you will say that to the Congress and the country, I will support you, and I believe that most of its members will do the same."[3] The House passed the aid package 287 to 107, the Senate, 67 to 23, and on May 22 Truman signed the law.

In terms of the rhetorical presidency, the packaging of Truman's speech merits consideration. At the February 27 meeting, the congressional leadership was willing to support Truman, but he had to present the case. According to Joseph M. Jones, who, as a speech writer for Acheson, was invited to attend a meeting of the State-War-Navy Coordinating Committee [SWNCC] Foreign Policy Information Subcommittee, the Congressional leadership indicated they would "support whatever measures should be necessary, *on the condition that* [emphasis in original] the President should explain the situation fully to Congress in a special message, and to the people by radio. They felt that they could support such a program only if the public were apprised of the grim facts. The President promised to go to the Congress and the people in this manner."[4] The only change from these original plans was that Truman decided to address the Congress and people with one speech that was broadcast live on Wednesday, March 12, 1947, at 1:00 P.M.

The SWNCC subcommittee met on Friday afternoon, February 28, "to consider the problem of how the question should be presented to the public." According to Jones, two thematic criteria were established: "formulation of intelligent opinions by the American people . . . furnishing full and frank information . . ."; and "to portray the world conflict between free and totalitarian or imposed forms of government."[5] The speech that Truman ultimately delivered did a reasonably good job of being straightforward on Greece, less so on Turkey, and it succeeded admirably well in painting the devil/angel polarities that the subcommittee must have realized would sell the program to the people.

THE EVOLUTION OF THE SPEECH DRAFTS

The speech staff set to work on the address on March 3, 1947. Jones, writing in Acheson's office, composed four drafts, dated March 3, 4, 6, and 8. Loy Henderson and Gordon Merriam also wrote separate drafts, but these were not used in the final speech.[6] Meanwhile, Clark Clifford and George Elsey were at work in the White House, where Elsey produced a draft that contained the core materials for a compelling introduction.

Marcus Tullius Cicero advised the orator to invent an exordium that made the audience disposed, attentive, and teachable. Such was not exactly the case with the introduction in the early drafts of the speech. In a suggested draft, March 7, 1947, Elsey wrote a tame but straightforward exordium: "I lay before you today for consideration and decision a grave problem affecting our foreign relations and our national security"; a second draft, March 9, added "I come to lay before you."[7]

When Clifford revised the introduction, he added drama, a latent fear appeal, and a sense of urgency; therefore, the audience would be inclined to give its full regard to the president's first words. Clark deleted Elsey's opening sentence, and handwrote a terse exordium. Notice, however, that Clifford borrowed heavily from Elsey's germinal thoughts and phrases (deletions are bracketed and additions italicized):

> The gravity of the situation which confronts the [country] *world* today necessitates my appearance before a joint session of the Congress.
>
> [Our basic]
>
> The [basic] foreign policy and the national security of this country are involved.
>
> One phase of the present problem, which I wish to present to you *at this time* for your consideration and decision, concerns Greece and Turkey.[8]

This draft was shown to the president.

Truman tended to join the speech staff toward the end of a speech's production. The general practice was sketched by David Lloyd: "The President would often be given a draft midway in this process, but usually the work would not be submitted to him until the drafting group felt that it was in pretty good shape. Then after the President had studied the draft we would meet with him and have what was known as a 'freezing session' [when the draft was finalized and typed for release]."[9] In this instance, Truman and the staff followed the normal practice. In conference, Truman, Clifford, and Elsey made some interesting emendations to improve the introduction.

In the first sentence, they considered whether to use the word "problem" or "situation." "Problem" denotes something to be solved, which was appropriate to the speech's purpose, but "situation" suggests images of a critical state of affairs. The word "situation" won out, probably because its connotations better frightened the audience.

Someone substituted "requires" for the original "necessitates." Without putting too fine a point upon it, the fine distinction between "requires" and "necessitates" is worth contemplating. Although "requires" has the sense of being called for, needed, or demanded, which certainly fits thematically with the speech, "necessitates" has the additional connotation of being unavoidable or inevitable. Thus, even though slightly different in meaning, "necessitates" was restored, probably because it communicated the sense of an inexorable force that must be addressed.

The last change, although a small one, is quite evocative of the care the participants in this freezing session gave to nuances of language. Clark had originally penned the word "phase." In conference with HST, this word was changed to "aspect," which was retained in the final speech. Given that the president sought money from the Congress, the word "phase" could connote negative implications to stingy congressmen and Americans. If Truman sought money for one phase, for one transitory state of affairs in Greece and Turkey, might he not return to Congress for more money when the phase changed there or in some other countries? The dreaded possibility of a give-them-an-inch-and-they-will-take-a-mile reading was remedied with the word "aspect." "Aspect" connotes a limitation of what is seen or considered. Thus, "aspect," when linked with "Greece and Turkey," implied that the consideration was circumscribed to those two countries, hence Truman would not be back for more money later.[10] Lest this exegesis seem too farfetched, consider that Richard Freeland claimed "Truman wanted a general principle of economic assistance, but confined the specific request to Greece and Turkey because Congress and the people might balk at a whole program at once."[11]

The conclusion of the speech artistically matched the introduction in tone and terseness. The interaction between Truman and his staff can be illustrated by the evolution of the one-sentence paragraph that closed the address. On the draft of March 10, the last sentence of the speech read, "We have had placed upon us, by the swift movement of events, great responsibilities"; HST personally penned a final appeal to the Congress: "I have full faith that the Congress will face these responsibilities squarely."[12]

However, on the final draft of the speech, the verbiage was changed, once for the better, once for the worst. It was an improvement to invert the order of the first sentence to stress "responsibilities" and to reinforce the image, by summoning it again, of the inexorable crisis with which Truman began the speech: "Great responsibilities have been placed upon us by the swift movement of events." But the alliteration, "full faith," that Truman had penned was excised and replaced with "I am confident," which vitiated the vigor of Truman's original version.[13]

THE TRUMAN DOCTRINE: SUPERNATION, CRISIS RHETORIC

Although the speech has been characterized as a "rambling address reflecting the many people who had a hand in its construction,"[14] the arrangement of the speech was problem-solution, which, baldly stated, was that Greece and Turkey needed U.S. aid, and the Congress should give it (and the people should support the Congress). The problem-solution configuration was candid enough, but within that rather prosaic pattern were some highly sophisticated appeals. Chief among them was Truman's reliance on dichotomized, supernation language, for, as Herman Ryan realized, Truman played to an American "tendency, resulting from our Puritan heritage, to view world affairs in Manichaean terms of virtue versus vice."[15]

Having garnered the attention of his listeners and made them receptive to him and his message, Truman wasted no time in discussing the New Facts, the first step in crisis rhetoric. He averred how the Greeks had requested an "urgent appeal for financial and economic assistance," from the United States, "if Greece is to survive as a free nation. I do not believe that the American people and the Congress wish to turn a deaf ear to the appeal of the Greek Government."[16] As a matter of fact, Hinds and Windt observed that Greece had not requested aid since the British decided to cease giving it, and only did so when "the U.S. government told the Greek government to request what the Americans thought it should request."[17]

The New Facts were narrated with compelling, yet clever, arguments. Although Truman wanted to step into the breech that was created by the British withdrawal, he portrayed the request as emanating from Athens, which it technically did. Thus, he created the illusion that the United States was responding to Greek pleas, when in fact he was seeking an active U.S. role that was portrayed as reactive. The fear appeal of Greece's surviving as a free nation was based on the enthymeme that the audience would supply to persuade itself: communism threatened Greece, therefore the United States must fight communism, therefore the United States must help Greece fight communism.

Unfortunately, Truman was not at pains to be forthright about Greece's so-called democracy. Although Greek Communists and leftists were contributing to the general disintegration of Greece, it is also true that the rightists, who comprised the monarchist government, which favored King George II, suppressed dissidents and the ensuing fighting between various factions threatened a civil war.[18] This is an instance of Germino's observation that in supernation rhetoric, freedom is defined merely as the absence of communism. Who, then, could turn a "deaf ear" to such an appeal?

Continuing in the devil/angel vein, Truman mentioned how a "military minority" had exploited the dreadful conditions after the Nazis left Greece in 1944, and how that cabal was also responsible for the lack of economic recovery in Greece to date. The military minority truly was communistic under General Markos Vafiadis, and it did receive supplies and training from Yugoslavia, Albania, and Bulgaria, behind whom stood the Soviet Union. However, Truman failed to tell the audience that the British had originally contributed to the Greek morass by demanding that King George II return to his throne after World War II, which polarized the country. The Greeks divided not so much along pro- or anti-Communistic lines as they did in their support of the monarchy, because they wanted a real democracy in Greece.[19]   But when dealing in black/white polarities, it is best not to confuse the audience with the troublesome grey areas that are bound to muddle stark portraitures.

What had begun in the speech as a discussion of the dire straits of the Greek economy was subtly but inexorably transformed as the speech progressed into a fear appeal concerning a Communist coup d'etat. "The very existence of the Greek state," Truman assured his audience, "is today threatened by the terrorist activities of several thousand armed men, led by communists, who defy the Government's authority at a number of points, particularly along the northern boundaries . . . . Meanwhile, the Greek Government is unable to cope with the situation. The Greek Army is small and poorly equipped. It needs supplies and equipment if it is to restore authority of the Government throughout Greece."   Again, Truman's narration was true by half. He understandably glossed over the facts that the Greek army vastly outnumbered the insurgents, that the army did not want to go on the offensive, that the government was rife with corruption, and that the economy contributed more to the problem than did the military factor.[20]

In narrating the problem in Greece, Truman stirred the audience's pity for Greece's travail during and after World War II, appealed to the audience's indignation that the Communists had contributed (Truman let it be inferred single-handedly) to the lack of economic progress, and aroused fear for an imminent Communist takeover in Greece. Thus fortified, the audience was ready for the supernation solution: "Greece must have assistance if it is to become a self-supporting and self-respecting democracy. The United States must supply that assistance. We have already extended to Greece certain types of relief and economic aid but these are inadequate."

But wait. The speech staff evidently reasoned that members of Congress and some of the people might still be reluctant to give U.S. aid.

Their reservations might be paraphrased thus: "Well, the Greeks might need aid, but cannot someone else help them? Why cannot the British continue to help? Or the United Nations? Why only the United States?" For those individuals who harbored such sentiments, Truman offered a classical *refutatio*, or refutation, to his opponents. Within his refutation, he marshalled the method of residues, sometimes called elimination order. Residual argumentation is a rhetorical application of the disjunctive syllogism: Given A, B, or C; not A, not B, therefore C, which is the residue or disjunct that the orator favors.

Truman proved his refutation with the method of residues. The claim to be warranted was: "There is no other country to which democratic Greece can turn. No other nation is willing and able to provide the necessary support for a democratic Greek Government." Notice that HST insisted on twice terming Greece "democratic," for rhetorical repetition and restatement can change reality through inculcation. Truman easily dispatched the first disjunct, which was the British government could no longer pay the bill, for it was true. To eliminate the second disjunct that the United Nations could not assist, Truman offered a one-sentence justification on why the United Nations could not function. The proof was an example of *petitio principii*, or begging the question, for the United Nations could not act because it could not act: "But the situation is an urgent one requiring immediate action, and the United Nations and its related organizations are not in a position to extend the help of the kind that is needed." Truman would never know whether it could have served because he never sought its help.[21]

From a persuasive perspective, if not a logical one, Truman did prove his method of residues, and hence this part of his refutation. Except for the Soviets, there was no other country able to perform the task, although the critic might question the cavalier fashion with which Truman dismissed the United Nations. But lest anyone have lingering doubts, Truman was at pains *again* to assure the audience that the "Greek Government has asked for our aid"; *mirabile dictu*, their first request in late December, 1946, before the British pull out, was for $1.2 billion![22] HST certified that the United States "would supervise the use of any funds," and that "each dollar will count toward making Greece self-supporting, and will help to build an economy in which a healthy democracy can flourish." Greece was again styled as a democracy; however, the fear of a Communist military takeover, which was the operative appeal in securing assent for aid to Greece, was transformed back to economic progress. Hence, albeit the audience was frightened into acquiescence, it could solace itself that it acted from altruistic motives. (After the act was passed, the Greeks requested and received significantly more military aid than economic aid,[23] which had been the original intent that had to be packaged by the speech staff as economic assistance.)

Truman offered another refutation to counter what intelligent people would have known about Greece. Perhaps realizing that the best defense is a good offense, Truman openly admitted, "The Government of Greece is not perfect," but he immediately countered with the proverbial yes-but response. Truman claimed the government represented "85 per cent" of the members in the Greek Parliament, and that 692 Americans (not 693 or 691) considered the "election to be a fair expression of the views of the Greek people." The part of the politics lecture that Truman left out was the fact that the Greek elections of March 1946, which had been urged by the United States, resulted in a boycott by the Left and anti-monarchists, thus resulting in an overwhelming victory for the monarchists.[24] But never mind, Truman told Americans that the U.S. had condemned "extremist measures of the Right or the Left." But the strong inference Truman left is that the U.S. would prefer the Right to the Left.

Before treating Truman's depiction of Turkey, a Ciceronian *digressio* is in order. A digression is when the orator strays from the flow of the speech in order to treat an ancillary, but meaningful, aside. Although the president did not utilize formally the classical organizational pattern that was first developed by Corax of Sicily (c. 467 B.C.) and later refined by Cicero, Truman did employ a *confirmatio*, or confirmation, and a *refutatio*, refutation, with regard to Greece.[25] This rhetorical one-two punch was well advised, because it gave proponents arguments (the dire economic situation and imminent Communist takeover in Greece) on which to base assent, and it preempted reservations that opponents might have (Can another country give aid? Is Greece really a democracy?). Nevertheless, as we have seen, Truman was not as forthcoming in either his confirmation or refutation as a rhetorical critic might desire. Moreover, the persuasive pains with which Truman portrayed Greece stood in stark contrast to his treatment of Turkey.

The second main head in Truman's problem-solution speech was Turkey. Frankly speaking, Turkey was not a momentous exigency, and people knew it. So did Truman, because he willingly admitted that Turkey, as juxtaposed to Greece, had been spared the prostration of World War II, had received material aid from Great Britain and the United States, and was not in danger of take over by the Soviets. Yet Truman had to make Turkey's case compelling. To influence his audience, he argued anew the method of residues, and introduced the halo effect. The halo effect is a technique whereby the orator associates a weaker case (Turkey) with a stronger case (Greece) in the hopes that some of the halo's celestial dust would settle on the less needy example. In short, Truman alleged a persuasive parallelism between Greece and Turkey without strictly proving it.

The New Facts briefly narrated the importance of "an independent and economically sound" Turkey to the "freedom-loving peoples of the world." Note, first, that if one loves freedom, as most Americans do, then one should favor a free Turkey as a patriotic American; and second, that although people throughout the world love freedom, in supernation rhetoric only the government of the United States acts. Whereas Greece had been depicted with heavily freighted fear appeals to tap the audience's emotions, a mere sentence sufficed: "[Turkey's] integrity is essential to the preservation of order in the Middle East." Only one sentence was necessary because Truman hoped the halo effect of Greece would transfer to Turkey: If one conjured Communists overrunning Greece, then it was a small mental step to behold them marching to Turkey. Thus, the audience completed a proportional enthymeme: As we should help Greece fight Communists, so we should help Turkey fight Communists.

As for the method of residues, Truman hurriedly recapitulated that Great Britain could no longer help, and, "as in the case of Greece," the United States is "the only country able to provide that help." (Truman trusted that the audience would supply the parallel enthymeme that since the United Nations could not help Greece, then it could not help Turkey.)

If amount of language is any indication of the drift of Truman's speech, it is instructive to recognize that Truman devoted about 433 percent more verbiage to Greece than to its neighbor. This skewed imbalance lends further credence that once Truman persuaded (via crisis, supernation rhetoric, and the method of residues) on the issue of Greece, then the audience would mentally shift that reasoning (via the halo effect) to Turkey. While on this subject, it is also enlightening to realize that Truman did not offer a refutation of reservations about giving aid to Turkey. The staff may have reasoned that the same argumentation for Greece was applicable to Turkey; that Americans understood the importance of Middle Eastern oil; or that most Americans realized that Turkey was a relatively sound democracy and, therefore, would not object as strenuously to helping that country.[26]

In a typical organizational fashion for Truman, he had an abrupt transitional device to what appeared to be a separate, unrelated argument. In the habit of stating his case and proving it, Truman averred: "I am fully aware of the broad implications involved if the United States extends assistance to Greece and Turkey, and I shall discuss these implications with you at this time." The use of the word "implications" was clever, if not misleading. On its face, the word suggests inferences or meanings that can be assumed from the facts in evidence. Thus, the word insinuated that

Truman would address issues, presumably financial, given Republican reluctance to contribute to an unbalanced budget, that would confront the United States if the aid package was passed. One could reasonably expect Truman to address related issues, such as whether the aid package would be enough, would more be needed later, would this kind of reasoning and aid package be applied to other similar cases, and so forth. But, as we have seen, Truman wisely steered clear of Scylla and Charybdis altogether.

Rather, Truman took another tack. Under the guise of "implications," he really offered a recapitulation of fear appeals and supernation rhetoric to support why the Congress should pass the aid legislation. The ramifications were not so much from a U.S. stance as they were from a worldwide perspective, because Truman broadly hinted at what would happen if the United States *did not* extend aid to Greece and Turkey.

As for the argumentative technique involved, Truman actually combined the classical confirmation and refutation in this section of his speech. That is, to partisans and perhaps neutrals, the "implications" served as additional warrants, which bolstered the ones he offered in the first part of the speech, to give assent to Truman's persuasive goal. For neutrals leaning against his proposal and for opponents, the "implications" functioned as a kind of refutation against their lingering reservations. Thus, the main head on "implications" served as a two-edged rhetorical sword to reinforce partisans while concomitantly assuaging adversaries.

"One of the primary objectives," President Truman proclaimed, "of the foreign policy of the United States is the creation of conditions in which we and other nations will be able to work out a way of life free from coercion. That was a fundamental issue in the war with Germany and Japan." The importance of this foreign policy pronouncement is that it moved the United States from a traditional public philosophy of the nation, which existed for the freedom and safety of the American people, to a new philosophy of the supernation, which implied that the United States now had a burden, in a Wilsonian sense, to make the world safe for democracy by fighting communism. Indeed, Truman's rhetoric was a far cry from President Roosevelt's reasons for declaring war on Japan, for FDR declared on December 8, 1941, "that our people, our territory and our interests are in grave danger." Truman simply could not make that case with respect to Greece and Turkey, but he would try.

So, unexpectedly, Truman's speech took yet another strange maneuver. Having a few minutes earlier dismissed the United Nations as ineffectual in giving the kind of aid (really military, not economic) that Truman wanted to give, he nevertheless tried to identify with the very organization that he had beforehand repudiated. Truman told his congressional and national audience that the United States had helped to found the United Nations for realizing "lasting freedom and independence for all its members," which was an honorable goal. But then Truman switched his pronouns. In a paragraph that led off by talking about the United Nations in the third person singular, Truman suddenly converted to the first person plural: "*We* shall not realize *our* objectives, however, unless *we* are willing to help free people to maintain their free institutions [my emphasis]." The change of pronouns was purposeful. Under the guise of acting with implied UN approval, Truman slyly shunted aside the United Nations, almost off stage, as the United States took center stage. With a distinct supernation appeal, Truman asserted that "totalitarian regimes . . . undermine the foundations of international peace and hence the security of the United States."

Then, in what Herman Ryan deemed a "superb presentation of the moralistic mission of the United States, and . . . the dualistic view of the world expressed with brilliant clarity,"[27] Truman waxed biblically on virtue versus vice:

> At the present moment in world history nearly every nation must choose between alternative ways of life. The choice is too often not a free one. One way of life is based upon the will of the majority, and is distinguished by free institutions, representative government, free elections, guarantees of individual liberty, freedom of speech and religion, and freedom from political oppression [One can almost hear in the background Kate Smith's rendition of "God Bless America."]. The second way of life is based upon the will of a minority forcibly imposed upon the majority. It relies upon terror and oppression, a controlled radio and press, fixed elections, and the suppression of personal freedoms.

Forsooth, a medieval morality play could not have made the dichotomies much clearer.

Having moved the audience to the plain of Armageddon, Truman sounded the supernation trumpet:

> I believe that it must be the policy of the United States to support free peoples who are resisting attempted subjugation by armed minorities or by outside pressures. I believe that we must assist free people to work out their own destinies in their own way. I believe that our help

> should be primarily through economic and financial aid
> which is essential to economic stability and orderly
> political processes.

With regard to the above quotation, Truman complimented himself by noting that "The key sentence . . . read 'I believe that it should be the policy of the United States . . .' I took my pencil, scratched out 'should' and wrote in 'must.' . . . I wanted no hedging in this speech . . . . It had to be clear and free of hesitation or double talk."[28] But, these leitmotifs sounded a bit strained. It is certainly debatable whether the Greek people were free in any sense that Americans would define as free. Turkey was not threatened with armed minorities, nor was the Soviet Union actively pressuring it. And the real reason to give aid, which was military, was misrepresented once more as economic aid. So much for double talk.

Mirabile dictu! Truman immediately summoned the United Nations back from oblivion. For an organization that could not act because it was never asked to help, Truman certainly paid lip service to its potency in foreign affairs. Although Greece and Turkey had not brought their cases to the United Nations, Truman claimed that the United States could not "allow changes in the status quo in violation of the Charter of the United Nations"; and in helping "free and independent nations," the United States will "be giving effect to the principles of the Charter of the United Nations." Thus, Truman appealed to the image of the United Nations as a world peacekeeping institution, while in truth he acted alone to actuate a supernation policy that was in the United States's, but not necessarily in the United Nation's interest, which was the real reason the UN was bypassed altogether in the first place.

But Truman was not finished with his one-two combination of confirmation and refutation argumentation for his proponents and opponents. In an attempt to clinch his point, HST summarized his position with some effective but fallacious conclusions. These passages will be given shortly, but his rhetoric, particularly the weaknesses, must be inventoried before it is quoted.

First and foremost, Truman committed the fallacy of begging the question, for he assumed the outcome of events that he needed to prove would occur, that is, Greece and Turkey faced an imminent threat from the Soviet Union. Second, and dovetailing neatly with his *petitio principii*, having enacted an earlier and successful role as a politics professor, Truman became an instructor in geography. In his lesson, he introduced the domino theory for his American pupils. The domino metaphor functioned as a powerful fear appeal, for the dominoes/countries were poised to fall one after the other into the communist camp. Third, HST employed a tricky grammatical construction. He exploited the conditional sentence, whose form is "If should . . . then would." Although conditional sentences are by their nature speculative, one can reasonably expect some supporting evidence, other than plain avowal, to warrant the probability of the conjectural condition. But, Truman offered no reasoning or proof, either here or earlier in his address, to adduce the probability of the conditional statement's becoming true. Stated another way, he used conditional assertions in default of actual proof, or, stated yet another way, the conditional sentences were predicated on the fallacy of begging the question.

For a president who professed to eschew double talk, note in the following quotation the fear appeal of the domino effect, the conditional statements, all of which were transformed from conjecture to reality by begging the question:

> *If* Greece should fall under the control of an armed minority, the effect upon its neighbor, Turkey, would be immediate and serious. Confusion and disorder *might well spread* throughout the entire Middle East. Moreover, the disappearance of Greece as an independent State *would* have a profound effect upon those countries in Europe whose peoples are struggling against great difficulties to maintain their freedoms and their independence while they repair the damages of war. It *would be* an unspeakable tragedy *if* these countries, which have struggled so long against overwhelming odds, *should lose* that victory for which they sacrificed so much. Collapse of free institutions and loss of independence *would be* disastrous not only for them but for the world. Discouragement and *possibly failure would quickly be* the lot of neighboring people striving to maintain their freedom and independence [my emphasis].

Then, like Gideon before the walls of Jericho, Truman melodramatically sounded the trumpet: "Should we fail to aid Greece and Turkey in this fateful hour, the effect will be far-reaching to the West as well as to the East. We must take immediate and resolute action." The problem presented, with its dire prophecies cast in Manichaean, supernation terms, Truman beckoned the Congress and country to cross the Rubicon.

His solution was simple at first blush, for he sought American aid to the tune of $400 million for Greece and Turkey. Whereas in the discursive statement of the problem area the real exigency was military aid, camouflaged as economic aid, Truman finally admitted in the solution of his speech that the aid was military. However, even here the request was packaged euphemistically. He asked Congress to authorize sending American civilian and military personnel to Greece and Turkey, for which he carefully added a technical caveat, "at their request"; and he alluded to the need for congressional authorization for "instruction and training of selected Greek and Turkish personnel." Truly, the solution part of his speech resembled more his treatment of Turkey rather than that of Greece. Whereas concrete and copious language characterized the Greek situation, Truman let a few succinct enthymemes suffice for Turkey. Likewise, in the solution part of his speech, Truman remained vague and terse, for he was not about to ruin the rhetorical efficacy of economic aid that was in reality military aid.

Although Truman indicated in his interview with speech professors White and Henderlider that he liked to close a speech with a summary of his main points, that pedestrian technique was not used for the Truman Doctrine. Owing to the importance of the address, Truman and his staff opted for a more dramatic, compelling culmination. Imbedded in the conclusion was an indirect appeal for support from the people, and a direct appeal for legislation from their Congress. To actuate his audience, Truman laced his peroration with an admixture of emotional appeals that stimulated their patriotism, pity, and fear. As for patriotism, Truman reasoned that the United States spent $341 billion in winning World War II, so the aid to Greece and Turkey amounted "to little more than one-tenth of 1 percent of this investment," which, according to the president, "is only common sense that we should safeguard this investment and make sure that it was not in vain." Thus, Americans were invited to complete the patriotic enthymeme that whereas it was fitting to spend money in World War II for freedom and democracy, the analogy applied to Greece and Turkey, and thus the money should be appropriated by the Congress.

As for pity, Truman reminded his audience that the "seeds of totalitarian regimes are nurtured by misery and want," they "spread and grow in the evil soil of poverty and strife," and they grow fully when "the hope of a people for a better life has died." Note that the Manichaean "evil soil" would easily be translated by the audience as communism. Note also that these justifications were grounded in humanitarian concerns that centered around economic themes, such as misery, want, poverty, and so forth. These and similar emotional appeals were also highlighted in the early parts of the speech where Truman found it expedient to stir them for a special effect. But unless one listened very closely, the actual aid that Truman requested from the Congress was for military purposes. Thus, Truman used a variation of the bait-and-switch selling technique. Applied to those who do not have *caveat emptor* engraved indelibly in their minds, the technique entails enticing buyers with one appeal, but turning them to another, higher priced product. Truman baited the American audience with a bill of goods that was ostensibly an economic aid package, but upon close examination, the product was actually military munitions.

The next to the last sentence in his conclusion reinforced the Manichaean, supernation rhetoric that was ubiquitous in his address: "The free peoples of the world look to us for support in maintaining their freedoms. If we falter in our leadership, we may endanger the peace of the world—and we shall surely endanger the welfare of our own nation. Great responsibilities have been placed upon us by the swift movement of events. I am confident that the Congress will face these responsibilities squarely." It did.

THE EFFECT OF THE SPEECH

On the whole, President Truman's delivery probably played a minor role in the impact of his speech. A Chicago policeman, who was arguably a better law enforcement officer than rhetorical critic, wrote that HST's "radio technique reached a new high—delivery, inflections and emphasis were perfect."[29] Other opinions were less charitable, for Joseph Jones, who helped write the speech, thought HST's voice "was flat and not impressive."[30]

As the speech had dealt in dichotomies, so did average Americans react to the speech in diametric ways. First, a sample of the public reaction pro-mail suggests that Truman struck some positive, responsive chords with his audience. These letters often mirrored the devil/angel rhetoric that made the speech so convincing. Someone from Norfolk, Virginia, appreciated the president's clarity of purpose, for this was a built-in strength of the speech: "You—Mr. President—make things so clear and understandable"; another listener from Washington, D.C., comprehended the Manichaeanism written into the address: "Anybody that disagrees with your speech does not like liberty and freedom, and is an ardent advocate of communism"; and a writer from St. Louis applauded Truman's strong stance: "Frankly, Mr. president, I did not think that you had the courage to make such a statement nor did I think your administration had the courage to finally adopt a firm, uncompromising, inexpedient moral stand on this most important issue."[31]

On the other hand, the con-mail suggested that some Americans were not distracted by Truman's anti-Communist themes. Instead, they looked beyond the rhetoric to the reality. A writer from Hollywood, California, reflected the view that the United States should restrain its foreign commitments: "It is not the function of our great country to act as the arsenal for the anti-democratic forces of the world." Two residents of the president's home state of Missouri complained that Greece was not a democracy—from Bennett, a writer protested "$400,000,000 to be sent to any such tyrannical set-up," and from St. Louis, an individual reminded the president that Greece was undemocratic: "The government in power in Greece is a reactionary government." Another writer caught the blatant hypocrisy in Truman's speech that is was acceptable for the United States to intervene in the internal affairs of Greece, but not for the Russians to do so: "Since when is intervention by us, Mr. President, in the internal affairs of other countries better than intervention by any other country?" And finally, a couple from New York City fully appreciated the unstated but operative reasons for U.S. intervention: "We believe that the real purpose behind this policy, which is not really only against communism, but against *any* change in the Greek and Turkish governments, is to insure that oil of the Near East to the United States rather than to Russia [emphasis in original]."[32]

(An early March polling of congressmen and senators who were willing to commit themselves reflected the same divisions as the public reaction letters. During the period March 12-14, twenty-seven lawmakers supported Truman, eight gave qualified support, twenty-two opposed, and eighteen gave non-committal statements.[33])

That the con letters had touched a sensitive nerve in the Truman administration can be discerned from the fact that Eben A. Ayers, assistant press secretary and special assistant in the White House, tried to spike the negative letters by implying that they were written by Communists and Communist-inspired sympathizers. Whether the con-mail writers were Communists is not the issue here. Rather, their letters confirm Windt's contention that crisis speeches are intended to diminish debate on the president's policy, and that those who would dare question the president's motives and policy are thereby cast as anti-American, anti-democratic. A writer from New York City rightly protested the administration's heavy hand on dissenters:

> In today's *New York Herald Tribune* I read that Mr. Eben Ayers, your assistant press secretary, said that many of the New York and Brooklyn protests against your plan to aid the governments of Greece and Turkey were "clearly inspired," the inference being that the writers were influenced by Communist propaganda.
>
> Mr. Ayers' statement was unworthy of the President's office. A fair inference would be that it was

his, or your, purpose to discourage those citizens who
believe your plan is wrong from saying so . . . . This, Mr.
President, is nothing short of intimidation.

You may count me among those who regard your
plan as shameful. You cannot make the governments of
Greece and Turkey "free" by saying so. And if we want
peace, why not go after it by helping the ordinary people
instead of the rotten fascists and monarchists who fatten on
war?[34]

Perhaps nowhere can this problem of rhetoric versus reality be
better understood than in a document originally stamped top secret. In the
White House meeting on February 27, Secretary of State Marshall and
Acheson endeavored to portray Greece and Turkey in an anti-Communist
expansionist light: "In the *public* [my emphasis] presentation the concept
of individual liberty is basic, and the protection of democracy everywhere
in the world."[35]

Hence, it is interesting to ponder the relationship between this
memorandum and speech writer Clifford's emendation on a draft. Did
Clifford change "country" to "world" on his March 9 speech draft as a
result of this meeting?[36] If so, this would reinforce Germino's thesis that
cold war rhetoric purposefully projects the United States as a supernation,
a theme as we have seen, that was forcefully recapitulated in the speech's
conclusion because only the United States could ensure the "peace of the
world."

Later critics also read in the speech the supernation, crisis rhetoric
persuasive appeals. William Pemberton portrayed the significance of
Truman's pitch to the people:

Although Truman's sketch of the nature of Greek and
Turkish society had little connection with the reality of
recent events there, it gave Americans a view of the world
that served them for decades. It mobilized public opinion
to resist the spread of communism, and prepared the way
for more extensive foreign aid programs necessary to keep
world trade flowing . . . . The Truman Doctrine trapped
Republican leaders by forcing them to choose between two
of their highest priorities, cutting the federal budget and
fighting communism. It also trapped Congress in a way
that has become a familiar political ploy. The administration secretly formulated a program, wrapped it in a cloak
of national security, and presented it to Congress as a fait

accompli. If Congress turned the president down, it not only would pull the rug from under him but might also, according to the administration, be the final blow to Greece, weaken Turkey and Iran, and start other dominoes falling.[37]

CONCLUSION

There are at least three ways to assess a speech. If one considers solely effect—Was the audience persuaded?—then one would have to pronounce Truman's speech a success. Granted, the causal link between Truman's giving the speech and the Congress's passing the legislation is tenuous, because the press weighed in with endorsements and the people approved in opinion polls. Nevertheless, the outcome is illustrative of the power of the rhetorical presidency with its constituent audiences.

The skeletal outline of the president's plan to contain communism had been known for a week before the address. The problem of "'Containment' of Communism," according to *Newsweek*, was "as plain as the gold star on Stalin's chest." However, when Truman appeared before the Congress in person, *Newsweek* noted that "the very stating of it made it the more awesome" and that his delivery "was somber; his pace, uncommonly slow—120 words a minute."[38]

As for the Congress, Senator Vandenberg's oral assurances to Truman at the February 27 meeting (if the president addressed the Congress, thus taking some of the heat on the crisis in Greece and Turkey, then the Congress would act), was tantamount to congressional approval. Although isolationists, such as Senator Robert Taft of Ohio, Senate Majority Leader Wallace White of Maine, and Speaker Joseph Martin of Massachusetts were on record as opposing the Truman Doctrine, the *New York Times* presciently headlined the eventual success of the Truman Doctrine speech: "TRUMAN ACTS TO SAVE NATIONS FROM RED RULE; ASKS 400 MILLION TO AID GREECE AND TURKEY; CONGRESS FIGHT LIKELY BUT APPROVAL IS SEEN."[39]

Newspaper editorials tended to support the president. To be sure, the *Cleveland Plain Dealer* justly complained about Truman's narration of the New Facts: "But the inference that the present Governments in Greece and Turkey are safely democratic, both in name and in fact, and that we can promote the broad aims of democracy by supporting them is hardly supported by the facts." This was seconded by the *Chicago Sun*: "The President's request should not be granted without adequate conditions which assure that we are really helping a free and democratic Greece and not a Fascist Greece . . . . If the Greek Government really represents its people, why is it in peril of collapse unless rescued by us?" The *San Francisco Chronicle* probably came the closest to the truth when it opined that the enemy was not Russia or communism, but "The real enemy is poverty"; and the *Chicago Tribune* taunted Truman for making "as cold a war speech against Russia as any President has ever made except on the occasion of going before Congress to ask for a declaration of war . . . . The outcome will inevitably be war." However, other presses sustained Truman's speech. One of the objections to the United States's assuming the British role was that the Truman was pulling British chestnuts from the fire; to this charge, the *St. Paul Pioneer Press* replied with the same metaphor: "There can hardly be any serious doubt in Congress over the answer that must be given to President Truman's request. These are our chestnuts that are in the fire." The *New York Herald Tribune*, the most influential Republican paper on the East Coast, even suffered Truman's speech: "And, when one considers the probable consequences of any other course, it is difficult to gainsay the conclusion." The *Philadelphia Inquirer* also cast its editorial support in Manichaean terms: "We must, it is plain, give the material aid the President urges, without which Greece and Turkey will swiftly be enveloped by that darkness."[40]

As judged by opinion polls, the American people apparently appreciated Truman's supernation, crisis rhetoric. Whereas Truman's personal popularity stood at 32 percent just after the 1946 elections in which the Democrats lost the House and Senate, his new stature showed over 60 percent of the people approved his presidency.[41]

One can also appraise a speech from a close reading of its text. Perhaps from a political perspective, the inherent ambiguity of the speech was, after all, persuasively expedient. Given two basic thrusts in the speech, which were strident anti-communism and/or blatant pity for the poor Greeks, the administration had unwittingly (wittingly?) built into the address two fallback positions for when the speech played in Peoria. If the anti-Communist line gave trouble, then the focus could be shifted to the pity appeals, and vice versa. Acheson did, in fact, adopt this approach in his later defenses of the doctrine. Acheson eschewed the anti-Communist tone of Truman's speech, which had alarmed American isolationists and leftists, and instead underscored in congressional hearings the pity-poor-Greece line that Truman had also used, for the *New Republic* reported that Acheson "was laying top stress on the unhappy situation in Greece and talking only about communism when forced to by the questions."[42]

If my line of analysis has any merit, then the underlying, bifurcating rhetoric of the Truman Doctrine speech becomes even more fascinating and functional than has hitherto been realized. The logical reasoning and consistency, which were lacking in the speech, that ethicists might require are in truth the crux of the speech's triumphant rhetorical appeal. Its ambiguity allowed listeners with different value systems to read into the address whatever appeals they found compelling. A speech is like a course of political action, for it is better to operate with the greatest latitude in policy and rhetoric than to be wedded to only one justification for a course of action or a speech.

One can also sample reasoned reactions, both from contemporary sources and later responses. Of that genre, three may suffice here. Two of them are from the liberal media of 1947. Freda Kirchwey, writing for the *Nation*, objected to Truman's characterization of the Greek guerrillas as Communist backed or inspired:

> Whether the guerrillas have received help—or if so, to what extent—from across the borders, the President obviously does not know, since he sprang his drastic program on the world without waiting for the finds of the United Nations commission now investigating the disturbances in northern Greece. But one thing is dead sure without any new evidence: the Greek guerrillas have received far less help from any source than the government's army has received from the British; and still they fight on. They fight, not because Russia orders them to, but because they have the backing of a large part of the Greek people who have suffered beyond endurance at the hands of right-wing irregulars and soldiers, armed and trained by the British. Terror has been practiced on both sides in Greece, but by ignoring the terror of the right Mr. Truman betrayed a shocking indifference to the human and political realities of the Greek struggle.[43]

The *New Republic* also understood the crux of Truman's supernation speech, and its sarcastic tone appropriately communicated its displeasure with his speech's problem of rhetoric versus reality:

> The Truman Doctrine's first magnificent gesture was to be the democratic Government's majestic undertaking on behalf of the survivors of an old and wretched order—the royalist office holders pledged to King George II of Greece and the authoritarian rulers of the Turkish police state. Its noble result would be to guarantee the politics of Europe against all forms of improvement. Repression, as long as it might represent itself as anti-Comintern, could count on

the support of Harry Truman's method of sustaining "free peoples everywhere."[44]

Lest these historical reactions to Truman's speech be dismissed as leftist propaganda, one might consider Lawrence Wittner's masterful and well-documented exposure of U.S. complicity with the Greek Right. His conclusion is worth considering:

> Yet, as indicated by their record in Greece—and in other lands subsequently "aided" by the United States—they felt a stronger commitment to Cold War concerns. Even the occasional constraints they demanded of their right-wing allies owed less to principle than to the need to placate public opinion. Little wonder, then, that despite their talk of freedom, American officials repeatedly acquiesced in or encouraged police state measures. Haunted by the spectre of Communist revolution, they moved ineluctably toward policies of repression.[45]

NOTES

1. Lynn Boyd Hinds and Theodore Otto Windt, Jr., *The Cold War as Rhetoric: The Beginnings, 1945-1950* (New York: Praeger, 1991), p. 129; Robert J. Donovan, *Conflict and Crisis: The Presidency of Harry S. Truman, 1945-1948* (New York: W. W. Norton, 1977), p. 283.

2. Quoted in Randall B. Woods and Howard Jones, *Dawning of the Cold War: The United States' Quest for Order* (Athens: University of Georgia Press, 1991), p. 144; Harry S. Truman, *Memoirs by Harry S. Truman*, vol. II, *Years of Hope and Trial* (Garden City, N.Y.: Doubleday, 1956), p. 103.

3. Donald R. McCoy, *The Presidency of Harry S. Truman* (Lawrence: University Press of Kansas, 1984), pp. 120, 122.

4. Memorandum for the file, The drafting of the president's message to congress on the Greek situation, March 12, 1947, papers of Joseph M. Jones, box 1, p. 1, HSTL.

5. February 28, 1947, Purpose of SWNCC foreign policy information subcommittee, papers of Joseph M. Jones, box 1, folder 1, p. 1, HSTL.

6. Papers of Joseph Jones, box 1, HSTL.

7. Papers of George M. Elsey, speech file, box 17, March 12, 1947, Truman Doctrine speech, draft of March 9, p. 1, HSTL.

8. Papers of Clark Clifford, presidential speech file, box 28, suggested draft, revised March 9, 1947, p. 1, HSTL.

9. Letter of David D. Lloyd to Wayne Grover, archivist of United States, September 30, 1957, p. 3, HSTL.

10. Papers of George M. Elsey, speech file, box 17, March 12, 1947, Truman Doctrine speech, draft of March 11, p. 1, HSTL.

11. Richard M. Freeland, *The Truman Doctrine and the Origins of McCarthyism* (New York: Schocken Books, 1974), p. 81.

12. Draft, March 10, 1947, papers of Joseph Jones, box 1, p. 14, HSTL.

13. Papers of George M. Elsey, speech file, box 17, March 12, 1947, Truman Doctrine speech, second draft of March 11, p. 9, HSTL.

14. Hinds and Windt, *The Cold War as Rhetoric*, p. 145.

15. Herman Butterfield Ryan, Jr., "The American Intellectual Tradition Reflected in the Truman Doctrine," *American Scholar* 42 (1973): 295.

16. *HST, 1947*, p. 176. All quotations from the Truman Doctrine speech are from this source.

17. Hinds and Windt, *The Cold War as Rhetoric*, p. 134.

18. McCoy, *The Presidency of Harry S. Truman*, pp. 118-119.

19. See, for instance, Terry H. Anderson, *The United States, Great Britain, and the Cold War 1944-1947* (Columbia: University of Missouri Press, 1981), pp. 159-160.

20. Woods and Jones, *Dawning of the Cold War*, pp. 137-141.

21. Woods and Jones, *Dawning of the Cold War*, p. 146; McCoy, *The Presidency of Harry S. Truman*, p. 120.

22. Anderson, *The United States, Great Britain, and the Cold War*, p. 162.

23. Truman, *Memoirs*, II, p. 108.

24. McCoy, *The Presidency of Harry S. Truman*, p. 119.

25. For an overview of classical Greek and Roman rhetoric, see my *Classical Communication for the Contemporary Communicator*, pp. 5-27.

26. William E. Pemberton, *Harry S. Truman: Fair Dealer and Cold Warrior* (Boston: Twayne, 1989), pp. 95-96.

27. Ryan, "The American Intellectual Tradition," p. 296.

28. Truman, *Memoirs*, II, p. 105.

29. President's personal files (PPF-200), public reaction files, box 305, HSTL. Hereafter cited as PPF-200.

30. Joseph Jones, *The Fifteen Weeks* (New York: Viking Press, 1955), p. 18.

31. PPF-200, box 305, HSTL.

32. PPF-200, box 305, HSTL.

33. "Confidential," congressional statements of President Truman's address asking for aid for Greece and Turkey, March 18, 1947, HSTL.

34. PPF-200, box 305.

35. Truman Doctrine, Important Relevant Papers, papers of Joseph M. Jones, box 2, folder 6, top secret draft, February 28, p. 3, HSTL.

36. See note 8.

37. Pemberton, *Harry S. Truman: Fair Dealer and Cold Warrior*, pp. 96-97.

38. "Policy: 'Containment' of Communism," *Newsweek*, March 17, 1947, p. 27; "Let the Nations Be Glad," *Newsweek*, March 24, 1947, p. 24.

39. "Truman Acts to Save Nations from Red Rule; Asks 400 Million to Aid Greece and Turkey; Congress Fight likely but Approval Is Seen," *New York Times*, March 13, 1947, p. 1.

40. See "Extracts from American Editorial Comment on President Truman's Message," *New York Times*, March 12, 1947, p. 4.

41. "After Two Years," *Time*, April 7, 1947, p. 23.

42. "Headwinds," *New Republic*, March 31, 1947, p. 5.

43. Freda Kirchwey, "Manifest Destiny, 1947," *Nation*, March 22, 1947, p. 317.

44. "Headwinds," p. 6.

45. Lawrence S. Wittner, "The Truman Doctrine and the Defense of Freedom," *Diplomatic History* 4 (1980): 187.

2
The Korean Quagmire

Whereas the Truman Doctrine had been foreshadowed by the press before the president dramatically announced it on March 12, 1947, the Korean War was sprung on Truman, the nation, and the world without warning. But, unlike FDR's "Day of Infamy" speech delivered on December 8 to immortalize December 7, 1941, and perhaps owing to the lack of skilled oratory by the thirty-third commander in chief, no one remembers Saturday, June 24, 1950, the day when the North Korean Communists invaded South Korea (the invasion began on Sunday, June 25, Korean time, but all dates hereafter will be given in U.S. time).

The military vagaries of the battlefield and the Manichaean philosophy of the war overwhelmed Truman, for he was restrained by the former and he created the latter constraint that came round to haunt him. Moreover, the famous encounter between HST and General Douglas MacArthur had its roots in the conduct of the war and, more importantly, in their diametrically opposed rhetorical justifications for the war and its envisioned outcome.

Aside from the invasion itself, the political motivations and rhetorical reasoning for the Korean War were stated in two documents. The formulation of these papers preceded the conflict, but they served as rationales when the war came. Although these papers were then top secret, they nevertheless motivated the administration's military responses to the war, and they especially molded its justifications for the public's consumption. The position papers were produced by the National Security Council (NSC), which was created by the National Security Act of 1947.

The first paper was NSC-48. It was signed by Truman at the end of 1949 on the heels of the Soviet's exploding an atom bomb in September and Mao Tse-tung's communist takeover of China in October from Chiang Kai Shek, who had to flee to Formosa. NSC-48 committed the United States to containing communism in Asia, and "where possible to reduce" the spread of communism.[1] The military significance of NSC 48, and for our purposes its rhetorical relevance, is that the Truman administration committed itself not only to containing communism, which had been earlier stated in the Truman Doctrine, but also to compelling Communists to retrench.

Unfortunately, the Truman administration sent mixed signals with regard to Korea. On January 12, 1950, Secretary of State Acheson addressed to the National Press Club with his famous "Defense Perimeter" speech, which was a public statement of the administration's secret position on NSC-48. In that address, Acheson purposefully excluded South Korea from the United State's defense perimeter that was vital to its interests, but implied that Formosa and South Korea could be defended under the aegis of the United Nations. Republicans later charged that Acheson's speech invited the North Koreans to invade the South. Whether it did is hard to determine, but James Stokesbury summarized the controversy: "[N]o one can say the speech was a green light, but it may safely be assumed that it was not a red or even a yellow one."[2] In any event, when a propitious moment presented itself, the Truman administration was prepared to act militarily and rhetorically if such intervention was warranted.

The second momentous document, NSC-68, was created in April 1950.[3] NSC-68 committed the United States to a military buildup to counter the Soviets in, according to Burt Cochran, a "Manichaean struggle adumbrated by the President in his Truman Doctrine speech."[4] The costs of such a program were stupendous and Truman was understandably reluctant then to present them to the Congress. However, the Korean War was a boon with regard to NSC-68, for it manifested the necessity of arming the nation on a war footing. The thinking was that behind North Korea stood China behind whom stood the Soviet Union. Thus, NSC-48 and NSC-68 gave the military and rhetorical warrants for the Korean War.

THE KOREAN WAR RHETORICS

President Truman's persuasive communications to the Congress and the people are an interesting case study in the evolution of justificatory rhetoric. Reflecting the worsening vagaries of the war, Truman escalated his rhetoric to steel the American people to stay the course with him. As such, his communications evolved from relatively simple, straightforward statements of facts to melodramatic morality plays replete with crisis, supernation appeals. The rhetorics under investigation are his written messages to the Congress, June 26 and 27, 1950; his press conference of June 29, 1950, in which Truman offhandedly claimed the Korean War was not a war at all but a police action; his address to Congress, and a similar, but more important speech to the nation, July 19, 1950, in which Manichaean rhetoric figured prominently; and his address to the nation, September 1, 1950, which was delivered in the depths of the war's worst worries in order to fortify the Congress and public opinion.

STATEMENT OF JUNE 26, 1950

The day after the invasion began, the Security Council of the United Nations met on June 25 to consider an American proposal. Owing to the absence of the Soviet representative, Jacob Malik, who was boycotting the Security Council because it refused to unseat Nationalist China for Communist China five months earlier, the Soviets were not present to veto (probably) the Security Council's resolution. The Council condemned the invasion, called for a cease fire, and demanded a withdrawal of Communist forces to the 38th parallel.[5] The 38th parallel was the boundary between the Democratic People's Republic of Korea, or North Korea, and the Republic of Korea, or South Korea.

President Truman's first response to the Korean invasion was a concise and candid communication to the nation on June 26, 1950:

> I conferred Sunday evening with the Secretaries of State and Defense, their senior advisers, and the Joint Chiefs of Staff about the situation in the Far East created by unprovoked aggression against the Republic of Korea.
>
> The Government of the United States is pleased with the speed and determination with which the United Nations Security Council acted to order a withdrawal of the invading forces to positions north of the 38th parallel. In accordance with the resolution of the Security Council, the United States will vigorously support the effort of the Council to terminate this serious breach of the peace.
>
> Our concern over the lawless action taken by the forces from North Korea, and our sympathy and support for the people of Korea in this situation, are being demonstrated by the cooperative action of American personnel in Korea, as well as by steps taken to expedite and augment assistance of the type being furnished under the Mutual Defense Assistance Program. Those responsible for this act of aggression must realize how

seriously the Government of the United States views such threats to the peace of the world. Willful disregard of the obligation to keep the peace cannot be tolerated by nations that support the United Nations Charter.[6]

The New Facts were not overblown. Truman correctly defined North Korean actions as "unprovoked aggression." The New Situation was also communicated forthrightly but with a little fanfare. Truman was pleased to inform the nation that the United States was acting in concert with the United Nations, which lent an air of legitimacy to the enterprise. (Ironically, the United Nations somehow could not act speedily in 1947 for the Greek and Turkey crisis when Truman wanted to act independently of the UN.)

However, sandwiched in the New Situation was a statement that was very important. As originally framed by the Security Council, the order was for "invading forces" to withdraw to "positions north of the 38th parallel" or, in other words, for the North Koreans to leave South Korea and to return to and stay in North Korea. Hence, Truman publicly committed himself and the United States to the UN's war aim of a return to the *status quo ante bellum*. It is extremely important to note that victory was not defined in terms of a traditional military triumph over North Korea, with a clearly demarcated winner and loser, but was defined narrowly as a return to the status quo, which would then be defined as a victory for the United Nations and United States.

Unlike the Truman Doctrine speech, incendiary language was kept to a minimum in this statement. "Unprovoked aggression," "invading forces," "serious breach of the peace," "lawless action," and "act of aggression" were words obviously meant to denigrate the North Koreans, but these characterizations were accurate and truthful descriptions.

Last, supernation rhetoric was present, but muted. In a sentence order that gave away whose war it really was, Truman stressed "how seriously" the United States viewed threats to "world peace," and then added, almost as an after thought, that disregarding the peace cannot "be tolerated by nations that support the United Nations Charter." Yet, despite the rhetorical bravado, the Commies kept coming.

STATEMENT OF JUNE 27, 1950

Truman's made his second response one day later on June 27, 1950:

In Korea the Government forces, which were armed to

prevent border raids and to preserve internal security, were attacked by invading forces from North Korea. The Security Council of the United Nations called upon the invading troops to cease hostilities and to withdraw to the 38th parallel. This they have not done, but on the contrary have pressed the attack. The Security Council called upon all members of the United Nations to render every assistance to the United Nations in the execution of this resolution. In these circumstances I have ordered United States air and sea forces to give the Korean Government troops cover and support.

The attack upon Korea makes it plain beyond all doubt that communism has passed beyond the use of subversion to conquer independent nations and will now use armed invasion and war. It has defied the order of the Security Council of the United Nations issued to preserve international peace and security. In these circumstances the occupation of Formosa by Communist forces would be a direct threat to the security of the Pacific area and to the United States forces performing their lawful and necessary functions in that area.

Accordingly, I have ordered the 7th Fleet to prevent any attack on Formosa. As a corollary of this action I am calling upon the Chinese Government on Formosa to cease all air and sea operations against the mainland. The 7th Fleet will see that this is done. The determination of Formosa must await the restoration of security in the Pacific, a peace settlement with Japan, or consideration by the United Nations.

I have also directed that United States Forces in the Philippines be strengthened and that military assistance to the Philippine Government be accelerated.

I have similarly directed acceleration in the furnishing of military assistance to the forces of France and the Associate States of Indochina and the dispatch of a military mission to provide close working relations with those forces.

I know that all members of the United Nations will consider carefully the consequences of this latest aggression in Korea in defiance of the Charter of the United Nations. A return to the rule of force in international affairs would have far-reaching effects. The

United States will continue to uphold the rule of law.

I have instructed Ambassador Austin, as the representative of the United States to the Security Council, to report these steps to the Council.[7]

The New Facts and New Situation were common knowledge by now, so Truman moved to a new plane. He infused the New Facts and Situation with more melodrama, and his supernation characterizations were transformed into saving the Far East from communism. Rather than North Korea's invading troops heeding the UN's call to "cease hostilities," Truman complained that they "on the contrary have pressed the attack." The answer why any country would be foolish enough to engage the United States and United Nations, if anyone needed an explanation, was cast in a Manichaean verity: "The attack upon Korea makes it plain beyond all doubt that communism has passed beyond the use of subversion to conquer independent nations and will now use armed invasion and war." Although this was the first time that the president mentioned the Communists, the term "communism" was kept purposefully vague. One could infer the Soviets, the Red Chinese, the North Koreans, or any combination of the above. For persuasive purposes, the precision of the term was not as important as its latitude: It allowed listeners to adduce whatever connotations suited best, because just as long as "Communists" were behind it, that was all that mattered.

As HST needed a Turkey in the Truman Doctrine speech to bolster the exigency of Greece, he turned in the Korean crisis to Formosa, which functioned as the analogical Turkey for the exigency of the Korean War. Indeed, Margaret Truman wrote that her father conceived Korea as the equivalent of Greece.[8] Although Formosa was not under imminent attack, Truman nevertheless used *petitio principii* to imply that it was. "In these circumstances," Truman averred, "the occupation of Formosa by Communist forces would be a direct threat to the security of the Pacific area and to the United States forces performing their lawful and necessary functions in that area." Again, the future subjunctive "would" is the giveaway for Truman's begging the question, for he never offered any proof that Formosa would be invaded (by the North Koreans? the Red Chinese? the Soviets?). Yet, the enthymeme was purposeful and powerful. Given that the United States lost China to the Communists in 1949, Americans would be loathe to lose Formosa; hence, they would support actions to save Formosa. But Truman overlooked one small detail. The Security Council's mandate was only for South Korea, but it did not hurt Truman's cause to introduce the canard of Formosa for good measure.

What had started out as an effort to contain communism in North

Korean was now transmuted into the United States-as-supernation to save the Far East and American interests there. Truman assured his audience that no more dominoes would fall. He ordered the Seventh Fleet "to prevent any attack on Formosa"; he "strengthened" the Philippines (would it be next?); and he furnished "military assistance" to "France and the Associated States of Indochina."

Truman then ended his statement with an admonition and some supernation bluster. He made a rhetorical sideswipe at the Soviet Union, which could be meant for none other because Red China's seat in the United Nations was held by the Chinese Nationalists on Formosa. Truman intoned: "I know that all members of the United Nations will consider carefully the consequences of this latest aggression in Korea." Immediately after offering that carrot, Truman then waved the stick: "The United States will continue to uphold the rule of law." Most Americans believed at the time that the Soviets were behind the communist invasion, so this belief actuated Truman's persuasive enthymemes. (But as we shall soon learn, the Soviets were not behind the North Korean invasion.)

Truman's message of June 27 was read to the House and Senate. In the Senate, the message prompted statements of support, which came from Republicans as well as Democrats, and in the House, members "rose to their feet and cheered" the president.[9] Governor Thomas Dewey of New York, whom Truman defeated in the 1948 election, telegraphed his support to the president. Truman replied in unusual religious phraseology: "We have taken our stand on the side of Korea and our pledge of faith to that nation is a witness to all the world that we champion liberty wherever the tyranny of communism is the aggressor."[10] It may have been that these early protestations of support for Truman's actions were misread in the White House as unqualified backing. When the war turned sour, the sunshine soldiers and summer patriots deserted the president.

PRESS CONFERENCE, JUNE 29, 1950

Aside from written messages ostensibly targeted for the Congress, Truman had yet to communicate with the American people, and this he did obliquely in a press conference. How to define the action in Korea evidently puzzled many Americans: "Mr. President, everybody is asking in this country, are we or are we not at war?" In a plain response, HST answered "We are not at war."[11]

Although it might appear absurd to claim that the United States was not at war, Truman in fact was constrained to answer in that fashion. One day earlier than the press conference, June 28, Senator Robert Taft (R-Ohio) told Truman that he had "no legal authority" for his actions in

Korea, and several other senators chimed in with their reservations.[12] Since HST had decided not to request a congressional declaration of war, he could not define the action as a war, because he did not want to validate a charge that he had circumvented his Constitutional responsibilities in not requesting war. Doubtless, Truman also dreaded terming the action a "war" for its psychological implications to a people committed to peace.

However, one reporter, not satisfied with the president's circumlocution, pressed the attack: "Mr. President, could you elaborate on this statement that—I believe the direct quote was, 'We are not at war.' And could we use that quote in quotes?" Truman authorized his negative definition: "Yes, I will allow you to use that. We are not at war." Then, in response to another question, which sought an elaboration on the meaning of the Korean action, Truman employed a metaphor. Truman characterized the assault on Korea as an unlawful attack "by a bunch of bandits" and averred that United Nations forces were "to suppress a bandit raid on the Republic of Korea." Swallowing the bait, a reporter asked an extension question in the phraseology of the president's metaphor: "Mr. President, would it be correct, against your explanation, to call this a police action under the United Nations?" Truman answered, "Yes. That is exactly what it amounts to."[13]

Because Truman had congressional backing, so far, for his actions in Korea, perhaps he reasoned that he did not need to define positively for the press, and hence the American people, what the action was, merely what it was not. However, his leaving the definition of the Korean military action to a reporter was probably a mistake, although it was not apparent at first blush, because a reporter, and not the president, managed the perception of the belligerency. Margaret Truman wrote about her father's definitional problem: "He accepted it, as a very rough estimate of what was being done in Korea, with no idea of how it would be misused by his critics in the months to come."[14]

In contravention to Truman's practice, for instance, Franklin D. Roosevelt wisely managed the press. He used his famous "neighbor's garden hose" metaphor in a press conference of December 17, 1940, to obfuscate successfully the legalities of his Lend-Lease program.[15] The "neighbor's garden hose" metaphor sufficed because it suggested a vague principle, but not an objective reality, which Roosevelt sought to camouflage from reporters and the people. On the other hand, the "police action" metaphor, which was a reporter's and not Truman's image, was ill-conceived and inappropriate. It featured, rather than cloaked, the semantic difficulty in which the Truman administration found itself. The "police action" metaphor underscored Truman's unwillingness to concede the obvious. Moreover, "bandits" are usually "suppressed" through capture and incarceration by the "police." But Truman mixed the metaphor: The Security Council's resolution called only for the "police" to ensure that the "bandits" withdraw to their hideout in North Korea. Thus, the inherent connotative contradictions in the "police action" metaphor would fester until General MacArthur finally challenged the logic and definition of Truman's limited war, "police action" theory in 1951.

TRUMAN ESCHEWS A WAR MESSAGE TO CONGRESS

After stunning successes in the surprise June invasion, the North Korean forces occupied Seoul, the capital of South Korea. Syngman Rhee, who headed the rightist forces under American tutelage, had to retreat southward. Rhee, whom Cochran termed "a fascist fanatic,"[16] is an example of the United States's enacting supernation rhetoric wherein it supports regimes that are not democratic but have as their only redeeming value a staunch anti-Communist government. On June 29, 1950, the United States received word from the Soviets that they would not intervene militarily. With these assurances, and having in its pocket the United Nations resolution to commit UN troops, Truman authorized General MacArthur to take several important military steps. But before treating the military strategy, we must digress in order to consider Truman's rhetorical tactics with the Congress.

Truman's refusal to seek some form of approval from Congress on the Korean War was a rhetorical mistake. A precedent for shared action was established with the Truman Doctrine speech. In that situation, Truman learned that the Congress would act if the president shouldered partial responsibility. With regard to the Korean War, HST might have reasoned to his advantage that the reverse would apply. The Congress should share with Truman partial accountability for the war. In fact, Acheson had recommended that Truman address the Congress on July 5, not so much to seek overt assent, but rather to rest his case for military actions on his Constitutional power as commander in chief. Burton Kaufman reasoned that Truman decided not to address the Congress because he had, initially at least, congressional backing, but was nevertheless fearful of extended debate; the timing for such a speech was not propitious; and Truman did not envision the full-scale war that ensued.[17]

However, as the months dragged on, the Korean War became Truman's War, a sobriquet that was to Truman's detriment. Although it was legal for Truman to act the way he did, for Congress had ratified the United Nations Charter, it was, according to Donald McCoy, not politic in the long run: "If the conflict in Korea had been ended successfully in a matter of months, Truman's calculations of the odds would have been correct; but the war stretched out for more than three years, and his administration consequently was to pay a heavy political price."[18] In this assessment, Cochran agreed: "Truman, however, never sought congressional approval—a tactical mistake that was to haunt him."[19] The reason, according to Robert Donovan, was that Truman misjudged congressional motivations: "Truman put too much reliance on the spirit of support he could sense in Congress without giving enough thought to how fickle it might become if the excitement turned to pain."[20] And when the pain came, Kaufman opined that a joint resolution of approval "would have made it all that more difficult for Truman's opponents later to criticize intervention."[21] Nevertheless, Truman relied on his presidential powers and ordered General MacArthur to initiate a United Nations military response in Korea.

TWO-PRONGED RHETORIC TO THE CONGRESS AND PEOPLE, JULY 19, 1950

Perhaps sensing a need to still troubled waters, as Acheson had wanted Truman to do on July 3, the president delivered his first broadcast to the nation. The two speeches, one to Congress and one to the people in the evening, were similar in their bent and flavor, but Truman did adapt to his different audiences. For instance, to the Congress, Truman claimed that the Communist attack "was naked, deliberate, unprovoked aggression, without a shadow of justification";[22] but for the people, the language ran closer to the ground: "The attack came without provocation and without warning. It was an act of raw aggression, without a shadow of justification. I repeat that it was an act of raw aggression. It had no justification whatever"; and a bit later Truman colloquially called it a "sneak attack."[23]

The preparation for the two speeches was similar. The address to the Congress, which was composed first, went through seven drafts, the speech to the people was finished in four drafts, which were begun on July 17 and finished on July 19, the day of the address. Charles S. Murphy, who assumed leadership of Truman's speech staff as special counsel, the position Clark Clifford held until his departure in February 1950, to return to private law practice, composed both drafts with the aid of David Bell, an assistant speech writer.[24]

President Truman gave this speech careful attention. One assumes he realized the importance of the address, and therefore he wanted it to reflect his best rhetorical efforts. As he was wont to do, HST underlined thoughts on the reading copy that he wished to stress orally. Examples of his practice are as follows. Note how he emphasized the short, punchy words: "This challenge has been presented squarely. We must meet it squarely" (the stylistic device that was employed here is epistrophe, which is defined as using the same word to end spoken thought groups, and Truman correctly realized that for the epistrophe to be communicated stylistically, it had to be stressed orally); and "This attack came without provocation and without warning. It was an act of raw aggression, without a shadow of justification. I repeat—it was an act of raw aggression" (again, although the epistrophe was separated by intervening verbiage, HST underscored orally its persuasive efficacy). Truman also added an insert that praised the South Korean army (his insert is italicized): "Now, however, the Korean defenders have reorganized, *and are making a brave fight for their liberty*, and an increasing number of American troops have joined them."[25] Assumedly, Truman wished to communicate that American troops would not have to bear the entire brunt of the battle.

Truman also contributed some interesting emendations on the preliminary drafts. Probably prompted by the speech draft's inherent Manichaeanism, "By their actions in Korea, Communist leaders have demonstrated their contempt for the basic moral principles on which the United Nations is founded," HST inserted on draft three a diatribe against the Soviets:

> It is a demonstration of the contempt which communists
> have for a moral code. They make agreements, they sign
> the United Nations Charter. They have broken every
> agreement made with us and our wartime allies. Now they
> have flouted the UN Charter.[26]

Truman's outburst was not used in the speech. Although perhaps too incendiary but emotionally inducing, there was no compelling evidence to suggest that the Soviets had flouted the UN Charter.

However, some of the president's emendations survived. One of Truman's inserts, a rather innocuous one, was retained, with slight modifications, in the final address:

> The Secretary of State called the President at
> Independence, Mo., and informed him that with the
> President's approval he was asking for a meeting of the
> United Nations Security Council. The Security Council
> met Sunday afternoon and just 24 hours after the
> Communist invasion of the Republic of North Korea it
> passed.[27]

On the fourth draft, Truman curiously careted an emendation that, one assumes, reflected the president's humor rather than his spelling (HST's addition is italicized): "Secretary of State *Atcheson* called me."[28] On this same draft, Truman changed a sentence to make it less technical and more understandable to the common man (his additions are italicized): "But many of our industries are ~~now operating at full capacity~~ *already going full tilt.*"[29]

Truman also paid particular attention to the peroration of his speech. As sections of the speech sought support for increased military expenditures and warned against speculation and profiteering, in addition to the general bid to champion the Korean War, Truman stirred American's patriotism in his ending. Truman strengthened the rhetorical appeal of his conclusion by rearranging for effect a paragraph that motivated the people to support the troops (the redeployment of the inserted paragraph is italicized):

> We know that the cost of freedom is high. But we are determined to preserve our freedom—no matter what the cost.
>
> *I know that our people are willing to do their part to support our soldiers and sailors and airmen who are fighting in Korea. I know that they can count on each and every one of you.*

Although it is impossible to determine which came first, Truman made a change in this redeployed insert. In place of the indefinite pronoun "they," Truman substituted "our fighting men," which made the line more concrete and compelling.[30]

However, the primary thrust of Truman's address, as a function of the rhetorical presidency, was to gain and maintain support from the American people for the Korean War. As may be expected, he touched on the major topics of crisis rhetoric.

First, Truman employed throughout his address Manichaean, supernation appeals to actuate the audience. In his introduction, Truman communicated good guy/bad guy polarities:

> This attack has made it clear, beyond all doubt, that the international Communist movement is willing to use armed invasion to conquer independent nations. An act of aggression such as this creates a very real danger to the security of all free nations.

If one subscribed to the domino theory, then Truman's pitch made good sense; otherwise, he did not adduce any evidence what the "real danger" was to all free nations. Rather, one had to wait until much later in the speech to realize Truman's reasoning. Truman argued by analogy. He urged Americans to learn from their past mistakes in reacting to the events prior to World War II, and then to apply those lessons to the Korean situation:

> These actions by the United Nations and its members are of great importance. The free nations have now made it clear that lawless aggression will be met with force. The free nations have learned the fateful lesson of the 1930's. That lesson is that aggression must be met firmly. Appeasement leads only to further aggression and ultimately to war. . . . We have done this [send armed forces to Korea] because we know that what is at stake here is nothing less than our own national security and the peace of the world.

Truman had stirred Manichaean, supernation rhetoric in his introduction, sprinkled it throughout his speech, and warmed to the theme again in his conclusion. Repetition and restatement were essential to Truman's drum beat. And, if the aphorism that the deity is a being who is mentioned in the last sentence of a political speech is valid, then Truman did not disappoint. In fact, Truman's closing remarks sound more ministerial than presidential:

> Our country stands before the world as an example of how free men, under God, can build a community of neighbors, working together for the good of all. That is the goal we seek not only for ourselves, but for all people. We believe that freedom and peace are essential if men are to live as our Creator intended us to live. It is this faith that has guided us in the past, and it is this faith that will fortify us in the stern days ahead.

Indeed, the keen reader would have perceived a paradox in Truman's Manichaean, supernation rhetoric: Why must the United States fight a war in order to have peace? This is an example of Theodore Windt's assertion that in crisis rhetoric, presidents indulge "in snatches of Newspeak" wherein war and peace are indistinguishable. Americans are unable to differentiate the terms, Windt holds, because they "are so sincerely committed to another symbolic battle with Communism. They can do so because they want to prove dramatically that they have character and courage in the wake of this latest threat. . . . They can do so because they have no alternative. War is peace; peace is war."[31]

Second, Truman carefully constructed his language with regard to the Soviet Union. In the above quotations from his address, Truman advisedly used the generic term "Communist," which could connote the Soviets, the Red Chinese, or the North Koreans. When he finally indicted the Soviet Union frontally, Truman let the audience infer that the Soviet Union was the proximate cause of the Korean War, but he never directly stated that thesis. Rather, he presented the case obliquely in the hopes that the audience would complete the reasoning. Truman vilified the Soviets for not supporting the United Nations, which, Truman wanted it inferred, implied that the Soviets started the war:

> Only a few countries have failed to endorse the efforts of the United Nations to stop the fighting in Korea. The most important of these is the Soviet Union. The Soviet Union has boycotted the meetings of the United Nations Security Council. It has refused to support the actions of the United Nations with respect to Korea.
>
> The United States requested the Soviet Government, 2 days after the fighting started, to use its influence with the North Koreans to have them withdraw. The Soviet Government refused.
>
> The Soviet Government has said many times that it wants peace in the world, but its attitude toward this act of aggression against the Republic of Korea is in direct contradiction of its statements.
>
> For our part, we shall continue to support the United Nations actions to restore peace in the world.

Although this excerpt is replete with Manichaean dualities, the last sentence culminates in an excellent example of an Aristotelian enthymeme: Since the Soviets do not support the United Nations, they must prefer war; therefore, the Soviets at least succor, and probably instigated, the war; therefore, they are wrong and the United States is right; therefore, the United States should fight in Korea. How or why the audience goes through the entire reasoning chain, or one similar to it, is not the issue; rather, the important point is that the audience should arrive at the argument's conclusion, which, as we shall see, it evidently did.

Third, Truman alluded to the United States' war aims. In a speech that stressed peace, Truman was not at pains to define for the American people exactly what "peace" was. In the middle of the speech, one sentence sufficed: "We know that it will take a hard, tough fight to halt the invasion, and to drive the Communists back." Thus, the aim seemed to be consistent with NSC-48 and NSC-68, as long as one assumed the preposition "back" meant back to the border between North and South Korea.

A little later in the speech, Truman also called on General MacArthur to testify. The commander in chief read a portion of the general's letter to the president, which assessed the military situation in Korea. In Olympian language, which was, incidentally, clearer than Truman's words on U.S. war aims, MacArthur recited perfectly for the president's persuasive purposes: "We are now in Korea in force, and with God's help we are there to stay until the constitutional authority of the Republic of Korea is fully restored."

Hence, between the president's one sentence and the general's more eloquent statement, the American people could gather that the United States was fighting in Korea to drive the invaders back. But Truman had done such an excellent job of reproaching the Soviets with Manichaean, supernation rhetoric that the enthymeme practically begged to be extended: If the Soviet Union could not be disciplined directly, could not the United States punish North Korea and thereby indirectly teach the Soviets a lesson? As we shall learn, it did not take long for this inexorable logic to seize the president, his advisers, MacArthur, and even the liberal media.

President Truman received qualified support for his speech. The target of his rhetorical presidency, the American people, wrote and telegraphed about 5 1/2 boxes of pro-mail, and 1 1/2 boxes of con-mail.[32] Realistically assessing the address, *Time* noted that Truman's delivery was not scintillating, gave the speech a yes-but approval, and skewered Truman's semantic problem on what to term the Korean War:

> The President's speech was carefully detailed, carefully delivered—but without inspiration that the occasion called for. It was a plan for defense, a competent one, but it was no compelling call to arms. It was a deliberately low-keyed speech—with none of the ringing phrases of a Churchillian or Rooseveltian performance.
>
> No longer did the President speak of "police action" in Korea, but nowhere in his speech did he call it war. (Of course, technically it wasn't, since Congress had not declared war.)[33]

Other considered reactions to Truman's responses to the Korean War were less heartening. Albeit not written with respect to a particular speech, George Kennan, on August 14, 1950, did capture the confusion and contradictions that were contained in Truman's rhetoric:

> Never before has there been such utter confusion in the public mind with respect to US foreign policy. The President doesn't understand it; Congress doesn't understand it; nor does the public; nor does the press. They all wander around in a labyrinth of ignorance and error and conjecture, in which truth is intermingled with fiction at a hundred points, in which unjustified assumptions have attained the validity of premises, and in which there is no recognized and authoritative theory to hang on to.[34]

A more recent reading of Truman's Korean War rhetoric confirms Kennan's observations, and it also warrants the findings of this study. Notice particularly Cochran's scoring of Truman's analogical reasoning for the Korean War: "The Cold War brought on the stage the children of light and the children of darkness; put its imprimatur on sanctions against heretics; produced an exegesis based on misplaced analogies; and a sociology of the Stalin regime that was questioned by the author of containment himself."[35] In fact, there has been no credible evidence that the Soviet's called for the attack; moreover, as we have seen, the Soviets signaled their intentions on June 29 not to intervene militarily in Korea, nor did they.[36]

ADDRESS TO THE NATION, SEPTEMBER 1, 1950

By August 1950, the North Korean army had captured about seven-eighths of the South Korean peninsula. President Truman again took to the airwaves to assure the American people. And at last, he got around to defining U.S. war aims at ten o'clock in the evening: "Tonight I want to talk to you about Korea, about why we are there, and what our objectives are."[37] True to form, the speech was organized topically around those three main heads.

Before discussing his aims and objectives, it might be appropriate to listen briefly, for by now it must be indelibly etched in the reader's mind, to Truman's broken record on Manichaean rhetoric. Paradoxically, Truman asserted that Americans were "fighting for the proposition that peace shall be the law of this earth"; stated a stark polarity, "the free and peace-loving nations of the world faced two possible courses"; raised the fearful specter of the domino theory, "We cannot hope to maintain our own freedom if freedom elsewhere is wiped out"; and denounced communism in artistic language that featured alliteration, "Communist imperialism preaches peace but practices aggression."

More importantly, however, Truman again asserted his historical analogy, which he first used in his July 19 speech, for military action in Korea. "If the history of the 1930's teaches us anything," and Truman assumed that it did, "it is that appeasement of dictators is the sure road to world war. If aggression were allowed to succeed in Korea, it would be an open invitation to new acts of aggression elsewhere." Later in the speech, HST reiterated that message: "Hitler and the Japanese generals miscalculated badly, 10 years ago, when they thought we would not be able to use our economic power effectively to defeat aggression." And then, as *Time* noted, "The President slowed down to let the next sentence sink in: 'Let would-be aggressors make no such mistake today.'"[38]

The logic of Truman's history lesson bears examination. Since Truman was not appeasing dictators, it may be reasonably assumed that he meant to prevent a third world war. In August, Navy Secretary Francis Matthews floated a trial balloon of his own for a so-called preventive war. With regard to the Soviet Union, Matthews urged the United States to "pay any price—even the price of instituting a war to compel cooperation for peace," for, according to Matthews, such a strategy would "win for us a popular title. . . . We would become the first aggressors for peace."[39] Needless to say, although it was a kind of a logical extension of Truman's inflated rhetoric against the Soviet Union and his ill-defined war aims, Matthew's prescription for peace was a veritable example of newspeak. Truman quickly disavowed the Navy secretary's speech, and did so again in his September 1 speech, to which we now turn.

In the latter part of his address, Truman listed eight points, in what might be termed HST's penchant for government by enumeration, that were "what we believe in and what we are trying to do. We also want the rest of the world to understand clearly our aims and our hopes." Truman's second point was a dramatic departure from the status quo, for he stated "We believe the Koreans have a right to be free, independent, and united—as they want to be. Under the direction and guidance of the United Nations, we, with others, will do our part to help them enjoy that right. The United States has no other aim in Korea." Since the North Koreans were attempting to unite the two Koreas under communism, Truman's vision of a united Korea was obviously a pro-United States government that professed anti-communism whether or not it was democratically free by U.S. standards of democracy (as was South Korea!).

Truman's third point was a statement of U.S. war aims, and more rhetorical bluster against the Communists. "We do not want the fighting in Korea to expand into a general war," Truman pledged, but he warned "It will not spread unless Communist imperialism draws other armies and governments into the fight of the aggressors against the United Nations." Thus, Truman held fast to his limited war, police action theory, but it was hard to reconcile his second point with the third point. If Truman did not want a general war, then why did he tempt fate in redefining the war to reunite the two Koreas?

And Truman's seventh point was a reiteration of his repudiation of Navy Secretary Matthew's trial balloon of a so-called preventive war. "We do not believe in aggressive or preventive war," Truman clarified for the people, "Such war is the weapon of dictators, not of free democratic countries like the United States." Whereas Matthews had advocated a kind of active-preventive war, wherein the United States would strike first against the Soviet Union, Truman's definition of a preventive war was a kind of reactive-preventive war that foiled Communist aggression after being initiated by them in Korea. However, Truman evidently overlooked the fact that his second point, which was to unite Korea under a non-Communist government, moved beyond a reactive-preventive war to an aggressive war.

And then, donning the ministerial mantle of Manichaeanism in his speech's peroration, Truman waxed priestly:

> The task which has fallen upon our beloved country is a great one. In carrying it out, we ask God to purge us of all selfishness and meanness, and to give us strength and courage for the days ahead. We pray God to give us strength, ability, and wisdom for the great task we face.

Assumedly, Americans would have affirmed an amen.

NSC-81

September was a watershed month in the Korean War. General MacArthur finally held the line at the Pusan Perimeter, and then on September 15, MacArthur invaded the port of Inchon, captured Seoul, and soon had the Communists back to the border from whence they came.

The Security Council's resolution of the *status quo ante bellum* had been achieved. In hindsight, the Truman administration could have proclaimed a joint United Nations-United States victory because North Korea had been expelled from the South. (Perhaps President George Bush remembered this historical precedent as a contributing motivation to end the Iraqi war without going to Bagdad for Saddam Hussein.)

At this juncture, though, the Truman administration took a fateful step. This step was previewed in his September 1 speech in which his second point pledged to reunite Korea. Truman signed NSC-81 in late September 1950. NSC-81 committed the United States to roll back communism in North Korea. NSC-81 was a logical extension of NSC-48, but applied to a specific purpose and location. NSC-81 was the rationale for removing the Communists altogether from Korea and uniting Korea under a non-Communist government that was favorable to the United States. General MacArthur had championed such a program, and the United Nations finally, but reluctantly, endorsed the plan. "Thus," as Bruce Cumings commented, "began the one serious attempt in postwar history to demolish an established Communist regime."[40]

But the Chinese, not the Soviets, stood behind the North Koreans, and gave intimations that China would enter the war if North Korea was invaded. The Truman administration disregarded these warnings as bluster. At Truman's behest, MacArthur ordered UN troops to advance toward China, and they reached the border at the Yalu River in late October, only to be pushed back by a combined Chinese-Korean army. MacArthur launched another counteroffensive, which was supposed to be his final thrust, and UN troops advanced back to the Yalu River in late November. But, true to their word, North Korean and Chinese forces struck back, hurled MacArthur's forces downward, recaptured the North Korean capital, and in early January 1952, retook Seoul. It was, according to Cochran, "the greatest defeat suffered by American arms since the Battle of Manassas."[41]

However, in the interim, Truman had been beating the war tocsin in speeches that merit attention. On September 9, Truman took to the airwaves to explain to the American people his domestic policies with regard to the war.[42] But his most significant speech during this time was delivered in San Francisco upon his return from Wake Island.

ADDRESS AT WAR MEMORIAL OPERA HOUSE, OCTOBER 17, 1950

In late August 1950, General MacArthur took it upon himself, at the coy invitation of the Veterans of Foreign Wars (VFW), to send a letter to the VFW's national convention. In that letter, MacArthur gratuitously criticized the Truman administration's position with regard to Formosa, which was to keep Chiang Kai-shek out of the war so as not to antagonize Red China. Truman ordered MacArthur to rescind the letter, which

MacArthur did, but it was too late, for the letter was made public before MacArthur could withdraw it. At the time, Truman considered relieving MacArthur of his Korean command.[43]

When Truman decided to visit MacArthur on Wake Island, October 15, many saw it as a political move. The November elections were looming, and Truman wanted to associate himself and the Democratic party positively with the highly esteemed MacArthur. In this respect, Truman was prescient, but hapless, for the Republicans cut the Democrat's majority in the Senate from twelve to two, one of whom was newly elected Senator Richard Nixon of California, and ninety-two to thirty-six in the House.[44] Truman left Wake Island with MacArthur's assurances that the Soviet Union and Red China would not intervene in Korea as UN forces pressed to the Yalu River.[45]

At San Francisco's War Memorial Opera House, according to Ray McKerrow, Truman "exuded confidence and unbridled optimism."[46] By now it is too tedious to recount the content of Manichaean rhetoric in Truman's Korean speeches, of which this address is no exception. Rather, the focus is on how NSC-81 functioned fully in this address.

Early in his speech, Truman told his audience that "I am confident that these [UN] forces will soon restore peace to the whole of Korea."[47] It was not just South Korea anymore, but the entire Korean peninsula. Lest anyone miss the point, Truman later spelled it out in full detail. Name dropping MacArthur for persuasive purposes, Truman allowed that "we talked about plans for establishing a 'unified, independent, and democratic' government" in Korea.

With sanguine assurances from MacArthur, who claimed "organized resistance throughout Korea will be ended by Thanksgiving,"[48] having disregarded Red China's public warnings, and, as we shall soon learn, egged on by even the liberal media, Truman, full of bravado, assured the American people that his supernation rhetoric would soon be reality:

> We seek no territory or special privilege in Korea or anywhere else. We have no aggressive designs in Korea or in any other place in the Far East or elsewhere. And I want that to be perfectly clear to the whole world. . . . The only victory we seek is the victory of peace. . . . They [North Koreans] continue to put up stubborn, but futile resistance. . . . The power of the Korean Communists to resist effectively will soon come to an end.

On the basis of an assumed military victory in Korea, Truman was emboldened to play semantic games. For all of his pious protestations to the contrary, it was the United States and the United Nations that now played the role of aggressor. Truman's definition of peace was in reality a war of aggression (NSC-81) to remove Communist North Koreans from power and to install an anti-communist regime in Korea. (Following this line of reasoning, President Bush's decision to stop the Iraqi war was justified, for to do otherwise would have opened him and the United Nations to a charge of aggression.)

On that article of faith of military success, elements of the liberal media promoted the unification of Korea. For instance, the *Nation* editorialized that North and South Korea should be unified under a UN trusteeship. To the *Nation*'s credit, it recognized the implications of Truman's supernation rhetoric because the "known facts about Syngman Rhee's unstable and unpopular regime" vitiated a unified Korea under his regime; nevertheless, the *Nation* misjudged the probabilities of Communist intervention: "But if the Russians or Chinese should commit their own forces to the struggle they would do so knowing that they were inviting general war, and that is a price Moscow is not prepared to pay."[49] The *Nation* was at least half correct.

The *New Republic*, another liberal organ, also called for a united Korea along the general lines envisioned by the *Nation*. Similarly, the *New Republic* misinterpreted Communist motives:

> If the Chinese refuse to replace them [North Koreans] as Soviet cannon fodder, Russia faces three choices: to negotiate a settlement; to watch MacArthur advance to the Siberian border; or to reoccupy North Korea at the risk of a third world war. Russian and China do not want a world war now.[50]

The *New Republic* was also correct by half.

Even more sanguine was *Life*, for it portrayed the Communists as smaller than life and the United States as larger than life:

> Any counsel of timidity is, in our opinion, quite worthless. . . . The danger of Chinese or Soviet intervention if the North Korean Communists are pressed close to the Manchurian border is, in our curbstone opinion, negligible. China's Mao Tse-tung has seen what American air and seapower can do; he might be quaking in his boots lest this power be placed at the disposal of Chiang Kai-shek on Formosa. As for the Russians, they

would hardly choose North Korea as the spot to touch off
a world conflagration unless they are immediately planning
to go to war with the West anyway.[51]

So much for curbstone opinions.

Ironically, Truman, MacArthur, and the media did not heed
Chinese Foreign Minister Zhou Enlai's public warning on September 29:
"The Chinese people absolutely will not tolerate foreign aggression, nor
will they supinely tolerate seeing their neighbor being savagely invaded by
the imperialists."[52] True to their word, the Chinese Communists joined
their North Korean comrades in November and sent the UN forces reeling
back.

But by February 1951, UN ground forces under the command of
General Matthew Ridgway recaptured Seoul. At this juncture, China
indicated that it was interested only in maintaining North Korea. The
Truman administration listened to China this time, and decided to forego
the rollback policy of NSC-81 in favor of a cease fire that would maintain
a divided Korea. In effect, the United States was back where it had been
in September 1950, where Truman might have left well enough alone.

CONCLUSION

The persuasive problem that Harry Truman had with the Korean
War was, according to McKerrow, a "juxtaposition of two incompatible
realities: a rhetoric of limited war and one of victory."[53] McKerrow did
not account for the two distinct stages, June to September 1950, and after
September 1950, that characterized Truman's Korean War rhetorics.
Rather, it was an instance, in the first stage, of Truman's rhetoric running
to catch up with military actions; and then, at a crucial juncture, it was a
instance, in the second stage, of HST's rhetoric running ahead of military
capabilities. In the first situation, the definition of limited war and victory
were linguistically consistent. But in the second circumstance, Truman
was constrained from changing the definition of limited war to achieve a
redefined victory. (If this assertion is not taken at its face value here, it
will be warranted in the next chapter on Truman versus MacArthur.)

Under the original UN Security Council's sanction, achieving the
status quo ante bellum was the victory that Truman talked about in his
early messages and speeches on the subject. When he achieved the
announced end of driving the North Koreans from the South in September,
Truman achieved his victory with a limited war (or police action), as he
had consistently defined the United Nation's aims. Truman uttered no
incompatible realities with respect to victory via limited war from June to

September 1950.

Truman created a new and altogether different persuasive problem when he decided to enact NSC-81. Although the National Security Council, the military, General MacArthur, the hawks in the Democratic and Republican party, the United Nations Security Council, reluctantly it might be added, and the media supported the transformation of a limited war (to achieve the *status quo ante bellum*) into an aggressive war (the destruction of the North Korean government), all figured that the Soviets and/or the Red Chinese would not enter the fray. On that assumption of a quick military victory, however misguided it was, Truman miscalculated. Without changing the constraints and definition of a limited war (there would be no UN attacks on China nor would Formosa enter the war), Truman escalated the definition of victory: Victory, redefined, now meant, under NSC-81, the capitulation of the Communists and the unification of Korea under a pro-U.S. government. All of this, as everyone hoped and agreed, could be achieved within the framework of the old definition of a limited war. When the military options were not escalated to match the increased rhetorical expectations, then the incompatible realities ensued, which is the subject of the next chapter. Therefore, McKerrow was only correct in his assessment of the second stage of Truman's Korean War rhetorical strategy.

Another point worth making, which has not been hitherto stated with regard to Truman's Korean War rhetoric, is how his Manichaean, supernation rhetoric played in Peoria. In a sense, Truman was a victim of his own success. In July 1950, over 80 percent of the people supported Truman's actions in Korea.[54] Although cause and effects are always tenuous, the case can be made that Truman achieved admirably well his aims from June to September 1950. The Truman administration assumed, the American people presumed, and Truman's Manichaean, supernation rhetoric reinforced such conjecture, that the Soviet Union, the villain, called the shots in North Korea. In hindsight, that assumption was mistaken, although Truman was advised that the Soviets would not intervene, which might have been the tip that they did not control the North Koreans as commonly thought. Nevertheless, the motivational nexus between Truman's denigration of the Soviets and the American people's willingness to assent to such characterizations clouded and controlled everyone's vision, and especially Harry Truman's, as to the real lead actors in the Manichaean morality play. Once the second act of the drama got under way in November 1950, there was little Harry Truman could do to disenthrall himself and his administration from a play he could no longer manage. Unfortunately for Truman, an increasing number of Americans became dissatisfied with the script, wanted it rewritten, and craved for their lead star, General Douglas MacArthur, to assume center stage. When Truman fired the prima donna, many Americans wanted to dismiss the director of America's most unsuccessful war.

NOTES

1. Bruce Cumings, "Korean War," in *The Harry S. Truman Encyclopedia*, p. 202.

2. James L. Stokesbury, *A Short History of the Korean War* (New York: William Morrow, 1988), p. 35.

3. Norman A. Graebner, "NSC 68," in *The Harry S. Truman Encyclopedia*, pp. 261-262.

4. Bert Cochran, *Harry Truman and the Crisis Presidency* (New York: Funk and Wagnalls, 1973), p. 289.

5. Robert J. Donovan, *Nemesis: Truman and Johnson in the Coils of War in Asia* (New York: St. Martin's-Marek, 1984), p. 49.

6. "Statement by the President on the Violation of the 38th Parallel in Korea," *HST, 1950*, pp. 491-492.

7. "Statement by the President on the Situation in Korea," June 27, 1950, *HST: 1950*, p. 492.

8. Margaret Truman, *Harry S. Truman* (New York: William Morrow, 1973), p. 461.

9. Harold B. Hinton, "Legislators Hail Action by Truman," *New York Times*, June 28, 1950, p. 1.

10. "Exchange of Messages with Governor Dewey Concerning U.S. Action in Korea," *HST: 1950*, p. 496.

11. "The President's News Conference of June 29, 1950," *HST: 1950*, p. 503.

12. Burton I. Kaufman, *The Korean War: Challenges in Crisis, Credibility, and Command* (Philadelphia: Temple University Press, 1986), p. 68.

13. "The President's News Conference of June 29, 1950," *HST: 1950*, p. 504.

14. Truman, *Harry S. Truman*, p. 467.

15. Ryan, *Franklin D. Roosevelt's Rhetorical Presidency*, pp. 35-36.

16. Cochran, *Harry Truman and the Crisis Presidency*, p. 314.

17. Kaufman, *The Korean War*, pp. 68-70.

18. McCoy, *The Presidency of Harry S. Truman*, p. 229.

19. Cochran, *Harry Truman and the Crisis Presidency*, p. 316.

20. Donovan, *Nemesis*, p. 53.

21. Kaufman, *The Korean War*, p. 70.

22. "Special Message to the Congress Reporting on the Situation in Korea," July 19, 1950, *HST: 1950*, p. 528.

23. "Radio and Television Address to the American People on the Situation in Korea," July 19, 1950, *HST: 1950*, pp. 538, 540.

24. "Message to Congress and People," July 19, 1950, files of Charles S. Murphy, presidential speech file, box 7, HSTL.

25. Papers of Harry S. Truman, speech file, box 29, July-Aug, 1950, original reading copy, pp. 3, 6, 14, HSTL.

26. President's secretary's file, speech file, longhand notes, box 49, third draft, p. 2, HSTL; see also *HST: 1950*, p. 537.

27. President's secretary's files, speech file, longhand notes, box 49, third draft, p. 4, HSTL; see also *HST: 1950*, p. 538.

28. President's secretary's files, speech file, longhand notes, box 49, fourth draft, insert, p. 4, HSTL.

29. President's secretary's file, speech file, longhand notes, box 49, fourth draft, p. 10, HSTL; see also *HST: 1950*, p. 540.

30. President's secretary's files, speech file, longhand notes, box 49, fourth draft, pp. 13-14 (the paragraph was moved from p. 13 to p. 14); see also *HST: 1950*, p. 541.

31. Windt, "The Presidency and Speeches on International Crises: Repeating the Rhetorical Past," p. 67.

32. President's personal file, PPF-200, box 334, HSTL.

33. "The Fabric of Peace," *Time*, July 31, 1950, p. 10.

34. George F. Kennan, *Memoirs: 1925-1950* (Boston: Little, Brown, 1967), p. 500.

35. Cochran, *Harry Truman and the Crisis Presidency*, p. 313.

36. McCoy, *The Presidency of Harry S. Truman*, p. 223.

37. "Radio and Television Report to the American People on the Situation in Korea," September 1, 1950, *HST: 1950*, pp. 609-614.

38. "The Days Ahead," *Time*, September 11, 1950, p. 22.

39. "Instituting a War," *Time*, September 4, 1950, pp. 11-12.

40. Cumings, "Korean War," pp. 202-203.

41. Cochran, *Harry Truman and the Crisis Presidency*, p. 324.

42. "Radio and Television Address to the American People Following the Signing of the Defense Production Act," September 9, 1950, *HST: 1950*, pp. 626-631; see also McCoy, *The Presidency of Harry S. Truman*, p. 230.

43. For background and a copy of MacArthur's letter, see "Two Voices," *Time*, September 4, 1950, pp. 9-10; see also Truman, *Memoirs, II*, pp. 354-358.

44. "The National Pendulum Swings," *Life*, November 20, 1950, p. 44.

45. Kaufman, *The Korean War*, pp. 89-92.

46. Ray E. McKerrow, "Truman and Korea: Rhetoric in the Pursuit of Victory," *Central States Speech Journal* 28 (1977): 4.

47. "Address in San Francisco at the War Memorial Opera House," October 17, 1950, *HST: 1950*, pp. 673-679.

48. Quoted in Donovan, *Nemesis*, p. 89.

49. "The Shape of Things," *Nation*, September 23, 1950, p. 257.

50. "Peace Aims for Korea," *New Republic*, September 25, 1950, p. 5.

51. "But What Comes Next?" *Life*, October 9, 1950, p. 38.

52. Quoted in Donovan, *Nemesis*, p. 89.

53. McKerrow, "Truman and Korea: Rhetoric in the Pursuit of Victory," p. 12.

54. John M. Fenton, *In Your Opinion* (Boston: Little, Brown, 1960), p. 89.

3
The President versus the General

At 10:30 P.M., April 11, 1951, President Truman took to the airwaves to deliver his Preventing a New World War speech, which was his response to preempt further attacks on his policy and to defend himself against the storm of protest that resulted from his dismissal of General Douglas MacArthur. Here are some of the more tepid letters and telegrams that Truman received after he gave his speech:

> Who are you trying to kid?
> And I use the 'dear' only as a form of salutation.
> Your speeches stink and you stink.
> I cannot help but feel you are 100% wrong.

Here is one letter that caustically communicated what many Americans felt about Truman (but not necessarily about his daughter, Margaret): "Your lousy speech over the radio trying to clear yourself of the blundering mistakes you made at the expense of General MacArthur are as stupid and dumb as your daughter's sand paper singing voice."[1] Barton Bernstein and Allen Matusow observed that "the public outcry against Truman's action was immediate, emotional, and rancorous"; Republicans in Congress actively considered impeachment; and Truman's effigy was hanged in San Gabriel, California.[2] Even before Truman delivered his speech, the White House received about 2,301 (67 percent) letters and telegrams against MacArthur's dismissal and only 1,126 (33 percent) for it.[3] In fact, Truman anticipated the attack because "he had thought for a long time and very heavily on the consequences of the action and determined that it was a necessary and proper action, and that he couldn't avoid the criticism that inevitably followed."[4]

PRECIPITATION OF THE CRISIS

One will recall that General MacArthur wrote a letter in August 1950, to the Veterans of Foreign Wars in which the general gratuitously criticized the president's policies with regard to Formosa. Although MacArthur complied with Truman's order to withdraw the letter (with the damage already done as it was published before MacArthur could retract it), the general could not abide silence.

In early March 1951, President Truman, with the concurrence of the Joint Chiefs of Staff (JCS) and to the particular relief of the British, determined to arrange a cease-fire with the Chinese on the basis of the *status quo ante bellum* of June 1950. MacArthur was appraised of Truman's initiative by the JCS. Hitherto, MacArthur had contented himself with issuing statements that countered Truman's policy,[5] but on March 24, MacArthur cast aside all caution. Perhaps he had read a Gallup poll in March that showed only 28 percent of Americans approved Truman's handling of his job.[6] He issued an unauthorized statement, amounting to an ultimatum, that called for the Chinese and Koreans to surrender immediately face annihilation of their forces. Rather than fire the general immediately, Truman reminded MacArthur of the president's December 6, 1950, directive to clear all statements with Washington, and reminded him not to make further unauthorized statements.[7]

The straw that broke the general's back was his letter to Representative Joseph Martin (R-Massachusetts), the minority leader of the House. In early March, Martin had requested a letter from MacArthur on his views in the Far East. MacArthur willingly obliged, but he did not indicate to Martin that his letter was not for public consumption. In fine, MacArthur urged, among other military maneuvers, unleashing Chiang Kai-shek's forces in Formosa to invade China, and then ended his letter with the now famous line: "As you [Martin] point out, we must win. There is no substitute for victory."[8] Martin read the general's letter on the floor of the House on April 5, and Truman thereafter decided to fire the general for insubordination.[9]

Whether Truman should have fired MacArthur is debatable, but the Constitutional issue has always been clear. Unless Truman relieved the general, a grave Constitutional precedent could have ennervated civilian control over the military. So, given the fact that Truman had the Constitutional power to fire the general, which was supported by the JCS and Truman's close advisers, the question arises: Why did President Truman bother to deliver his speech on April 11, 1951?

From the perspective of the rhetorical presidency, it was to gain and maintain support for his policy. But which policy? Since Truman was under attack for firing MacArthur, one would resonably expect Truman to defend the dismissal in his speech. Yet, an exmination of the production of the relevant speech drafts will demonstrate why that was not the case. In studying Truman's interaction with his speech staff and Secretary of State Dean Acheson, one can evaluate the preparation of this address with an eye toward its success.[10] The thesis is that Truman should have forthrightly defended MacArthur's dismissal but was partially dissuaded from doing so by Acheson. As delivered, the speech basically defended the Truman-Acheson Korean War policy, and not Truman's dismissal of the general. Truman would have been more persuasive if he allowed his speech staff to give specific reasons in the speech for relieving MacArthur. The firing demanded from Truman a direct defense for that action, and not a general justification of the Korean War.

THE PRODUCTION OF THE SPEECH DRAFTS

On Friday afternoon, April 6, one day after Martin read his letter on the floor of the House, Truman requested Acheson, Secretary of Defense George Marshall, General Omar Bradley (chairman of the JCS), and Averell Harriman to confer with him on the crisis. On Saturday morning, April 7, they informed Truman that MacArthur should be relieved of his command, a decision that Truman had already and independently reached.[11]

Robert Walrath Tufts produced the first draft, which reached the White House on Tuesday morning, April 10. The draft was probably prepared at Acheson's request, for Tufts was a member of the policy planning staff in the State Department.[12] Tufts outlined the history and defended the rationale for the administration's Korean War policy in a nineteen page legal-sized draft, but he never mentioned nor defended MacArthur's firing. Acheson also worked on this draft and urged Truman to accept it.

David Bell, speech writer and administrative assistant to the president, recalled from a 9:30 A.M., Wednesday, April 11, speech staff meeting with Truman that HST's reaction to the Tufts-Acheson draft was not favorable. Truman wanted his own staff to rework the Tufts-Acheson draft:

> He said he had read it, and Mrs. Truman had read it, and
> then he read it again. As far as he could see, it was just
> a lot of words. Murphy mentioned that Acheson had

worked on it himself, and felt it was in pretty good shape.
The P. said yes, he knew that, but he told Acheson we'd
have to work it over to suit ourselves. This was a
considerable relief to us, as we had been afraid we'd have
to battle Acheson down to the wire.[13]

Truman's reaction was no doubt unfavorable because Acheson did
not justify the firing. Acheson wanted the speech to focus solely on
Korean War policy: "The decision to relieve MacArthur was Truman's
alone; however, in terms of policy, the decision had for its prime
consequence the removal of Acheson's only formidable opponent to
keeping the war in Korea limited."[14] Accordingly, Acheson specifically
advised Truman not to mention MacArthur: "Murphy then brought up the
subject of mentioning MacA—asking if the President had made up his
mind, recalling that Acheson had recommended against it the previous
afternoon, and the President had tentatively agreed to that course, and
saying that he (Murphy) felt strongly enough about it that if it was felt that
MacA couldn't be mentioned, he would recommend that the Pres. not give
the speech at all."[15]

The speech staff was correctly concerned over battling Acheson
down to the wire over mentioning MacArthur. They sensed a need for the
president to defend the general's firing rather than HST's being the
mouthpiece for justifying a limited war policy in Acheson's own words.
Accordingly, the staff had produced its own draft in the interim because it
handed Truman its draft to read: "The President said he wasn't sure he
should make the speech, and felt we should defer the question of
mentioning MacA, till 3:15, when he would meet with us and settle the
whole thing. In the meantime, he would read our draft (which Murphy
had just handed him)."[16] In line with the thesis question asked earlier,
observe that Truman wondered why he should deliver the speech at all,
which probably hinged on whether, and to what extent, he should mention
the general.

Because Truman was dissatisfied with the Acheson-Tuft draft, he
directed his staff to produce a draft. David Bell and Charles Murphy,
speech writer and special counsel to the president, were the White House
writers for this purpose. In overview, each wrote his own drafts and then
they collaborated on some drafts to furnish Truman with a finished draft
that they handed him to read at their meeting.

Murphy produced two drafts that had his initials on them. His first
draft, dated April 10, 1951, was based on the Tufts-Acheson draft, but
Murphy added six pages of handwritten materials plus many
emendations.[17] Even with these changes, Murphy still retained their basic

history and rationale for the Korean War policy, and he did not mention MacArthur. On a clean typed copy of draft one, Murphy produced a second draft, dated 4-11-51.[18] Upon reflection, Murphy wrote an insert about MacArthur's dismissal to be placed at the very end of the speech. He indicated that MacArthur was relieved because he did not agree with the administration's Korean War policy, and because Truman did not want anyone to be confused about its strategy in Korea:

> I have thought long and hard about this question of extending the war in Asia. I have discussed it many times with the ablest military advisors in the country. I believe with all my heart that the course we are following is the best course. I believe that we must try to limit the war to Korea for these vital purposes: To make sure that the precious lives of our fighting men are not wasted; to see that the security of our country and the free world is not needlessly jeopardized; and to prevent a third world war.
>
> A number of recent events have made it evident that General MacArthur did not agree with that policy. I have therefore considered it essential to relieve General MacArthur so that there would be no doubt or confusion in the minds of anyone what our high purpose is.
>
> I took the action with the greatest reluctance, but the cause of world peace is more important than any individual.[19]

It was certainly better to mention MacArthur at the end of the address than not at all. However, by placing the dismissal justification at the end, Murphy succeeded in stressing, with the primacy effect, the Korean War policy, and minimizing, by burying it in the end of the speech, why MacArthur was fired. Also, Murphy's language implied that MacArthur was dismissed only because he differed with the administration's policy, which played to those who claimed that Truman's policy was wrong, which only exacerbated Truman's problems! Murphy also failed to mention that the JCS, the general's boss after the president, also agreed that MacArthur should be dismissed. As when Truman decided to go it alone in the Korean War without a congressional imprimatur, this is a case where Truman should have shared the responsibility with, and hence deflected some of the blame to, the JCS. At any rate, a much stronger case could have been made against MacArthur. Bell made such a indictment in his draft.

Bell produced two drafts. He composed the first one on April 10.

Bell based his draft on Murphy's first typed draft. But most significantly, Bell added an introduction that stated a detailed rationale for MacArthur's dismissal. His introduction immediately arrested the audience's attention, in the context of the dismissal crisis, by indicating that the president would explain why he fired the general. Bell stressed MacArthur's insubordination to his commander in chief:

> My Fellow Americans:
>
> Two days ago, I relieved General of the Army Douglas MacArthur of his command in the Far East, and appointed Lieutenant General Matthew Ridgway to succeed him. I want to tell you why I did that.
>
> General MacArthur is a very great soldier. If he had confined himself to his duties and responsibilities as a military commander, I would have been glad to have him in command as long as he would stay.
>
> But General MacArthur did not confine himself to his job as a military commander. Instead, time and time again, in violation of direct orders, he made official pronouncements on foreign policy—pronouncements which, if carried out in my judgment, would spread the conflict in Korea into a full-scale war in Asia. Such a course is in direct conflict with the policy of the United States and the United Nations. We are doing our utmost to prevent the Korean conflict from growing into a third world war. We will do everything we can to make this policy succeed. The issue of peace is far greater than any individual.
>
> General MacArthur's place in history as one of our greatest commanders is fully established. The Nation owes him a debt of gratitude for the distinguished and exceptional services which he has rendered his country in posts of great responsibility. For that reason, I deeply regret the necessity for the action I felt compelled to take in his case.
>
> Full and vigorous debate on matters of national policy is essential under the constitutional system of our free democracy. It is fundamental, however, that military commanders must be governed by the policies and directives issued to them in the manner provided by our laws and Constitution.[20]

Bell's justification for the dismissal was better than Murphy's. Bell captured the essence of HST's plain speaking when he stated the problem and then had Truman tell the audience why he solved it in that manner. Bell's introduction stated clearly that MacArthur's policy was insubordinate and inimical to American interests. He then used Murphy's Korean War history to reinforce the wisdom and correctness of MacArthur's dismissal by starkly contrasting Truman's policy with MacArthur's in Korea, which would cause a third world war. By placing the defense at the very beginning, Bell met the dismissal crisis forthrightly, for it was justified on Constitutional grounds, which were not debatable, rather than on whether the administration's policy was correct, which was quite disputable. Moreover, Bell's discussion of the insubordination charge was more direct than Murphy's watered-down version. Bell produced a second draft, but the MacArthur paragraphs remained the same.[21]

From the third draft (actually the second draft) a fourth draft (actually the third draft) was produced on April 11. This draft was probably a joint effort by Bell and Murphy because neither's initials are on this draft. One page is significant with regard to MacArthur. It is a typed insert to replace the original page, and several emendations on it are worth noting (deletions are bracketed and additions are italicized):

> I have therefore considered it essential to relieve General MacArthur so that there would be no doubt or confusion in the mind of anyone as to [what our high purpose is] *the real purpose and aim of our policy.*
>
> [I took this action with the greatest reluctance.] *It was with the deepest personal regret that I found myself compelled to take this action.* General MacArthur is one of our greatest military commanders. But the cause of world peace is more important than any individual.
>
> [Now that he has been relived from active duty, I wish the General well. He will, of course, be free to state his personal views on our foreign policy to whatever extent he desires.][22]

Bell produced this page because the paragraph beginning "Now that he has . . ." appears *de novo* in this draft and it comes from Bell's first draft, but it was not used in his second draft. Note that in the first paragraph, there was evidently a Freudian slip: "our high purpose," replete with supernation evocations, became "the real purpose and aim," which smacked of expediency over principle.

Bell's forthright speech introduction must have been vetoed by the staff because it wished to honor Truman's tentative agreement with Acheson on not mentioning MacArthur. The passive voice ("I found myself compelled") was probably an effort to diffuse HST's responsibility that the active voice ("I took this action") implied. Nonetheless, the effort to disperse accountability could have been accomplished adroitly by alluding to the JCS, which had concurred with the commander in chief. Bell then attempted to work in a paragraph to show that as a civilian, MacArthur could state his foreign policy views without reprisal. But that paragraph was excised, too, probably because it inadvertently validated the conservative's charge that Truman fired MacArthur for his views, and it unfortunately diverted attention from the real issue: The general was insubordinate.

With the specter of Acheson's being against mentioning MacArthur, and with the president in tentative agreement, the speech staff must have believed that Murphy's watered-down version would be more palatable than Bell's version. This draft was retyped as the fourth draft (actually the fourth draft). Truman was handed the smooth copy of the fourth draft. This is the only draft that he corrected in his own handwriting, and all of his corrections appear in the final reading copy and no other changes were included in it.[23]

PRESIDENT TRUMAN'S EMENDATIONS

HST was satisfied with the speech and its minimal mentioning of MacArthur because he accepted it:

> You will recall that at the beginning of the afternoon conference the Pres. said he didn't see how he could make this speech—he had a date Thursday night, and Friday would be too close to the J-J dinner. When we all urged him to make it that night (Wed.) he laughed, and said something about us all ganging up on him but put up no real argument. I don't recall whether he said anything about our draft, but obviously he wouldn't have agreed to make the speech if he hadn't felt fairly comfortable about it.[24]

Truman made several changes on the draft, and they are significant because they illustrate his thinking at a critical time in American history. He crossed out words and substituted new ones, he made punctuation changes, and he excised whole sentences. Several emendations are worth noting. Truman underlined words and phrases that were important to him:

"to meet the attack in Korea and defeat it <u>there</u>"; "<u>The door is always open</u>"; "<u>But the cause of world peace is more important than any individual</u>"; "<u>We are only interested in real peace</u>"; and "That war can come if the communist rulers want it to come. <u>But this Nation and its allies will not be responsible for its coming.</u>"[25] He also communicated to his audience that the Communists were at fault for widening the war, and he took specific pains to denigrate them: "These were the troops they threw into battle when the North Korean [army was driven back] *communists were beaten*" and "The question we have to face is whether [this] *the communist* plan of conquest can be stopped without a general war."[26] Truman simplified the meaning in the following phrase: "If we were to do these things, we would [be enmeshed] *become entangled.*" He tried to make the text more optimistic by changing certain words to a more positive tone: "that it is the most [hopeful] *effective* course of action we can follow"; "these vital [purposes] *reasons*"; "But we [are] *will* not [interested] *engage* in appeasement"; and "for a practical way of [maintaining] *achieving* peace and security."[27]

These changes demonstrated that Truman made his speech staff's draft his own text by his final emendations. The staff still had ample time to prepare the reading copy from Truman's corrections in time for the late evening broadcast at 10:30 P.M. Truman also paid some minimal attention to the delivery of the speech because he practiced it at least once: Elsey remembered that Truman was alone in the Fish Room "reading the speech aloud to himself" before he went to the Oval Office to deliver it.[28]

The speech staff won a minor victory over Acheson with the mention of MacArthur at the end of the speech. Yet, the basic theme and rationale for the address derived from the Tufts-Acheson draft. Bell was thwarted in his attempt to focus the speech on defending the dismissal, for, as delivered, the speech accomplished the opposite effect.

THE SPEECH'S EFFECT

President Truman's dismissal of General MacArthur has been vindicated on Constitutional grounds. General Matthew Ridgway, who replaced MacArthur in Korea, analyzed the negative political-military outcome of MacArthur's "Grand Design"; Richard Rovere wrote that HST's "recall of General MacArthur, probably the one larger piece of work in his entire Administration where the initiative was clearly his own . . . was one that took considerable courage"; and Averell Harriman praised Truman's decision in the crisis: "President Truman was the one man who had the courage to step up and deal with it. It was one of the most courageous acts that any president did."[29]

Yet, contemporary support for the president's speech was weak. The White House mail statistics showed some favorable movement from the initial pro-con ratio of 32 percent to 68 percent, but the final figures were not reassuring: pro, 37,708 (45 percent) and con, 46,389 (55 percent).[30] Harris concluded the speech was not a success: "The speech did not produce a great volume of personal mail for the President nor did it create a wave of protest against MacArthur"; although MacArthur's dismissal was received quite favorably by the allies, David Rees observed that "the President was unable to project the historical necessity of his policy in political terms that would appeal to the public."[31]

By Truman's own standards, his speech was not successful. Irving Perlmeter, assistant press secretary to the president, indicated that Truman and his speech staff were cognizant of how they might best address the American listener: "He spoke for a purpose; to get some idea across; to get some result to occur and the impact of the speech, whether it would be understood, how it would be understood, and by whom it would be understood, were always central in the discussions."[32] Truman observed that the speaker should accomplish his persuasive goal: "I would say that the effective speaker is one who accomplishes what he sets out to do" and he believed Cicero's method was efficacious to do that: "I believe an audience approves of Cicero's method, which was to state his case and then prove it."[33] But no one has attempted to explain how the speech might have been more successful, which, James Andrews argued, is a function of the rhetorical critic: "The critic who is trained in rhetoric knows what *is* persuasive; when that critic enters into a controversy, it is to argue the question of what *should* be persuasive [Andrew's emphasis]."[34]

Borrowing the language from Cicero, Truman stated and proved the wrong case. His relative failure as a rhetorical president is attributable to his misdirected defense for firing MacArthur. HST should have stated and proved his case against the general. The defense should have primarily justified MacArthur's dismissal on Constitutional grounds. Bell's draft rightly emphasized the primacy of the Constitutional crisis. Truman later wrote that he fired MacArthur "because he wouldn't respect the authority of the President."[35] That was the real case that Bell realized had to be communicated to the American public in the context of the dismissal crisis. Howard K. Smith wisely perceived this necessity when he wrote that Truman's best defense for relieving the general depended on who was to be commander in chief: "But if he sticks doggedly to the point—do his opponents favor altering the basis of American government from Republicanism to Bonapartism—and reiterates it each time his enemies shift the conflict to other grounds, no honest American can do anything but

admit that Mr. Truman's decision was right."[36]   But the persuasive
problem was intensified with Truman defended the limited war policy first
and his firing of MacArthur second.

HST later assessed the salience of the topics in his speech. "I went
on the air on the evening of April 11," Truman wrote, "to restate the
government's policy to the American people. I explained why we were in
Korea and why we could not allow the Korean affair to become a general
all-out war. . . . I explained why it had become necessary to relieve
General MacArthur."[37] Since the speech stressed the limited war policy,
it was construed by the public to be a defense for that strategy rather than
as a primary defense for dismissing the general: "Harry Truman went on
the air with the best defense that Lawyer Acheson could give him.
Truman's argument gets it appeal from the fact that all sane men prefer
peace to war and a small war to a big war.   Truman's speech was
constructed to give the impression that MacArthur was in favor of
unlimited war while Truman was for limited war."[38]

In the context of the rhetorical situation of the dismissal
controversy, Americans tuned to their radios to learn why Truman fired
MacArthur. That situation demanded a defense for the dismissal and not
necessarily a broader defense for the limited war policy. Truman's speech
would have been better received by his American audience if Bell's rather
than Murphy's version of the Tufts-Acheson draft would have been
accepted. But it was not. Truman's delivered Acheson's speech that
stressed the limited war concept, and secondarily mentioned in a few lines
late in the speech why MacArthur was fired.

PREVENTING A THIRD WORLD WAR, APRIL 11, 1951

By now, the drone of supernation, Manichaean rhetoric that one
encounters in Truman's Korean War speeches must be deadening. So,
only the most egregious examples, and only a few of them, will be offered
to sustain the thesis. With these quickly dispatched, other and more
interesting rhetorical features of the speech will then be explicated.

Although by this time it was plainly clear to everyone that the
Chinese Communists were the culprits in Korea, Truman still insisted on
denigrating the Soviets: "The Communists in the Kremlin are engaged in
a monstrous conspiracy to stamp out freedom all over the world"; "Notice
that he [a Communist officer] used the word 'liberation.'   This is
Communist double-talk meaning 'conquest'"; a few lines later HST
repeated the charge in more colloquial language, "Again, liberation in
Commie language means conquest"; when, for good measure, it suited his
purposes, Truman vilified the whole Communist lot: "The dangers are

great. Make no mistake about it. Behind the North Koreans and Chinese Communists in the front lines stand additional millions of Chinese soldiers. And behind the Chinese stand the tanks, the planes, the submarines, the soldiers, and the scheming rulers of the Soviet Union."[39] Truman also alluded to supernation verities: "[I]t becomes a clear and present danger to the security and independence of every free nation"; "the ability of the whole free world to resist Communist aggression has been greatly improved"; and "Our resolute stand in Korea is helping the forces of freedom now fighting in Indo-China and other countries in that part of the world. It has already slowed down the time-table of conquest."

However, the speech contained other salient rhetorical features. As he had argued in his July 19 and September 1, 1950, speeches, Truman pressed the historical analogy to World War II as applicable to the Korean situation:

> The best time to meet the threat is in the beginning. It is easier to put out a fire in the beginning when it is small than after it has become a roaring blaze.
>
> And the best way to meet the threat of aggression is for the peace-loving nations to act together. If they don't act together, they are likely to be picked off, one by one.
>
> If they had followed the right policies in the 1930's—if the free countries had acted together, to crush the aggression of the dictators, and if they had acted in the beginning, when the aggression was small—there probably would have been no World War II.

Truman also used rhetorical repetition and restatement to inculcate his message, which lawyer Acheson gave him. Lest there be any confusion in Truman's Korean War policy, he stated his theme, with variations, at least ten times throughout the speech:

> We are trying to prevent a third world war.
>
> [B]efore they can result in a third world war.
>
> [T]he best way of stopping it without a general war.
>
> So far, we have prevented World War III.
>
> We are trying to prevent a world war—not to start one.

[W]e would be running a very grave risk of starting a general war.

[A] full scale war with Red China.

[T]o avoid an all out war.

[T]o prevent a third world war.

The free nations have united in their strength in an effort to prevent a third world war.

The president also marshalled a refutation section in his speech to preempt attacks on his Korean War policy. Taking the objections from MacArthur's mouth, Truman paraphrased the general and the objections of MacArthur's supporters: "But you may ask why can't we take other steps to punish the aggressor? Why don't we bomb Manchuria and China itself? Why don't we assist the Chinese National troops to land on the mainland of China?" This was a master stroke in rhetorical refutation, because these were the very steps that MacArthur advocated. Truman twice answered that such activities would start a third world war, but he offered no proof to warrant his claims. It just was the president's word against the general's, and many preferred MacArthur's. HST then concluded his refutation section with an appeal to traditional American values: "It may well be that, in spite of our best efforts, the Communists may spread the war. But it would be wrong, tragically wrong—for us to take the initiative in extending the war."

Mirabile dictu! What hypocrisy it must have seemed to the American people for Truman to assert piously in April 1951, that it would be wrong to extend the war a la MacArthur's plan, but Truman had no compunction in extending the war, back when the military situation looked rosier, in activating NSC-81! Indeed, without Truman's willingness to escalate the military equation, which he would not, then there was no hope of fulfilling the rhetorical expectations he had created, and the tiger devoured its rider.

Nor was Truman very clear about those rhetorical expectations of his war aims, so that there would be no MacArthurian confusion. Either Truman was confused in his own mind as to the war aims, or he purposefully tried to obfuscate what they were in an effort to appeal to different stripes of listeners; whatever the motivation, the war aims were chameleon-like. At the beginning of the speech, the June-September 1950, military aim was to defend South Korea: "And they warmly supported the decision of the Government to help the Republic of Korea against the

Communist aggressors. Now, many persons, even some who applauded our decision to defend Korea, have forgotten the basic reasons for our action." Toward the middle of the speech, Truman reiterated the original intent, which was "to resist the attack." But then, in the conclusion of his speech, Truman muddied the waters by metamorphosing the war. First, he listed three aims that suggested the June-September 1950, war aims: the fighting must stop, fighting must not break out again, and "there must be an end of the aggression." But then Truman immediately followed that sentence with the war aims of NSC-81: "A settlement founded upon these elements would open the way for the unification of Korea and the withdrawal of all foreign forces." But, Truman had already agreed to a cease-fire at the 38th parallel, so holding out this false hope was a crass political ploy or a shot in the foot. In the last few sentences of his speech, Truman finally defined the military aim: "That is our military objective—to repel the attack and to restore peace." But even this definition is problematical because the attack had been repelled once, in the fall of 1950, and then once again in early 1951. Since NSC-81 was unobtainable without the military commitment that Truman would not make, and for good reasons, he could not restore peace with a united Korea.

Hence, the speech as delivered, rather than defending Truman's firing of MacArthur, raised more problems than it solved. Truman could not have it both ways. In answer to the question posed at the beginning of this chapter, he probably would have done better not to deliver the speech as a general defense of the Korean War; or, wishing to explain his firing of MacArthur, Truman should have used Bell's draft.

CONCLUSION

One remaining issue must be considered, which concerns contemplating, from another perspective, whether Truman gave the best speech that could have been delivered.

As a consequence of being dismissed, General Douglas MacArthur returned to the United States a national hero. Hoping to needle the Truman administration, and with an eye toward the presidential elections in 1952, Republicans invited the general to address a joint session of Congress on April 19, 1951. MacArthur did not disappoint. He reached several rhetorical climaxes in his speech, entitled Don't Scuttle the Pacific, but the one that sent the Asia-first Republicans to their feet in jubilant cheering and applause was a line evocative of MacArthur's letter to Joe Martin, which had motivated Truman's final decision to fire MacArthur. With all of the smoldering emotion of which the general was capable, he implored the Congress:

But once war is forced upon us, there is no other
alternative than to apply every available means to bring it
to a swift end. War's very object is victory, not prolonged
indecision. In war there is no substitute for victory.[40]

The general was quite the orator, and he obtained a shortrange success that
was phenomenal, but not so with Harry Truman.

Truman's speech was in part an explanation for his firing of the
general and part an accusation against the general's policy, which Truman
thought would trigger a third world war. As delivered, it is advanced,
Truman's speech invited MacArthur to debate the president before
Congress on military policy, and it allowed the general to ignore the
insubordination issue. The claim is that Bell's draft would have forced
MacArthur to confront a rhetorical dilemma: He would have been
constrained to address the issue of insubordination, or to underscore, by
its conspicuous absence, his finessing the problem.

Against this thesis, Bernard Duffy argued that Truman wisely
avoided attacking the general frontally. Albeit, Duffy did recognize, "As
Ryan indicated, direct allegations of MacArthur's insubordination or
affirmation of the president's constitutional authority over the military were
obtrusively absent in Truman's speech."[41] Nevertheless, Duffy claimed
that Truman's releasing to the press, through Joseph Short, his press
secretary, documents at 1:00 A.M. on April 11 that detailed the five
instances in which MacArthur disobeyed orders, was sufficient: "Thus,
Truman presented both the reasoning for his decision and the supporting
evidence. For those who wanted to listen, Truman's legal case against
MacArthur was both clearly expressed and fully substantiated."[42] In fact,
Duffy invoked Truman himself who opined that "these papers stated the
case."[43]

If all Truman was interested in doing was stating his case, then
these released documents sufficed. Even so, Truman went easy on the
general, who was unable "to give his wholehearted support . . . in matters
pertaining to his official duties," because Truman believed it was
fundamental that "military commanders must be governed by the policies
and directives issued to them in the manner provided by our laws and
Constitution."[44] If one deems the release of the documents as efficacious,
then HST's political instincts were perhaps better than his speech staff's,
for, as will be recalled, Truman did not want to deliver a speech. But,
Truman acquiesced in delivering an address (one assumes that the staff did
not reason that the documents sufficed to state the case). Therefore, we
turn to the second subject of whether the address was the best one that
could have been given.

Ironically, Duffy confirmed the thesis that Truman should have frontally attacked the general. The contention is that such an attack would have forced MacArthur's hand. "Thus," Duffy wrote, "MacArthur evaded the very issue that Ryan says would have been Truman's best argument: that in firing MacArthur, Truman had exercised appropriately his constitutional authority after the general had exceeded his. It was fortunate for MacArthur that a great many people were as willing to blame the president for the Korean stalemate as he was and that the constitutional issues was not one that seemed to concern most people at the time"; moreover, later in his essay Duffy acknowledged that "MacArthur skillfully shaped his speech to exploit the audience's frustrations with the Korean War and their strong identification with him, while ignoring the narrow issue of his Constitutional right to oppose the Truman administration."[45] Thus, it seems that Duffy inadvertently validated the thesis he meant to dispute.

The closing remarks are left, not to Truman, but to two five-star generals. The first is General Douglas MacArthur. In testifying before the Congress, he indicated who better understood the nature of the Korean War—the president or the general:

Senator Brien McMahon [D-Connecticut].   You see, General, what I want to find out from you is this—that if you happen to be wrong this time and we go into all-out war, I want to find out how you propose in your own mind to defend the American Nation against that war.

General MacArthur.   That doesn't happen to be my responsibility, Senator. My responsibilities were in the Pacific, and the joint Chiefs of Staff and the various agencies of this Government are working day and night for an over-all solution to the global problem.

Now I am not familiar with their studies.   I haven't gone into it. I have been desperately occupied over on the other side of the world, and to discuss in detail things that I haven't ever superficially touched doesn't contribute in any way, shape, or manner to the information of this committee or anybody else.

Senator McMahon. General, I think you make the point very well that I want to make; that the Joint Chiefs of Staff, and the President of the United States, the Commander in Chief, has to look at this thing on a global basis and a global defense.

You as a theater commander by your own

statement have not made that kind of study, and yet you advise us to push forward with a course of action that may involve us in that global conflict.

General MacArthur. Everything that is involved in international relationships, Senator, amounts to a gamble, risk. You have to take risks.

Senator McMahon. I couldn't agree with you more.[46]

The second, well known statement is from General Omar Bradley, Chairman of the Joint Chiefs of Staff:

Red China is not the powerful nation seeking to dominate the world. Frankly, in the opinion of the Joint Chiefs of Staff, this strategy would involve us in the wrong war, at the wrong place, at the wrong time, and with the wrong enemy.[47]

NOTES

1. Selected letters and telegrams, president's personal files, box 340, HSTL.

2. *The Truman Administration*, edited by Barton J. Bernstein and Allen J. Matusow (New York: Harper Colophon Books, 1966), p. 455; "President on Radio," *New York Times*, April 12, 1951, p. 7; "Dismissal Angers South California," *New York Times*, April 12, 1951, p. 7.

3. Merne Arthur Harris, "The MacArthur Dismissal--A Study of Political Mail," (Diss: University of Iowa, 1966), pp. 250, 203.

4. Irving Perlmeter, oral history interview, May 23 and 24, 1964, p. 55, HSTL.

5. "MacArthur on War," *The Truman Administration*, pp. 452-454.

6. "All Time Low," *Time*, March 19, 1951, p. 25.

7. Cochran, *Harry Truman and the Crisis Presidency*, pp. 325-27; Kaufman, *The Korean War*, pp. 156-160. For MacArthur's statement and Truman's orders, see Truman, *Memoirs*, II, pp. 440-443.

8. Truman, *Memoirs*, II, pp. 445-446.

9. "Letter of Joseph Martin to MacArthur," in *The Truman Administration*, pp. 454-455.

10. For the need to determine "To what degree did he [Truman] rely upon others to prepare his speeches? How did he decide what should be in them? Which speeches were effective, and which were not," see *The Truman Period as a Research Field*, edited by Richard S. Kirkendall

(Columbia: University of Missouri Press, 1967), pp. 12-13.

11. "The MacArthur Dismissal," April 28, 1951, president's secretary's files, box 129, pp. 1-2, HSTL; Truman, *Memoirs*, II, p. 448.

12. *Biographic Register of the Department of State*, Department of State Publication 4131, p. 444.

13. Letter from David Bell to George Elsey, April 16, 1951, papers of George Elsey, box 74, pp. 1-2, HSTL.

14. David S. McClellan, *Dean Acheson: The State Department Years*, (New York: Dodd, Mead, 1976), p. 313.

15. Letter from David Bell to George Elsey, p. 2., HSTL.

16. Ibid.

17. "Draft, CSM, 4-10-51," tab 3, papers of George Elsey, box 74, pp. 1-20, HSTL. A typed copy of this draft is in tab 4, which mistakenly was taken as a so-called second draft: see note 18.

18. This draft is titled "Third Draft, CSM, 4-11-51," but I count it as a second draft because it is merely a smooth copy of draft one in tab 3.

19. "Third Draft [second], CSM, 4-11-51," papers of George Elsey, box 74, p. 13, HSTL.

20. "Draft, 4-10-51, DEB," tab 5, papers of George Elsey, box 74, pp. 1-2, HSTL. This draft was thirteen pages.

21. "Draft of 4-11-51, D Bell," tab 6, papers of George Elsey, Box 74, pp. 1-2, HSTL.

22. "Fourth Draft, 4-11-51," tab 9, papers of George Elsey, box 74, p. 11, HSTL. This draft was thirteen pages.

23. "Fourth draft, 4-11-51," tab 10, papers of George Elsey, box 74, pp. 1-13, HSTL. The reading copy is in tab 13, pp. 1-5.

24. Letter from David Bell to George Elsey, p. 2, HSTL.

25. "Fourth Draft, 4-11-51," tab 10, papers of George Elsey, box 74, pp. 5, 10, 11, 12, and 13, HSTL.

26. Ibid., p. 5.

27. Ibid., pp. 8, 9, 11, 12, and 13.

28. "Memorandum Re General Ridgway," April 17, 1951, papers of George M. Elsey, tab 14, box 74, p. 1, HSTL.

29. Matthew B. Ridgway, *The Korean War* (Garden City: Doubleday, 1967), pp. 145-148; Richard H. Rovere, "Truman after Seven Years," *Harpers*, May 1952, p. 29; W. Averell Harriman, "Mr. Truman's Way with Crisis," in *The Korean War: A 25-Year Perspective*, edited by Francis H. Heller (Lawrence: The Regents Press of Kansas, 1977), p. 235.

30. Memorandum, William J. Hopkins to the president, May 8, 1951, president's secretary's files, HSTL.

31. Harris, "The MacArthur Dismissal--A Study of Political Mail," p. 207; Memo to Sec. of State, April 14, 1951, selected records relating to the Korean War, Dept. of State, box 10, folder 37, HSTL; "Relief Felt in U.N. on the Dismissal," *New York Times*, April 12, 1951, p. 1; David Rees, *Korea: The Limited War* (New York: St. Martin's Press, 1964), p. 223.

32. Perlmeter, oral history transcript, p. 53.

33. White and Henderlider, "What Harry S Truman Told Us About Speaking," p. 39.

34. James R. Andrews, *The Practice of Rhetorical Criticism* (New York: Macmillan, 1983), p. 11.

35. Merle Miller, *Plain Speaking: An Oral Biography of Harry S Truman* (New York: G. P. Putnam's Sons, 1973), p. 287.

36. Howard K. Smith, "Thou Art Soldier Only," *Nation*, April 21, 1951, p. 363.

37. Truman, *Memoirs*, II, p. 450.

38. "MacArthur vs. Truman," *Time*, April 22, 1951, p. 32.

39. "Radio Report to the American People on Korea and on U.S. Policy in the Far East," April 11, 1951, *HST: 1951*, pp. 223-227.

40. For a text of this speech, see *Vital Speeches of the Day*, May 1, 1951, pp. 430-433.

41. Bernard K. Duffy, "President Harry S. Truman and General Douglas MacArthur: A Study of Rhetorical Confrontation," in *Oratorical Encounters: Selected Studies and Sources of Twentieth-Century Political Accusations and Apologies*, edited by Halford Ross Ryan (Westport, Conn.: Greenwood Press, 1988), p. 80.

42. Duffy, "Truman and MacArthur," p. 82. See *HST: 1951*, pp. 222-223, for the documents that indicted MacArthur.

43. Truman, *Memoirs*, II, p. 450.

44. "Statement and Order by the President on Relieving General MacArthur of His Commands," April 11, 1951, *HST: 1951*, p. 222.

45. Duffy, "Truman and MacArthur," pp. 89, 92.

46. "Military Situation in the Far East," *Hearings before the Committee on Armed Services and the Committee on Foreign Relations*, United States Senate, 82nd Congress, 1st session, (Washington, D.C.: GPO, 1951), Part 1, p. 76.

47. "Military Situation in the Far East," Part 1, p. 76.

4
Doing Unto Dewey

Occasionally, an orator delivers a speech that is definitive in his or her career. Abraham Lincoln's A House Divided speech set him on the road to the White House. Franklin D. Roosevelt's Teamsters' Union address innervated a flagging 1944 campaign. Richard Nixon's 1952 Checkers speech saved his political career. And Barbara C. Jordan delivered a keynote address at the Democratic National Convention in 1976 that serves as a benchmark for that genre of oratory. Harry S. Truman also delivered a pivotal persuasion, for it energized him and his party, and it probably had some lingering effect with the electorate: "My most successful speech? I believe it was my acceptance address at the Democratic National Convention. That speech was something of a personal spiritual milestone, From that time on, I never doubted that we would win."[1] Others were not so sure, so a major effort was underway to make Truman's speech a good one.

THE PRODUCTION OF THE CONVENTION ADDRESS

The institutional speech team for this address consisted of Clark Clifford, Charles Murphy, David Bell, and George Elsey. Although Samuel Rosenman had left the Truman team in January 1946, he rejoined the speech staff and generated some major contributions.

The rhetorical blueprint for the speech was supplied by William Batt, Jr., director of the research division of the Democratic National Committee. In a July 9 memorandum, Batt advocated that "the words and phrases should be short, homely, and in character. This is no place for Churchillian grandiloquence," and he suggested that the speech juxtapose the liberal measures with "how the 80th Congress killed them all."[2] As we shall learn, the speech accomplished both aims admirably well. But before turning to the text of the speech, two issues need to be resolved.

The first query is whether Rosenman was responsible for the famous unsigned memorandum, dated June 29, 1948, that suggested the president call the Congress back for a special session.[3] Underhill understood the difficulty in assigning authorship for this memorandum. He was inclined to think that it originated with William Batt of the Democratic National Committee and that Clifford was persuaded to adopt the idea.[4] Rosenman acknowledged that the actual memo was Clifford's, but Rosenman claimed that he made the suggestion to Clifford "*before* [emphasis in original] June 29, 1948."[5] It is impossible to determine whose memo it was, but the line about Truman's "leading his party in a crusade for the millions of Americans ignored by the 'rich man's Congress'" is certainly reminiscent of the crusade that FDR promised to lead in the peroration of his 1932 acceptance speech at Chicago; and it was certainly evocative of FDR's sobriquet of the "economic royalists" that denigrated the Republicans and their rich constituents in the 1936 campaign.[6]

The second point is to determine authorship for the final speech. A number of writers worked on preliminary drafts. Murphy composed a draft that was not used and Rosenman wrote two drafts that were undated, but one became the core for the eventual speech.[7]

The speech process congealed when Truman resolved not to read his speech, but to deliver it off-the-cuff, which was HST's terminology for an extempore speech that was well conceived and outlined, but delivered in an ad libitum fashion. Sometime before Tuesday, July 13, President Truman resolved that he would deliver the convention speech off-the-cuff.[8] His decision was motivated, in part, by his success with some extempore remarks before the American Society of Newspaper Editors on April 17 in Washington, D.C. in which he experimented with that format, and in speeches that Truman gave later in his western tour in early summer.[9] The modus operandi was for Truman to have a bare-bones speech outline to follow to which he would add flesh as he spoke.

With Truman's decision to deliver the speech off-the-cuff, Clifford, Murphy, and Rosenman gathered in the Cabinet Room on Tuesday, July 13, to compose a draft for the speech. These men took Rosenman's original outline and reshaped it. On July 14, Bell and Elsey produced a second draft, which was evidently edited on the run by Murphy and Clifford, after a meeting with Rosenman and Truman. From this second draft a final reading copy was typed.[10]

Truman took to the rostrum a twenty-one page, quadruple-spaced speech outline. (The one exception to this practice was the speech's peroration. Written by Rosenman, the conclusion was actually a paraphrase of FDR's peroration for his 1932 acceptance speech, and this paraphrase was triple-spaced.) To appreciate Truman's feat, Murphy estimated that HST ad-libbed two-thirds to three-fourths of the outline, and that the speech, as delivered, was about one-half of the outline.[11] For instance, one can compare Truman's outline for his first page, reproduced below, with what he actually said in his convention speech that is given in Part II: Collected Speeches. Here is his outline, which was quadruple-spaced on the reading copy, and it had only one major point per page:

1. Introduction
   (a) Thanks for the nomination.
   (b) Acceptance.
   (c) Reference to Vice Presidential candidate.[12]

THE TURNIP SPEECH: VICTORY FROM THE YAWNS OF DEFEATISM

"What Mr. Truman implied was that seeds of legislation sowed on July 26 would make a good autumn harvest. That is the way of the turnip."[13] Eschewed by children and adults alike, Truman decided to make the Republican-controlled Congress eat the loathed vegetable.

Truman approached the rostrum that had a bank of microphones attached to it. Reacting to shouts from the audience to move the microphones, Truman ad-libbed his memorable beginning. It was a harbinger of things to come, because Truman, it seems especially so in hindsight, *was* able to see what he was doing:

> I am sorry that the microphones are in the way, but I must leave them the way they are because I have got to be able to see what I am doing—[slight pause for effect] as I am always able to see what I am doing [applause].[14]

The rhetorical efficacy of Truman's convention speech ensued from several factors (including his delivery that will be discussed shortly) but the motivational method of his address bears special examination. Truman's acceptance speech can be best understood in terms of a schema that was developed originally by Kenneth Burke.[15] Streamlined and adapted here for critical purposes, the paradigm involves three steps or stages in a speech: Guilt—> Victimization—> Salvation. Succinctly stated, the speaker first induces guilt, anger, frustration, and associated emotions, in the audience. The speaker then channels the audience's emotions onto a person or group, which has, according to the speaker, victimized the audience; thus, the victimizer becomes the scapegoat for the audience's guilt and anger. Last, the speaker shows the audience how it can gain salvation, which is obtained by following the orator's solution in vanquishing the victimizer. In the context of his acceptance address, Truman stirred the Democratic audience's guilt by chastising those who might not vote Democratic, and then addressing their anger and frustration with the Republican party; he then identified the Republican-controlled Congress as the scapegoat for the country's ills; and he then offered the convention audience salvation only if it supported and voted for the Democratic party and Harry S. Truman in the fall. The same persuasive method also worked for the radio audience and the American people: Only Harry S. Truman would battle the villains on behalf of the victimized people.

The guilt trip began early in the address. "Now is the time," Truman admonished the audience, "for us to get together and beat the common enemy. And that is up to you." And a few lines later, the president laid guilt on two of the Democratic party's important constituencies, farmers and laborers:

> Never in the world were the farmers of any republic or any kingdom or any other country as prosperous as the farmers of the United States; and if they don't do their duty by the Democratic Party, they are the most ungrateful people in the world!
>
> Wages and salaries in this country have increased from $29 billion in 1933 to more than $128 billion in 1947. That's labor, and labor never had but one friend in politics, and that is the Democratic Party and Franklin D. Roosevelt.
>
> And I say to labor what I have said to the farmers: they are the most ungrateful people in the world if they pass the Democratic Party by this year.

Having instilled some shame in Democrats who might not support the party, Truman wisely turned, still in the guilt stage, to stirring their anger. He did this by ticking off the accomplishments of the Democratic party: turning away from isolationism, removing trade barriers, and starting foreign aid programs.

Abruptly, with the transitional device, "I would like to say a word or two on what I think the Republican philosophy is, and I will speak from actions and from history and from experience," Truman moved to the victimization stage. Truman clearly delineated the villain:

> The Republican Party, as I said a while ago, favors the privileged few and not the common everyday man. Ever since its inception, that party has been under the control of special privilege; and they have completely proved it in the 80th Congress. They proved it by the things they did *to* the people, and not *for* them. They proved it by the thing they failed to do. [Emphasis in original.]

Truman then listed all of the legislation and programs that he had requested but the Republican Congress had failed to pass. Sandwiched in the long litany of Republican perfidy, Truman flung some effective rhetorical barbs. Skewering the Republicans on the hypocrisy of their platform, Truman inveighed: "They promised to do in that platform a lot of things I have been asking them to do that they have refused to do when they had the power." And, in language that ran close to the ground, Truman compared Republican rhetoric with reality on social security: "I wonder if they think they can fool the people of the United States with such poppycock as that!"

   The salvation step was the logical completion of the victimization stage. Calling the Republican's poker hand, Truman delivered his rhetorical coup de grace:

> I am therefore calling this Congress back into session July 26th. . . . I am going to call Congress back and ask them to pass the laws to halt rising prices, to meet the housing crisis, which they say they are for in their platform. . . . Now, my friends, if there is any reality behind that Republican platform, we ought to get some action from a short session of the 80th Congress. They can do this job in 15 days if they want to do it. They will still have time to go out and run for office.

Truman's sarcasm had a ring of truth, for the enthymeme the audience easily completed was that since the Republicans did not pass their platform earlier, they will not pass it later. And they did not!

   Having dispatched the duplicity of the Republican platform, Truman animated the salvation stage by indicating how the audience could save itself. Waving the bloody shirt of "attacking the citadel of special privilege and greed" in 1932 and the image of FDR's driving "the money changers from the temple" in his 1933 inaugural address,[16] Truman delivered Rosenman's peroration that quoted Roosevelt's acceptance speech in Chicago. As FDR called on the people to support him in 1932 to vanquish the Republicans, so did Truman in 1948. But in case Democrats did not get the message, Truman made a direct appeal in the salvation stage. It was vintage Truman:

> Now my friends, with the help of God and the wholehearted push which you can put behind this campaign, we can save the country from a continuation of the 80th Congress, and from misrule from now on.
>
> I must have your help. You must get in and push, and win this election. The country can't afford another Republican Congress.

PRESIDENT TRUMAN'S CONTRIBUTIONS TO THE SPEECH

Although it is widely accepted that Rosenman, Clifford, and Murphy, with the help of Bell and Elsey, were responsible for Truman's convention address, it is nevertheless worthwhile to demonstrate the hand that Truman had in the speech. Since no one has paid any attention to his contributions, a new finding can be advanced.

The president was a better writer than has been supposed. In a handwritten, penciled draft, Harry Truman constructed some diatribes against the Republicans that were quite elegant. The stylistic device he used was anaphora, the repetition of the same or similar phrases at the beginning of successive thought groups. Delivered effectively, anaphora gives the speech force and polish. FDR was famous for that stylistic device, but Truman understood how to employ it, too. In response to reading the Republican platform, Truman wrote out what he wanted to do in his speech; note the elegant anaphora, "I shall ask them," that he composed (the misspellings are Trumans's):

> I shall call this 80th (worst except one in history [Truman did not supply the other parenthesis, and I assume it belongs here] on ~~Sept 1~~ July 19 and I shall ask them to pass the Taft-Ellender-Wagner Housing Bill which their platform says they are for.
>
> I shall ask them to control prices.
>
> I shall ask them for Aid to Education.
>
> I shall ask them for increased benefits under Social Security.
>
> I shall ask them for an increased minimum wage.

I shall ask them for Civil Rights legislation.

I shall ask them for the Loan to United Nations for headquarters.

I shall ask them for T.V.A. steam plant.

I shall ask them to amend their anti-semitic anticatholic [sic] displaced person act.

And then we'll see whether the greatest agregation [sic] of political fakers, special privelege [sic] stooges and demagogues will act.

The people will believe me when I tell them the truth and the result can only be one way. Continuation of a peoples [sic] government.[17]

The speech staff took Truman's notes and worked them into the speech immediately after the turnip day paragraph.

Unfortunately, the staff's bare-bones outline did not contain the anaphora. Here is Truman's outline from which he spoke:

19.   I am, therefore, calling the Congress back into Session to reconvene on July twenty-sixth.

    (a) I shall ask them to pass laws -

        1 - to halt rising prices - and

        2 - to meet the housing crisis.

    (b) At the same time I shall ask them to act upon other vitally needed measures, such as:

        (1) aid to education

        (2) a national health program

        (3) civil rights legislation

        (4) an increase in the minimum wage

        (5) extension of social security coverage and increase in benefits

        (6) funds for projects needed in our program to provide public power and cheap electricity

        (7) an adequate and decent displaced persons law

        (8) funds for United Nations headquarters

    (c) If there is any reality behind the Republican platform, we can get action from the Congress now.[18]

The original, stylistic anaphora that Truman wrote was watered-down and its oratorical effect was lost. HST could have delivered an FDR-like cadenced attack against the Republicans. He could have spoken the anaphora of his "I shall ask" lines, and after three or four phrases delivered in that fashion, the audience probably would have responded to the attack, much as 1940 campaign audiences reacted to FDR's famous "Martin, Barton, and Fish" anaphora, and as the Washington, D.C., audience rejoined to the anaphora in Dr. Martin Luther King's 1963 I Have a Dream speech.

The point is that Truman's initial instinct on the anaphora was better than his staff's. It would have been an easy matter for the staff to write "I shall ask the Congress for" before each of the topics. As actually delivered (see "Collected Speeches"), Truman lumped all of these important pieces of legislation together, probably because he did not remember, at the time of utterance, to deliver the style of his handwritten note. On the other hand, the staff's highlighting each legislative piece with "I shall ask the Congress for" would have charged the speech with an unmistakable elegance, force, and emphasis.

However, Truman did remember one issue from his handwritten note. The staff had deleted Truman's reference to the anti-Catholic and anti-Jewish displaced persons law (see above). On the reading copy, Truman wrote "anti-Jewish anti-Catholic" next to the seventh point (see above). And Truman delivered his insert in the actual speech (see "Collected Speeches").

THE SPEECH'S EFFECT

Truman's speech motivated positive and negative responses from average Americans. A New Haven, Connecticut, listener evidently remembered President Franklin D. Roosevelt's blaming the Supreme Court in 1937 for the lack of progress with the New Deal, and therefore complained about Truman's ploy a decade later with this comparison: "It was bad enough for a President to try to discredit the Supreme Court when it opposed him, but for one to discredit Congress for the same reason is an infinitely greater disservice to our country." A Brooklyn, New York, resident indulged in some colloquial name-calling: "Of all the blasted puffed up nincompoops you beat them all." However, partisans appreciated Truman's brand of rhetoric. Reacting to the logical impact of Truman's speech, a lawyer from Detroit, Michigan, advised: "Repetition on these two points [prices and housing], constantly drumming it in that the Republican Congress is to blame, should have a telling effect upon the average independent middle class voter." Audience members also appreciated the visceral impact of Truman's convention oratory. Someone telegraphed the president: "Last night you began the process of ripping the mask of hypocrisy from the Republican countenance." A person from

Kansas City, Missouri, relished HST's rhetoric: "I listened to the President's acceptance speech last night and that was the real Capt. Harry talking. . . . He got up on his hind legs and let'em have it." And someone caught the efficacy of Truman's fighting speech: "Everyone who heard the President talk, including some who thought he didn't have a good chance in November, now seem to believe that anything can happen."[19]

National newspaper editorials also took sides along partisan lines. The fourth estate, with Republican leanings, decried Truman and his attack on the 80th Congress. The New York *Herald Tribune* defined Truman's calling the Congress back into session as a "shoddy partisan trick on his opponents"; the Minneapolis *Star* sneered: "Whether this proves to be 'smart politics' will depend on what the American people think of such cynically partisan use of presidential power"; the Portland *Oregonian* opined that when Truman "stepped down from the rostrum his stature was at a new low"; and the Chicago *Tribune*, which wanted Senator Robert Taft rather than Governor Dewey, circuitously complained that Truman was really attacking Taft, not Dewey, and therefore, "Once more, the Republicans have been caught with the wrong candidate." However, Democratic dailies generally hailed Truman's feat: "A special session," the Baltimore *Sun* sensed, "is likely to prove a source of acute embarrassment to Mr. Dewey"; the *Washington Star* realized the persuasive efficacy of Truman's gesture: "[T]here is not a chance in the world that the special session will act on the long list of measures enumerated by the President, but it will put the Republicans on an uncomfortable spot and give Mr. Truman a good sounding board against which to make some political speeches"; the St. Louis *Globe-Democrat* defined Truman's action as "an adroit dare"; and the Cleveland *Plain Dealer* caught the real purpose of Truman's speech: "By common consent it was a political maneuver designed for the purpose of putting the Republican opposition on the spot and for rallying the Democrats for the campaign."[20]

TRUMAN'S DELIVERY

Samuel Rosenman, who wrote and heard his boss FDR deliver many of those fine addresses, believed that Truman's delivery in Philadelphia was impressive: "It was one of the best deliveries I ever heard him make."[21] In Truman's situation, the term "best" is a relative term that is grounded in the historic, rhetorical situation.

From a purely technical standpoint, the speech was not delivered effectively. Truman's rate was too fast, which was always his major problem, and his phrasing was poor. However, speaking technique must be adapted to the occasion and measured thereby: It is worth considering whether FDR's measured, mellifluous rate would have stirred delegates at 2:00 A.M. The fact is that Truman's rat-a-tat-tat rate, even poorly phrased, excited the delegates from the beginning of his address. For instance, he rushed some of the important introductory lines. Here is how Truman delivered them (dashes indicate a pause for phrasing): "Senator Barkley and I will win this election / and make these Republicans like it—don't you forget that. / We will do that because they are wrong and we are right, and I will prove it to you in just a few minutes." FDR would have spoken slower, and might have inserted a pause, accompanied by a vocal cue of an upward inflection, after "like it" and "we are right" to milk the audience; nevertheless, Truman evoked spirited cheering from his listeners.[22]

Truman's gestures were also hackneyed. True to form, he overused his famous (infamous?) two-handed wood-chop-gesture. Moreover, it was often jerky and ill-timed, which gave the speech an undignified air. But, as a speech to rouse the delegates, perhaps his otherwise lamentable delivery was useful, for Clark Clifford thought in "punching the air with a high-pitched staccato instead of his usual droning style, President Truman roused the sluggish audience."[23] For instance, HST used his two-handed chop to punctuate this line that he delivered increasingly quickly, yet, the audience was innervated: "Victory has become a habit of our party. / It has been elected four times in succession [hand chops], / and I am convinced it will be elected a fifth time next November." Truman also tended to rock back and forth on his feet. Usually *verboten*, this banal platform movement, in Truman's case, communicated a certain cockiness as he battled the Republicans. He appeared as the prize fighter, rocking on his feet from almost uncontrolled energy, just waiting to wade into his Republican opponents. Indeed, Roy Jenkins opined that Truman "was a sergeant-major telling his squad to get off their backsides. It worked rather well. They sat up. The listened. They cheered. For a moment they almost thought they might win."[24] Considering that Truman had been kept waiting for four hours because of a poorly managed convention; that he had been denied the unanimous ballot, which had been accorded FDR, because Southerners, who were angered by Truman's strong civil rights record, would not support it; and that he had to wait until the doves of peace, which had been released just before his appearance and had made their own mayhem in the convention hall, finally settled down; considering all of those factors, Robert Donovan decided: "In these seemingly hopeless circumstances Truman went before the bedraggled delegates and did the last thing anyone would have imagined possible at that wretched hour of 2 A.M. He electrified the convention."[25] Having secured the nomination, Truman had to win the election.

THE MIRACLE OF '48

At Columbus, Ohio, June 17, 1948, at 11 P.M., returning from a whistle-stop tour from the West Coast, on what Truman tongue-in-cheek told his audiences was a nonpolitical tour, HST sounded the leitmotif of his 1948 campaign: "Only one-third of the qualified voters of the Nation voted in November 1946, and you elected the 80th Congress; and you got just what you deserved, when 66 2/3 per cent of you stayed at home. . . . And if you are gullible enough to be fooled twice in a row, you will still deserve what you get."[26]

After clinching the nomination, Truman went on whistle-stop tours of the United States. The statistics are impressive: He travelled nearly 20,000 miles by train, made 7 whistle-stop tours, delivered from 26 to 34 major addresses (depending on how one defines a major address), and delivered close to 250 impromptu remarks from the rear of his railroad observation car (see "Chronology of Speeches").[27]

The whistle-stop talks were arduous. Rising early and retiring late, Truman usually spoke seven or eight times a day from the train. Sandwiched between his informal, impromptu remarks from the rear platform of the armored presidential observation car *Ferdinand Magellan*, which was originally built for FDR, Truman delivered formal addresses in cities and towns where he would speak in an auditorium or armory. His two busiest whistle-stop days were: sixteen speeches in Oklahoma and Missouri on September 29, and sixteen speeches in Massachusetts, Rhode Island, Connecticut, and New York City (where he made six separate appearances) on October 28. Two days tied for second place: September 30 with thirteen stops in Illinois, Indiana, and Kentucky, and October 8 with thirteen stops in New York state, which was Dewey's bailiwick. One should also realize that Truman delivered a major address in the evening on each of these long days!

The format for the whistle-stops varied, but Truman usually professed surprise that so many folks came out to see him (which also surprised the pollsters because it was a foregone conclusion that Dewey would win); thanked the people for attending, which sometimes was in the very early morning or late evening; made some local color remarks that were targeted to the particular locale; boosted Democratic candidates that were running for office; and then lambasted the Republicans and their good-for-nothing, do-nothing 80th Congress.

For the whistle-stops and his major addresses, Truman recapitulated many of the themes from his convention address. For instance, he induced guilt in his audience at Burbank, California, September 23, when he proclaimed, "Now, if you stay at home this time you will get just what you deserve. I don't think your are going to do it—I don't think you are going to do it!"; at Yuma, Arizona, September 24, he preached self-interest: "I am not only asking you to vote for me, I am asking you to vote for yourselves in your own selfish interests," which was a theme he reiterated at Crawfordsville, Indiana, the home of Wabash College: "Therefore, I want every one of you to go to the polls on November 2nd and vote in your own interests." At Worchester, Massachusetts, October 27, 1948, Truman lectured on Republican economic theory: "The Republicans believe in what they call the 'trickle down' theory. They want the big, rich, and wealthy, privileged special interest groups to get the lion's share of the income and let the scraps fall down to the rest of us." He also joked in innumerable places that voters should return him to the White House so that he would not have to worry about the Republican-sponsored housing shortage. From time to time, the president could wax eloquently. At Oklahoma City, September 28, he constructed a series of seven accusing clauses that began with the anaphora of "I charge that," and at Akron, Ohio, October 11, Truman began seven clauses of anaphora with "I believe."[28]

Nor was Truman above borrowing from FDR's rhetoric for effect. For a major campaign address at Philadelphia, October 6, HST borrowed themes and similar language that Roosevelt had used so impressively in his campaign oratory. Attacking the "me too, me better" Republican strategy in his second canvass, FDR sarcastically skewered the Republican party at Syracuse, New York, September 29, 1936:

> Of course we believe in all these things; we believe in social security; we believe in work for the unemployed; we believe in saving homes. Cross our hearts and hope to die, we believe in all of these things; but we do not like the way the present Administration is doing them. Just turn them over to us. We will do all of them—we will do more of them—we will do them better; and most of all, the doing of them will not cost anybody anything.[29]

This passage is also illustrative of FDR's artistry with language, because it contains instances of the anaphora and epistrophe for which he was famous; moreover, one can easily phrase his speech if one follows the punctuation. And in Philadelphia, October 23, 1940, FDR repeated, although not as eloquently, his attack on Republican "me too, me better" campaign promises: "If they could only get control of them, they plead, they would take so much better care of them, honest-to-goodness they would."[30]

Although the attacks against the Republican "me too, me better" stance were quite similar, compare FDR's treatment to Truman's at Philadelphia, October 6, 1948. Note that HST's sentences were too long for cadenced phrasing, and that opportunities for anaphora and epistrophe were overlooked:

> They tell you, "We know the Democrats took you out of the great depression that we created, but they didn't do it very well. We can do it better."
>
> The Republicans tell you, "We are all for labor's rights to collective bargaining, which the Democrats gave you, but we know how to make it work better."
>
> They say to the farmer, "We know you are better off than you ever have been before, and the Democratic farm program is so good that we are not against it anymore, but we could run it a lot better." . . . They just say, "Turn all these Democratic programs over to us, and we will take care of everything. Just leave everything up to the Republican Party and you won't have anything to worry about."[31]

DOCTOR DEWEY AND THE REPUBLICAN RECORD

Although never mentioned in the speech by name, Governor Thomas Dewey has been indelibly linked to one of Truman's best major campaign addresses, which he delivered in Hunt Armory, Pittsburgh, Pennsylvania, on October 23, 1948. The rhetorical situation was ripe for a ripping rebuttal against the Republican candidate and the 80th Congress because Dewey had delivered an address in Pittsburgh at the same venue on October 11. Truman's speech was a composite of his generic rhetoric in the campaign, but it has always been a favorite for it contained Truman's first foray into dialogue. It also had some other persuasive techniques, which have not been examined hitherto, that make the speech worthy of close scrutiny.

Charles Murphy wrote the draft for the speech. A major metaphor that Murphy invented was the famous "cracked record." In order to juxtapose the lack of legislation from the 80th Congress versus the platform promises of Dewey, which called for many of the programs his own party's Congress refused to pass, Murphy hit on an excellent stylistic technique to dramatize the difference. Murphy had Truman say:

This year the same candidate is back with us, and he is saying much the same thing; that he likes the Democratic laws, but that he can run them better than we can.

It sounds to me like the same old phonograph record; but this year the record has a crack, and the needle gets stuck in that crack every once in a while.

Now the crack in the soothing syrup of that record was provided by the Republican 80th "do-nothing" Congress.

Now, in 1948, every time the Republican candidate says, "I can do it better," up comes an echo from the crack which says, "We're against it."[32]

Thus, Murphy set the verbal stage for Truman to tick off all of the programs (minimum wage, social security, old-age insurance, collective bargaining, and so forth) that the Democrats favored but that the 80th Congress failed to pass, and that now Dewey had endorsed; thus, the broken record metaphor highlighted the hypocrisy in the Republican campaign. The audience loved it, but one disgruntled person, from Kimberly Heights, Tennessee, wrote the president and turned the broken record image against him: "Speaking of cracked records as you suggested in your speech, I believe you just run over and over the same things time after time."[33] In truth, the person was correct! Truman's speeches were highly repetitive; nevertheless, the persuasive efficacy of restatement cannot be dismissed. Perhaps Truman and his staff were aware of the potency of rhetorical redundancy, which Adolph Hitler recognized: "Only constant repetition will finally succeed in imprinting an idea on the memory of a crowd."[34]

David Lloyd wrote out in longhand the now-famous dialogue between Doctor Dewey and the American patient-voter. Lloyd wanted the dialogue to commence in the introduction so that it would serve as an extended and humorous metaphor for the issues. Ironically, Murphy was on the verge of dropping the dialogue. Luckily, he talked with Clark Clifford, who stated that the staff needed "to get some life into our speeches," so Murphy showed the dialogue to Clifford. Clifford liked it, made a few changes, and submitted it to Truman, who accepted the idea.[35]

Lloyd's colloquy has every bit the stature of FDR's famous dialogue about his little dog Fala given in the Teamsters' Union address, Washington, D.C., September 23, 1944. Here are FDR's famous words about his little dog Fala:

These Republican leaders have not been content with attacks on me, or my wife, or on my sons. No, not content with that, they now include my little dog Fala [laughter and applause for twenty seconds]. Well, of course, I don't resent attacks, and my family don't [sic] resent attacks, but Fala does resent them [laughter and applause for fifteen seconds]. You know, Fala is Scotch [laughter], and being a Scottie, as soon as he learned that the Republican fiction writers in Congress and out had concocted a story that I had left him behind on the Aleutian Islands and had sent a destroyer back to find him—at a cost to the taxpayers of two or three or eight or twenty million dollars—his Scotch soul was furious [laughter and applause for ten seconds]. He has not been the same dog since [laughter and applause for fifteen seconds].[36]

Now compare this with Lloyd's dialogue, which might just be better. If there is any difference in audience reaction, it is surely due to Truman's delivery. When he played the role of Doctor Dewey, Truman did try to lower slightly the pitch of his voice in order to differentiate the Democratic patient from the Republican doctor. The following excerpt is from a recording of the speech, and audience reactions are included in brackets; moreover, Truman did make a mistake in rendering one of the lines, which is not given in his public papers, and the ad-libbed remarks are italicized:

My opponent is conducting a very peculiar campaign. He has set himself up as some kind of doctor with a magic cure for all the ills of mankind.

Now, let's imagine that we, the American people, are going to see this doctor. It's just our usual routine checkup which we have every four years.

Now, we go into this doctor's office.
And "Doctor," we say, "we're feeling fine."

"Is that so?" says the doctor [laughter]. [Truman was supposed to say next, "You been bothered much by issues lately?" but he made a mistake and ad-libbed] *"I've been bothered much by issues lately."* [Then, sensing his mistake, he ad-libbed] *"Have you been bothered much by issues, lately, too?* [laughter])"

"Not bothered, exactly," we say. "Of course, we've had a few. We've had the issues of high prices, and housing, and education, and social security, and a few others."

"That's too bad," says the doctor [laughter]. "You shouldn't have so many issues [laughter]."

"Is that right?" we say. "We thought that issues were a sign of political health."

"Not at all," says the doctor [laughter]. "You shouldn't think about issues. What you need is my brand of soothing syrup [laughter]—I call it 'unity.'"

Then the doctor edges up a little closer.

And he says, "Say, you don't look so good [laughter]."

We say to him, "Well, that seems strange to me, Doc. I never felt stronger, never had more money, and never had a brighter future. What is wrong with me?"

Well, the doctor looks blank and he says [laughter], "I never discuss issues with a patient. But what you need is a major operation [laughter]."

"Will it be serious, Doc?" we say.

"Not so very serious," he says. "It will just mean taking out the complete works and putting in a Republican administration [prolonged laughter]."[37]

Truman delivered the speech convincingly, for the *New York Herald Tribune*, one of Dewey's influential supporters, granted that "Mr. Truman, who often hurries through a speech, read tonight's speech slowly and with good effect."[38]

Truman made some interesting changes on the reading copy that illustrate his management of language for effect. Murphy had constructed a series of indictments against Dewey with regard to Democratic achievements, and then concluded ironically each paragraph with the epistrophe of "Maybe that's what he calls a failure." Truman changed Murphy's epistrophe to "Is that what he calls a failure?" This change was felicitous, for it asked a rhetorical question, in the repeated form of epistrophe, that the crowd was bound to answer "No." Truman also made an interesting change in the speech's peroration. Murphy had summarized the speech with "These two phrases, 'me too,' and 'we're against it,' sum up the whole Republican campaign. My friends, that's not funny," to which Truman added: "It's tragic, tragic for the everyday citizen." And, illustrative of Truman's ad-libbing, he vocally added the following at Pittsburgh (his insert is italicized): "Our side—the Democratic side—doesn't say, 'We're against it.' It says, 'We can do it.' *And we will do it—if you will give us a chance.*"[39]

And the voters did. The popular vote was about 24,100,00 (49.5 percent) for Truman versus Dewey's 21,900,000 (45.1 percent), and the electoral vote was 303 against Dewey's 189 and Strom Thurmond's 39.[40]

CONCLUSION

This chapter has pointed the way toward a revision of Harry S. Truman as an orator. Of course, his delivery was his major distraction, which might be a reason one hesitates to term Truman a "great" American orator. However, the 1948 campaign was Truman's finest oratorical hour, for it proved conclusively that he could energize crowds with his appeals, especially when he relied minimally on his manuscript and instead spoke extempore, or ad-libbed his addresses. Unfortunately, but inexplicably, Truman reverted to his wooden style of delivery for the rest of his presidency. Moreover, Truman possessed a substantial mastery over the grand rhetorical strategy of the campaign. His handling of language for purposeful effect, as illustrated by his emendations on various drafts, was more artistic than has hitherto been granted.

Harry Truman won the 1948 campaign on his own merit and against substantial odds, which Franklin D. Roosevelt did not have to confront in 1932 and 1936, and certainly not in 1940 and 1944, although the race with Dewey was FDR's closest. HST's political instincts were prescient, for he correctly forecasted, in his undated manuscript penned on White House stationery after the Republican convention but before the Democratic convention, that "The American people will believe me when I tell them the truth and the result can only be one way. Continuation of a peoples [sic] government."[41] Such Jacksonian faith, from a Jackson County Democrat, was rewarded by the American people in 1948.

NOTES

1. White and Henderlider, "What Harry S. Truman Told Us About His Speaking," p. 39.

2. "Memorandum from William Batt, Jr., July 9, 1948," papers of Clark Clifford, presidential speech file, Box 34, HSTL.

3. "Should the President Call Congress Back?" June 29, 1948, papers of Samuel I. Rosenman, box 9, HSTL.

4. Underhill, *The Truman Persuasions*, pp. 270-271.

5. Rosenman, oral history transcript, September, 1969, p. 86.

6. "Should the President Call Congress Back?" HSTL.

7. Files of Charles S. Murphy, presidential speech file, accepting presidential nomination, July 15, 1948, box 1, HSTL; Campaign 1948—HST acceptance speech, papers of Samuel I. Rosenman, box 9, HSTL; David E. Bell, oral history transcript, August, 1972, p. 144, HSTL.

8. Papers of George Elsey, speech file, 1948 Campaign, July 14, president's acceptance speech, box 24, HSTL.

9. Underhill, *The Truman Persuasions*, pp. 264-265; *HST: 1948*, pp. 221-224.

10. "Some Aspects of the Preparation of President Truman's Speeches for the 1948 Campaign, December 6, 1948," papers of Charles S. Murphy, Truman administration file, box 82, pp. 3, 6-7, HSTL.

11. "Some Aspects of the Preparation of President Truman's Speeches for the 1948 Campaign, December 6, 1948," p. 10, HSTL.

12. "Acceptance Speech of the President at the Democratic National Convention, Convention Hall, Philadelphia, Pa.," papers of Harry S. Truman, speech file, box 27, p. 1, HSTL.

13. "Missouri's 'Turnip Day' Is Explained by Truman," *New York Times*, July 16, 1948, p. 2.

14. Cassette, "Convention Address," speeches of Harry S. Truman, 1948-1951, HSTL.

15. Kenneth Burke, *Permanence and Change*, (2d ed. Indianapolis: Bobbs-Merrill, 1965), pp. 274-294.

16. For a discussion of this important speech and its utilization of anger—>victimage—>salvation, see my *Franklin D. Roosevelt's Rhetorical Presidency*, pp. 76-86.

17. "Republican Platform," undated, president secretary's files, box 8, pp. 3-5, 8, HSTL.

18. "Original Reading Copy, Acceptance Speech of the President at the Democratic National Convention, Convention Hall, Philadelphia, Pennsylvania," papers of Harry S. Truman, president's secretary's files, speech file, box 27, p. 19, HSTL.

19. Selected letters, PPF-200, box 323, HSTL.

20. "Excerpts from Editorials on the President's Nomination," *New York Times*, July 16, 1948, p. 2.

21. Rosenman, oral history transcript, p. 83.

22. Cassette, side 1, "Address upon receiving the Presidential Nomination at the Democratic National Convention," 7-15-48 (25 minutes), selected speeches of Harry S. Truman, 1948-1951, HSTL.

23. Clifford, *Counsel to the President*, p. 222.

24. Roy Jenkins, *Truman* (New York: Harper and Row, 1986), p. 130.

25. Donovan, *Conflict and Crisis*, pp. 406-407.

26. *HST: 1948*, p. 374.

27. For the best descriptions of the entire whistle-stop campaign, see Underhill, *The Truman Persuasions*, pp. 274-288; and Donovan, *Conflict and Crisis*, pp. 432-437.

28. *HST: 1948*, pp. 555, 564, 753, 878, 609, 747.

29. Franklin D. Roosevelt, *The Public Papers and Addresses of Franklin D. Roosevelt: 1936*, edited by Samuel I. Rosenman (New York: Macmillan, 1937), pp. 388-389. Hereafter given as *FDR* with the year.

30. *FDR: 1940*, p. 490.

31. *HST: 1948*, p. 678.

32. *HST: 1948*, p. 840.

33. PPF-200, box 324, HSTL.

34. Quoted in Alan Bullock, *Hitler: A Study in Tyranny* (New York: Bantam Books, 1961), p. 45.

35. Files of David Lloyd, box 25, HSTL; "Some Aspects of the Preparation of President Truman's Speeches for the 1948 Campaign," p. 67, HSTL.

36. *FDR: 1944*, p. 290.

37. *HST: 1948*, pp. 838-839; recording SR61-25, 10/23/48, address at Hunt Armory, Pittsburgh, Pennsylvania, HSTL.

38. "Truman Calls Dewey's Labor Plan 'Me Too,'" *New York Herald Tribune*, October 24, 1948, p. 1.

39. President's secretary's files, president's campaign speeches, box 2, pp. 5, 23, 24, HSTL.

40. Donovan, *Conflict and Crisis*, p. 437.

41. "Republican Platform," (undated) president's secretary's files, box 8, p. 8, HSTL.

5
Point Four

Harry S. Truman had the distinct rhetorical disadvantage of following in the footsteps of perhaps the greatest presidential orator in American history. The differences were conspicuous with regard to the classical canons of rhetoric. When inventing (*inventio*) a typical address, Franklin D. Roosevelt often drafted firsthand his speech whereas Truman usually relied on his speech staff to present him with a finished product. Samuel I. Rosenman, who was FDR's best writer and who stayed on with Truman until January 1946, noted that President Roosevelt "wrote and dictated a great deal more than President Truman."[1] FDR also attended to the arrangement (*dispositio*) of his addresses for persuasive effect, but Truman was not usually given to such rhetorical attentions. As for the canons of style (*elocutio*) and delivery (*actio*), FDR significantly surpassed his successor. FDR had a personal hand in the styling of his speeches, and he often penned memorable phrases himself; likewise, FDR carefully considered how he should deliver his speeches for maximum impact on his audiences. On the other hand, HST gave little notice to styling his speeches; moreover, he generally disliked practicing and delivering addresses at all. For instance, Clark M. Clifford, who was Rosenman's counterpart on the Truman speech staff, hinted that the staff had to urge Truman to "read the entire speech aloud to get the whole feel of it."[2]

But the most telling comparison was the artistry of the two presidents' speech staffs. FDR had first-rate writers in Rosenman, Robert Sherwood, Harry Hopkins, and, until his death in 1936, Louis Howe. Truman allowed himself to be served by conventional speech writers. As special counsel, Clifford headed a team whose major players were George Elsey, Clifford's assistant, and Charles S. Murphy, administrative assistant to the president. Rosenman thought Clifford's writing was prosaic: "He did not write well. He was quite a pedestrian writer . . . [and] he did not write with facility or with any great inspiration or imagination."[3] Although Rosenman's depiction might be a jealous colleague's opinion, Clifford admitted as much when he opined that upon Rosenman's departure, "Unbelievably there was no professionally qualified speech writer around the White House to fill the vacuum,"[4] and that no one would place Truman's "unexperienced speech writer [Clifford] in a class with great speech writers" like those of Roosevelt's or John Kennedy's.[5]

Consequently, FDR, the consummate phrasemaker, intimately associated "The only thing we have to fear is fear itself" with his First Inaugural Address and "I see one-third of a nation ill-housed, ill-clad, ill-nourished" with his Second. Truman's Inaugural was known as Point Four.

THE GENESIS OF HARRY TRUMAN'S INAUGURAL ADDRESS

President Harry S. Truman beat Governor Thomas E. Dewey of New York by running against the Do-Nothing Eightieth Congress in the 1948 election.[6] The Republican-controlled House and Senate were loath to pass the president's domestic agenda, for Republicans and conservative Democrats were intent on dismantling as much as possible of the Roosevelt-Truman New Deal, so Truman ran frontally against the Congress and incidentally against Dewey. In truth, Truman only followed the lead of FDR who ran against Hoover in 1932, 1936, 1940, and 1944, although the Republican stand-ins were Alf Landon, Wendell Willkie, and Dewey.[7]

On the other hand, the president's forte had been in foreign policy. Addressing a joint session of Congress on March 12, 1947, Truman delivered his so-called Truman Doctrine speech that committed the United States to the containment policy against communism, which was passed by a bipartisan Congress. Thus, the political auguries of Truman's caretaker administration and of the 1948 campaign impinged on the inaugural address by anyone skilled enough to read them.

Enter George Elsey, Clifford's assistant, who had a profound impact on the development of the inaugural address. In a November 16, 1948, memorandum to Clifford, Elsey endorsed the inaugural's purview:

> I suggest that the State of the Union Message be confined
> insofar as possible to domestic matters and that all foreign
> policy issues be reserved for the Inaugural Address. . . .
> No other occasion in the foreseeable future offers the
> President so great an opportunity to speak to the entire

world . . . and I believe that his words on January 20
should match the dignity and responsibility of that role
[leader of the free world].[8]

Elsey's perception made preeminent rhetorical sense. Whereas it would be
difficult for Truman on inaugural day to speak as the *vox populi* (the voice
of the people, to use Andrew Jackson's conception of the presidency) on
domestic issues that were divisive, Truman could address a fairly united
country on foreign affairs, for anti-communism was growing and
containment was accepted as the Soviets expanded in Europe.

Thus, Truman made a clean break with his 1948 campaign, which
was devoted to lambasting Congress and the Republican party for not
passing Truman's domestic agenda, and instead focused on foreign issues
where he had some prior successes and would be less constrained by
Congress.

Although Elsey charted the course, it was quite another task to
compose a speech. The speech invention process lurched along. Clifford
notified the State Department that he could use some help on the
inaugural.[9] Joseph Jones obliged. Jones, a speech writer in the State
Department, sent a January 6, 1949, draft and a January 11, 1949, revision
to David Lloyd. Lloyd, who joined the Truman speech team at Clifford's
behest, was helping with the inaugural. These drafts, in conjunction with
another undated State Department draft were evidently rejected by Clifford
in conference with Lloyd.[10]

Early in this process, President Truman agreed to Elsey's
memorandum of November 16, 1948, concerning the inaugural's treating
foreign rather than domestic affairs. Elsey noted, in conference with HST,
that the speech was "not to exceed 15 minutes @ 120 words = 1800
words"; that the speech should be "exceedingly simple in language and
concrete not abstract"; and that the "President stated that the Inaugural
would be on Foreign Policy."[11]

Then, the process took a fortuitous turn. Benjamin Hardy, a junior
officer in public affairs at the State Department, had read Clifford's call for
suggestions from the State Department. Hardy tried to present his idea
through normal diplomatic channels, but the State Department was
uninterested. Persevering, he contacted George Elsey, in what Elsey later
characterized as an "entirely unofficial and off-the-record visit."[12] Hardy
presented Elsey with the outline of Point Four, and Elsey then conferred
with Clifford, who immediately seized upon the idea. Clifford remarked
in chiasmus: "[W]e had a speech in search of an idea, Hardy had an idea
in search of a speech."[13]

Hardy's germinal ideas are as follows:

1. Political institutions
    a. UN [United Nations]
    b. Respect for the rights of all peoples
2. Economic betterment
    a. ERP [European Recovery Program, or Marshall Plan]
    b. World trade
    c. Technological development
3. ~~Military Security~~ Preservation of Law and Order
    1. Regional defense pacts
    2. Military aid and advice to other nations
    3. Our own military strength

Fourth, we will join with other nations in reducing barriers to international trade because world trade is one of the foundations of world peace.[14]

These four points, with only slight modifications, were the innervating components of the speech as delivered.

A first draft was written, but it is unsigned and undated. A second draft, January 14, 1949, finally had Hardy's four points in it. Evident in the second draft was the numbering for five points, but the fifth point was never developed.[15]

Point Four proceeded on to a third draft dated January 15, 1949. Clark Clifford, David Lloyd, George Elsey, Charlie Ross, and Matt Connelly all gathered in the Cabinet Room as President Truman read aloud the draft. Although Truman made some suggestions for this draft, none of them were significant.[16]

Clifford sent Dean Acheson at the State Department a fourth draft, dated January 16, for his perusal. Acheson would replace George Marshall as Secretary of State on January 20, 1949. Acheson made a suggestion that was used in the final address. His insert was an example of the classical concept of apophasis, or affirmation-by-denial. If Acheson did not wish "to draw issues," then why make the point? Indeed, the apophasis neatly masked his real intent:

> I state these differences, not to draw issues of belief as such, but because the actions resulting from the Communist philosophy are a ~~result~~ [in original] threat to the efforts of free nations to bring about world recovery and lasting peace.[17]

Acheson's juxtaposition of communism and the free world is supernation rhetoric, which will be examined in the next section.

The draft of January 16 also exhibited some last minute stylistic polishing. For instance, "conciliation and accommodation in the settlement" became "peaceful settlement," for the changes were "Shorter, more punch, means the same, and is not [emphasis in original] gobbledegook," moreover, the following emendation was made in order to make the thought easier to speak: "In addition we must complete our plans for reducing the barriers to, and increasing the flow of, world trade" became orally more manageable with "In addition we must carry out our plans for reducing the barriers to world trade and increasing its volume."[18]

The president made some insignificant changes on a fifth draft dated January 20, 1949. The reading copy was twenty-four pages long. On it, Truman underlined words for emphasis, but he emphasized so much verbiage that his practice made little sense for vocal pacing.[19]

PRESIDENT TRUMAN'S INAUGURAL ADDRESS: SUPERNATION RHETORIC

Prior to the end of World War II, perhaps with the exceptions of imperialism in the Philippines and in various gunboat diplomacies in Central America, the people of the United States and their presidents were committed to a public philosophy of a reified nation. Among the many aspects of this ideology was one that conceived the nation as the embodiment of freedom and justice for the American people.[20] Consequently, American domestic issues tended to dominate in pre-World War II inaugurals.[21]

After World War II, according to Dante Germino, a new kind of rhetoric emerged, which he called supernation rhetoric: "[T]he rhetoric of inaugurals stressed . . . the new note of the quasi-apocalyptic transformation of the world in a final battle with demonic communism."[22] Two trains of thought characterized this Supernation rhetoric: (1) the president depicts the supernation in Manichaean terms, which is "to view one's own side as the repository of all goodness and the other of all evil"; and in using this kind of rhetoric, (2) the president distorts the connotative and denotative meanings of freedom:

> The result has been the arbitrary division of the world into that of the "free" and the "enslaved," even though a majority of the countries with whom the United States has made alliances can scarcely be called "free" in the American public philosophy's understanding of freedom. Instead of being defined in relation to that philosophy,

freedom becomes defined as non-Communist.

> Regimes formerly seen as unfree in terms of the American public philosophy (military dictatorships and feudal autocracies) now become bastions of "liberty" if they appear to be threatened by Soviet expansion.[23]

Since Truman was the first president to deliver an inaugural after World War II, his address is a prototype of supernation rhetoric.

Indeed, one might expect as much, for Kenneth W. Thompson wisely observed the nexus between a president, an inaugural speech, and an historical context:

> It would be false . . . to suggest that the role of inaugural addresses by Presidents is everywhere the same. The context of such addresses is the spirit of the times. While the President imposes himself upon the form of the address, it is the times in part that shape the President's outlook, and what he feels called on to say. Moreover, each historical era brings with it social and intellectual tendencies that influence contemporary thought.[24]

The argument in this section is that Truman made a clean break with historical inaugural addresses by focusing almost entirely on foreign issues. Specifically, his inaugural was cast in supernation rhetoric, which now remains to be explicated.

President Truman sounded the leitmotif of supernation rhetoric in the second sentence of his Inaugural Address: "I accept it [the presidency] with a resolve to do all that I can for the welfare of this Nation and for the peace of the world."[25] Truman spoke not only as the *vox populi* but also as the *vox populi libri mundi* (the voice of the people of the free world); hence, Truman enacted the president-as-the-speaker-of-the-free-world role that Elsey envisioned in his memorandum. Truly, the rhetoric was as much for the people of the world as for U. S. citizens, because Truman inextricably linked the welfare of the United States to world peace. He declared: "It is fitting, therefore, that we take this occasion to proclaim to the world the essential principles of the faith by which we live, and to declare our aims to all peoples."

At their face value, the "essential principles of faith" were traditional exponents of nation rhetoric. Although Truman delivered the following words, they could just as appropriately be spoken by any previous chief executive:

> The American people stand firm in the faith which has inspired this Nation from the beginning. We believe that all men have a right to equal justice under law and equal opportunity to share in the common good. We believe that all men have a right to freedom of thought and expression. We believe that all men are created equal because they are created in the image of God. From this faith we will not be moved.

Stylistically, the anaphora of "We believe" communicated some elegance to an otherwise pedestrian patriotism.

Yet, a classical Aristotelian enthymeme was at work in Truman's nation rhetoric. An enthymeme is a truncated rhetorical syllogism in which the audience completes the logic of the argument without the orator's proving all of the premises. In the historical context of Soviet expansionism, democratic principles, such as "equal justice under law" and "freedom of thought and expression," assumed a salience that transcended traditional lip service to domestic verities. Truman invited domestic and foreign audiences to complete his enthymeme by making an inference and then by applying that conclusion to a political course of action: Communism denies and subverts U.S. values, therefore communism is bad; ergo, communism should be contained.

If some obdurate listeners did not perceive Truman's drift, he reiterated it in subsequent paragraphs. These passages also signaled the transition to supernation rhetoric. "[T]he United States and other like-minded nations," Truman averred, "find themselves directly opposed by a regime and a totally different concept of life." Here, his enthymeme was so clear that Truman did not have to identify the regime as the Soviet Union and the philosophy as communism.

Truman used the stylistic device of antithesis to juxtapose communism with democracy. Four pairs of antithetical units starkly communicated Manichaean divisions.

1. Communism believes "that man is so weak" that he "requires the rule of strong masters," but democracy believes "that man has the moral and intellectual capacity . . . to govern himself."
2. Communism "subjects" individuals to invidious state controls whereas democracy protects "the rights of individual."
3. Communism "maintains that social wrongs can be corrected only by violence" whereas democracy achieves "social justice . . . through peaceful change."
4. "Communism holds that the world is so widely divided into

opposing classes that war is inevitable," but "Democracy holds
that free nations can settle differences justly and maintain a
lasting peace."

The anaphora of "Communism" and "Democracy," which juxtaposed each
of the four thought units, verbally reinforced the antithesis. Truman's dual
role—the voice of the people and the voice of the free people of the
world—coalesced in the conclusion he drew concerning the antithesis of
communism with democracy:

> These differences between communism and democracy do
> not concern the United States alone. People everywhere
> are coming to realize that what is involved is material
> well-being, human dignity, and the right to believe in and
> worship God. [And then he used Acheson's insert:] I state
> these differences, not to draw issues of belief as such, but
> because the actions resulting from the Communist
> philosophy are a threat to the efforts of free nations to
> bring about world recovery and lasting peace.

By now, most listeners would have appreciated Truman's point, but
he was not finished with his verbal portraiture of Communist perfidy.
Continuing in the Manichaean vein, he warranted more evidence of the
United States as hero versus the Soviet Union as villain. The antithesis
was present, but in the form of an enthymeme: The audience easily
supplied what nation was the opposite of the United States. The listing had
four paragraphs that began with the anaphora of "We have." First, "We
have sought no territory." Americans, and free peoples of the world,
would recall the Soviet Union's violating the Yalta agreements in Rumania,
Bulgaria, and Poland, Russian pressures on Turkey and Iran, as well as the
Berlin Blockade and the fall of Czechoslovakia in 1948. Second, "We
have constantly and vigorously supported the United Nations." And
Americans would have remembered that the Soviet Union often used its
veto power to stymie world peace. This was one of the reasons why
Truman bypassed the United Nations for the Truman Doctrine and the
Marshall Plan, which probably would have been vetoed by the Soviets.[26]
Third, "We have made every effort to secure agreement on effective
international control of our most powerful weapon [the atom bomb]." The
fact that the Soviet Union vetoed in the Security Council in 1946 a plan for
international control of atomic energy warranted Truman's claim.[27]
Fourth, "We have encouraged . . . the expansion of world trade on a
sound and fair basis." The 1947 Geneva agreement had produced the

General Agreement on Tariffs and Trade [GATT].

Truman could have continued the anaphora of "We have" to list additional anti-Soviet evidence. But the speech team ceased using that elegant stylistic device; nevertheless, the Manichaean enthymeme marched forward. "Almost a year ago, in company with 16 *free nations* [my emphasis] of Europe, we launched the greatest cooperative economic program in history." Truman alluded to the Marshall Plan, and he allowed in supernation rhetoric that "We have saved a number of countries from losing their liberty."

The Manichaean juxtapositions, used once in four units of clear antithesis, and once in four units of implied antithesis, were masterful rhetorical enthymemes. Truman's supernation rhetoric presented the evidence, and Americans and foreigners supplied the inferences.

As a U.S. solution to combat Soviet perfidy, Hardy's outline of Point Four remained remarkably intact. His first point was political institutions, with the United Nations as a subpoint. As delivered, Truman pledged: "First, we will continue to give unfaltering support to the United Nations." Hardy's other subpoint of "respect for the rights of all peoples" became more narrowly defined by HST as "lands now advancing toward self-government under democratic principles." Hardy's second point, economic betterment with subpoints of the ERP, world trade, and technological development, remained complete, except for the technology part. "Second," the president intoned, "we will continue our programs for world economic recovery." Specifically, he mentioned the "European recovery program," and reducing the barriers to world trade because "Economic recovery and peace itself depend on increased world trade."

Hardy's third point was preservation of law and order, which included regional defense pacts, military aid and advice, and U.S. military strength. It was a serviceable blueprint, for Truman announced, "Third, we will strengthen freedom-loving nations against the dangers of aggression." Truman acknowledged that a "collective defense arrangement," which would become known as NATO (North Atlantic Treaty Organization), was close to fruition and that the Rio Pact was a fait accompli. Truman sold the fledgling NATO alliance with supernation rhetoric while employing the fallacy of *petitio principii*. Without bothering to prove that the United States was faced with imminent armed aggression, Truman assumed that premise, and then argued that the aggression could be deterred by providing "unmistakable proof of the joint determination of the free countries to resist armed attack from any quarter . . . [then] the armed attack might never occur." Incidentally, the inaugural audience's "applause was perhaps the strongest" for this appeal.[28] Additionally, Truman pledged to "provide military advice and equipment to free nations" who would cooperate with the United States.

Hardy's fourth point was the reduction of trade barriers to international trade and peace. Of the four points, this one was redirected in the final address toward technological aid to developing countries. However, the theme of international trade and peace were still the end products of the revised rhetoric.

"Fourth," Truman proclaimed, "we must embark on a bold new program for making the benefits of our scientific advances and industrial progress available for the improvement and growth of underdeveloped areas." Truman listed the miserable living conditions of more than half the people in the world, and then offered U.S. "technical knowledge" that was "inexhaustible." However, this aid was circumscribed. The problem was worldwide, which included Communist countries, but the solution was limited to anti- or non-Communist nations, for U.S. aid would be made "available to peace-loving peoples," which excluded Soviet satellites. Later in his address, Truman again assured Americans that "Our aim should be to help the free peoples of the world." And Truman summarized his four points with a Manichaean appeal:

> Democracy alone can supply the vitalizing force to stir the peoples of the world into triumphant action, not only against their human oppressors, but also against their ancient enemies—hunger, misery, and despair. On the basis of these four major courses of action we hope to help create the conditions that will lead eventually to personal freedom and happiness for all mankind.

Incidentally, Truman's summary also warrants the interpretation that he viewed his speech as four points, not Point Four.

The conclusion of Truman's Inaugural could be termed a classical peroration, an ending of unusual elegance and force. Truman constructed a series of five sentences that began with the anaphora of "We are aided by." His language was reminiscent of FDR's famous "Four Freedoms" speech (freedom of speech, worship, want, and fear), January 6, 1941, for Truman proclaimed "We are aided by all who wish to live in freedom from fear . . . who want relief from lies and propaganda . . . who desire self-government . . . who long for economic security . . . [and] who desire freedom of speech, freedom of religion, and freedom to live their own lives for useful ends." To bolster the Manichaean, supernation rhetoric that recurred throughout the speech, Truman waxed Biblically: "Our allies are the millions who hunger and thirst after righteousness." To motivate Americans to gird up their loins in the ongoing battle of good against evil, the president preached that it would "test our courage, our devotion to duty, and our concept of liberty." And, as if to verify the cliche that God is a being mentioned in the last sentence of a political speech, Truman intoned: "With God's help, the future of mankind will be assured in a world of justice, harmony, and peace."[29]

TRUMAN'S DELIVERY

Although Elsey's November 16, 1948, memorandum noted that the inaugural should be 1800 words and fifteen minutes long, it lasted twenty minutes and contained about 2200 words. Hence, HST delivered the speech at 110 wpm. Given that Truman's rate was normally around 150 wpm,[30] he made a conscious effort to slow the rate in order to dignify the occasion.

Truman delivered his speech in a typically Truman fashion. His eye contact was poor because he read his speech. He evidently did not practice it enough, for he made numerous mistakes in simple pronunciations, such as "I ask for your encour...encouragements"; "It may be our lot to experience, andn [HST slurred "and" and "in" together, paused slightly, and then spoke the words separately]"; "The difference...the differences between communism and democracy do not concern the United States alone"; and he muffed one of the principal lines in the speech: "From this fai...uh...faith we will not be moved."[31] His voice was nasal, which he could not help, and it became more so whenever he raised his pitch; however, his nasality was less objectionable when he spoke in lower pitches. His vocal pacing was uninspired, for he was unwilling or unable to change it.[32]

Truman had little feeling for how to manage his voice for effective speaking. He lacked any sense of rhetorical timing. He gave few vocal cues to stress salient ideas, and he did not use the rhetorical pause for effect. Hence, HST often expected applause for a line, but was perplexed when he heard none. Yet, what Truman truly lacked in the techniques of speaking seemed to be recompensed by Truman-as-president: "Without eloquence or command of speech, he lights fires among crowds who sense that Roosevelt was for them and that Truman is one of them."[33]

Truman's speech was the first inaugural to be broadcast on television, and that medium highlighted Truman's strengths and weaknesses on the platform. With a fresh hair cut, he looked like a sheep just shorn. As a television presence, Truman's delivery was lackluster: "Truman's speech was the slow movement in the spectacle."[34] Jack Gould noted that when the "Star Spangled Banner" was sung to open the festivities, people watching TV at home "instinctively followed the action of the spectators in Washington and rose promptly to their feet."[35] One assumes that the home viewers reacted as empathetically to Truman as the live audience did when it clapped its approval of his speech.

REACTIONS TO THE ADDRESS: FOUR POINTS AND POINT FOUR

Point Four was an example of amphiboly, or ambiguous meaning. In this case, the uncertainty is in the number: Should the address be called Four Points or Point Four? Alonzo Hamby observed that Truman "proclaimed four basic points for American foreign policy" and that HST "dwelt longest on the fourth point."[36] Harold Gosnell noted that Truman's foreign policy address "outlined four major policies," but that "the last of these policies came to be called 'Point Four'"; moreover, Roy Jenkins noted that the address "was christened Point Four (by the press, not by Truman) and was the beginning of Third World Aid."[37] Although a fine point, the nomenclature of Point Four or Four Points is significant. Point Four captured the initial limelight, but the Four Points (actually, the first three points minus the fourth) were the epicenter of Harry Truman's presidency in foreign policy from 1949 to 1953. And all four points were communicated in Manichaean, supernation rhetoric.

With regard to Four Points, the public reaction to Truman's Inaugural was favorable. The Truman Library contains five pro-folders and one con-folder. A self-confessed Republican wrote from Providence, Rhode Island: "Its simplicity, its directness, its lack of class or partisan ill will place it high in the hearts of our people."[38] Incidentally, this Republican voter appreciated that Truman eschewed in his inaugural the discord of the 1948 campaign that propelled him to the White House.

A few writers reacted specifically to Truman's supernation rhetoric. Truman's Manichaean, holier-than-thou attitude in the inaugural was discomforting to some Americans. A writer from Rochester, Minnesota, complained that Truman's heated rhetoric was "a declaration of war." In less hyperbole, a writer from Wilton, Connecticut, scored Truman's Cold War idealogy:

> [I]t is neither true, nor safe to believe, that all the virtue
> is on our side and all the evil on our opponents' [emphasis
> in original] . . . . Finally, I notice that Wall Street, to
> which you alluded unfavorably in your appeal to the
> electorate, reacted favorably to this speech, which in itself
> is an indication that you are off on the wrong boat.[39]

Perhaps one of the reasons the business community initially reacted so favorably to the fourth point was that it presented an opportunity to make money. *Tass*, the Soviet news agency, taunted that it ensured "the maximum possibilities for penetration by American capital into backward nations"; lest this be perceived as Communist propaganda, Ernest K. Lindley correctly noted: "Yet, obviously, capital will not go abroad unless it is protected against confiscation and permitted to earn interest or a profit. This is what the president had in mind when he spoke of 'guarantees to the investor.'"[40]

Moreover, a writer from Chicago, Illinois, objected to HST's helping governments whose only virtue was being non- or anti-Communist, for the writer protested "the support of governments that are fascist and corrupt such as those of Greece and China. Finally, it does not seem that nations are being considered as equals when they are preached to and when they are told that our ways are better than theirs."[41]

These anecdotal letters were also mirrored by national figures. Henry Wallace—who was vice-president under Roosevelt from 1941 to 1945, who was dumped by Roosevelt in favor of Truman in 1945, who, as secretary of commerce, was fired by Truman in 1946, and who waged an unsuccessful bid against Truman as the Progressive candidate for president in 1948—complained that his former boss's speech came "closer to a declaration of war than the inaugural address of any peacetime President in our history."[42] But no less a sophisticated critic of American politics than Walter Lippmann observed the inherent problems with Truman's Manichaean, supernation appeals: "For while a good democrat will certainly be an anti-Communist, those who are solely anti-Communist are not likely to be good democrats. They are likely to think that if only they hate the false philosophy enough, then automatically and ex-officio so to speak, they are the exemplars of the true philosophy."[43] Likewise, the *New Republic* rejoined Truman's rhetoric with a stinging rebuttal:

> His remarks about the Communist philosophy and what America proposes to do about it appear to call this country to a holy crusade against Russia . . . which could have no conclusion but war. . . . [I]n pursuit of our containment of Russia we have made friends with every other dictatorship everywhere—with Chiang, Peron, Franco—if it was only willing to be, or to say it is, anti-Communist. . . . Greece sinks from one level of corruption and incompetence to another, and we do nothing about it, since the corrupt leaders are our allies against Moscow and its friends.[44]

Indeed, these objections about the United States's supporting anti- or non-Communist countries are warranted. Robert Packenham determined that "At no time since the end of World War II has the proportion of democracies in the Third World been greater than 25%; most of the time it has been between 10 and 20%."[45]

Four Points prompted international approval. The Italian and British press reacted favorably, and the conservative *Daily Telegraph* caught the spirit of Truman's supernation pitch:

> In this speech the President makes ridiculous the rumors
> that he is over-susceptible to Communist advances, for no
> more devastating commentary on Communism has ever
> been made than his contrast between that faith and true
> democracy.[46]

However, as may be expected, the Communists carped in *Tass* that Truman's speech was an "enraged attack" on Communism.[47]

Point Four—the fourth point—originally attracted the most notice. *Newsweek* noted that "The President was calling on the nation to reinforce the cold war against Communism with a worldwide recovery program."[48] But the president's new program "caught nearly everyone by surprise . . . . Most foreign observers were delighted; most U.S. Congressmen were confused."[49] This paradox is resolved in the summary section.

CONCLUSION

"President Harry Truman's inaugural address," James Reston reasoned, "was generally interpreted in the capitol as one of the most ambitious pronouncements on foreign affairs every made by an American President."[50] HST's speech has been assigned the sobriquet of Point Four, but its historical importance and rhetorical efficacy were in its Four Points.

Originally, Hardy gave Elsey four thematic components. Their raison d'etre ensured peace and security for the United States under the free world leadership of President Truman. Indeed, the Manichaean, Supernation appeals inherent in all four points made little rhetorical sense if they did not seek acquiescence from the audience for supporting the United Nations, economic recovery, military security, and technological aid. All of these four points, but especially the first three, maintained the United States as the leader of the non-Communist world and strengthened the free world against Soviet domination.

The first three points in Truman's Inaugural Address remained cornerstones in American foreign policy against Communism until the early 1990s. However, the result of the fourth point was less favorable. William Pemberton observed that Truman's "proposal reaped great propaganda rewards, but the much lauded plan never amounted to much except as a publicity device," and he observed that although the fourth point was intended for Third World countries, most of the money went to Europe.[51]

The fourth point of Point Four is an example of how rhetoric is not easily translated into political action. Hardy's four points were an idea in search of a speech, and the fourth point was a speech in search of a program.

In his press conference on January 27, 1949, President Truman was asked how he would implement the fourth point. HST candidly admitted: "I can't tell you just what is going to take place, where it is going to take place, or how it is going to take place. I know what I want to do." One of the reasons the State Department was not receptive to Hardy's idea was that no such program was being studied. The fourth point, an Act for International Development, was passed by Congress in May, 1950, more than a year after its dramatic announcement on inaugural day.[52] Sensing that Point Four was a prosaic label for a major foreign policy initiative, a reporter asked "for lead purposes, is there any other title we could give to point four?" Truman answered: "I think it speaks for itself. All you need to do is read the speech; it is perfectly plain. Doesn't seem to have confused any foreign government. The only people who seem to be confused about it are our own newspapers here at home. [Laughter]"[53]

When explaining why the fourth point failed to meet expectations, Thomas Patterson said it best:

> Hastily announced, originally neglected by the State Department, lost in the turmoil of more dramatic Cold War issues, hampered by limited congressional appropriations, resisted in many parts of the Third World, spurned by American businessmen, and ultimately diverted to military purposes and strategic materials stockpiling, Point Four faltered early.[54]

NOTES

1. Rosenman, oral history transcript, p. 52.
2. Clark M. Clifford, oral history transcript, April 1977, HSTL, p. 297.

3. Rosenman, oral history transcript, p. 30.

4. Clifford, *Counsel to the President*, p. 73.

5. Clifford, *Counsel to the President*, p. 74.

6. Ryan, "Harry S Truman," p. 401.

7. Ryan, *Franklin D. Roosevelt's Rhetorical Presidency*, p. 73.

8. George Elsey to Mr. Clifford, November 16, 1948, papers of George Elsey, speech file, box 36, HSTL, pp. 1-2.

9. Clifford, *Counsel to the President*, p. 249.

10. The drafts upon which I based my inference concerning their rejection are in the papers of David Lloyd, presidential speech file, box 13, HSTL.

11. Notes on Inaugural Address, January 27, 1949, papers of George Elsey, speech file, box 36, HSTL. For some inexplicable reason, twentieth-century Democratic presidents tend to be less longwinded than Republican presidents, and Truman was not an exception; see Donald L. Wolfarth, "John F. Kennedy in the Tradition of Inaugural Speeches," *Quarterly Journal of Speech* 47 (1961): 126.

12. Memorandum for Mr. Clifford, July 17, 1963, papers of Clark Clifford, box 39, HSTL.

13. Clifford, *Counsel to the President*, p. 250.

14. Files of David Lloyd, box 13, HSTL. One would observe that "Preservation of Law and Order," which is a Godterm in American polity, is perhaps more palatable than "Military Security," which was crossed out; yet, the three subpoints under the main heading clearly indicate the concern for U.S. military security.

15. Inaugural Address, 1949, papers of David Lloyd, presidential speech file, box 13, HSTL.

16. Draft of January 15, papers of George Elsey, speech file, box 36, HSTL.

17. Draft of January 16, papers of George Elsey, speech file, box 36, HSTL.

18. Draft of January 16, papers of Clark Clifford, box 39, HSTL, pp. 5, 7.

19. See president's secretary's files, speech file, box 48, and Inaugural Address, reading copy, HSTL.

20. Germino, *The Inaugural Addresses of American Presidents*, pp. 2, 15-19.

21. Wolfarth, "Kennedy in the Tradition of Inaugural Addresses," p. 130.

22. Germino, *The Inaugural Addresses of American Presidents*, p. 21.

23. Ibid., pp. 23, 25.

24. Ibid., p. x.

25. *HST, 1949*, p. 112.   All subsequent quotations of HST's Inaugural Address are from this speech text.

26. George T. Mazuzan, "United Nations," in *The Harry S. Truman Encyclopedia*, edited by Richard S. Kirkendall (Boston: G. K. Hall & Co., 1989), pp. 369-370.

27. Truman, *Memoirs*, II, p. 11.

28. "Truman Sworn in, the 32d President," *New York Times*, January 21, 1949, p. 2.

29. Germino, in *The Inaugural Addresses of American Presidents*, p. 21, opined that one could read Truman's Inaugural "uncharitably as calling on God to be the incidental helper of American technology."

30. Underhill, *The Truman Persuasions*, p. 337.

31. Cassette, Side 2, Inaugural Address, selected speeches of Harry S. Truman, 1948-1951, HSTL.

32. Underhill, *The Truman Persuasions*, pp. 334-338.

33. "Harry Truman on His Own Now," *New Republic*, January 24, 1949, p. 5.

34. "Hail to the Chief," *New York Times*, January 21, 1949, p. 55; Jack Gould, "10,000,000 Viewers See the Ceremony," *New York Times*, January 21, 1949, p. 6.

35. Gould, "10,000,000 Viewers See the Ceremony," *New York Times*, January 21, 1949, p. 6.

36. Alonzo L. Hamby, *Beyond the New Deal: Harry S. Truman and American Liberalism* (New York: Columbia University Press, 1973), p. 354.

37. Harold F. Gosnell, *A Political Biography of Harry S. Truman* (Westport, Conn.: Greenwood Press, 1980), p. 441; Jenkins, *Truman*, p. 146.

38. Papers of Harry S. Truman, president's personal file, PPF-200, box 326.   The writer from Providence was a stylist, for this passage contains the stylistic devices of anaphora and asyndeton.

39. PPF 200, box 326, HSTL.

40. "World Fair Deal", *Newsweek*, January 31, 1949, p. 18; Ernest K. Lindley, "The President's Fourth Course," *Newsweek*, January 31, 1949, p. 19.

41. PPF-200, box 326, HSTL.

42. "Wallace Calls Talk of Truman Warlike," *New York Times*, January 21, 1949, p. 5.

43. Walter Lippmann, "The Inaugural," *Washington Post*, January 24, 1949, p. 3.

44. "President Truman's Global Plans," *New Republic*, January 31, 1949, pp. 5-6.

45. Robert Packenham, *Liberal America and The Third World* (Princeton: Princeton University Press, 1973), p. 41.

46. See "President's Talk Encourages Italy" and "Message Praised by British Papers," *New York Times*, January 21, 1949, p. 6.

47. "World Fair Deal," *Newsweek*, January 31, 1949, p. 18.

48. Ibid.

49. "Bold New Program," *Time*, January 31, 1949, p. 16.

50. James Reston, "Speech Seen as Aid to Western World," *New York Times*, January 21, 1949, p. 1.

51. Pemberton, *Harry S. Truman: Fair Dealer and Cold Warrior*, p. 160.

52. Packenham, *Liberal America and The Third World*, p. 43.

53. *HST: 1949*, pp. 118-119.

54. Thomas G. Patterson, *Meeting the Communist Threat: Truman to Reagan* (New York: Oxford University Press, 1988), p. 157.

Conclusion

On May 8, 1945, at nine o'clock in the morning from the radio room in the White House, Harry S. Truman, the thirty-third president of the United States broadcast words that war-weary Americans yearned to hear: "This is a solemn but a glorious hour. I only wish that Franklin D. Roosevelt had lived to witness this day. General Eisenhower informs me that the forces of Germany have surrendered to the United Nations. The flags of freedom fly over all Europe."[1]

When Truman delivered his valedictory on January 15, 1953, he was unable to utter the words that a war-weary nation yearned to hear: that the United States was at peace in Korea. Moreover, when HST left the presidency in 1953, the flags of freedom did not fly over all of Europe, but the Truman Doctrine did save Greece, Turkey, and, if one ascribes to the domino theory, the oil-rich Mideast from falling under the domination of the Soviet Union. Thus, Truman's valedictory speech serves as a fitting recapitulation of the selected themes of his presidential rhetoric that were treated in this book.

TRUMAN'S VALEDICTORY

Truman wrote out in longhand an undated eighteen page draft, which became the core of the address.[2] Charles Murphy worked almost all of Truman's handwritten materials into a fifty-two page first draft, which is undated. Richard Neustadt composed a draft on January 10, 1953, parts of which were incorporated into the final address. Interestingly, Neustadt termed this speech a "final fireside," a sobriquet that never gelled with Truman's speech making. The address then went through six drafts, with the final completed on January 14.[3]

The speech was broadcast over national radio and television at 10:30 P.M. Truman's delivery was not effective. He read the speech, whose pages were on a small stand on his desk, and he would turn them as he finished each one. His eye contact, which did not matter over the radio, but was terribly important on the television, was practically nonexistent, for he only occasionally looked up from his text for fleeting moments. Nor was his voice management impelling: His phrasing was poor, he read too quickly, and there were unnatural pauses in his rate. Yet, after nearly eight years in office, Americans evidently did not expect their president to be eloquent; rather, if the following two letters can suffice as warrants for the claim, Americans reacted favorably to Truman-the-man and not to Truman-the-orator. From Washington, D.C., a listener thought Truman's homey address "was the finest speech you ever made, and it was given the best"; and a listener from Long Island complimented the president: "and as always you spoke in your wonderful human, down-to-earth way."[4]

Even the media caught something of the poignancy in Truman's valedictory. Dorothy Thompson, writing in the Washington *Evening Star*, praised the wide-ranging address: "President Truman's Farewell address was one of the ablest and most comprehensive speeches he has made during the presidency"; Richard L. Strout, writing for the *Christian Science Monitor*, caught the speech's rhetorical motive that was disguised in the rest of the verbiage: "It was just the speech to efface some of the rancor of the recent election, to make a lot of people proud to be Americans, to strengthen faith abroad in the moral and spiritual values of the United States, and finally, also, to make a lot of fellow citizens feel better about Mr. Truman"; and the *New York Times* noticed the subtle appeals to posterity for Truman's ethos, which it thought would be kindly remembered: "But when any number of years have passed and when the weaker and all-too-human side of Harry S. Truman has fallen out of mind, we think that for the high hopes he had and for the bravery with which he tried to realize them, he will be remembered and respected."[5]

The speech was a rambling, discursive account of Truman's presidency. He discussed a variety of topics, from General Eisenhower's impending presidency to such trivial points as how he had to take an automobile from Blair House to the White House, which Truman personally penned on the fifth draft, dated January 13, 1953 (his deletions are bracketed and additions are italicized):

The Secret Service wouldn't let me walk across the street,
[so I had to get in a car every night and drive home—even

though it was just one block.] *so I had to get in a car in the morning to cross the street to the White House office, again at noon to go to the Blair House for lunch, again to go to the office and finally take an automobile at night to return to the Blair House.   Fantastic isn't it?   But necessary so the guards thought—and they are the ones exposed to danger.*[6]

However, for our summary purposes here, Truman's argumentation on the two major themes of this book must be the remaining focus.

Bert Cochran, writing in the early 1970s, claimed: "In his farewell address, Truman tried to justify his fateful decision to the ages. 'When history says that my term of office saw the beginning of the cold war,' he opined, 'it will also say that in those eight years we have set the course that can win.' That is precisely what history will not say."[7]   As of the early 1990s, with the collapse of Soviet communism, perhaps that judgment needs to be revised.

Truman's "course that can win" was based partly on Manichaean rhetoric.   Consistently, from the Truman Doctrine to his valedictory, Truman preached against the evil empire:

I suppose that history will remember my term of office as the years when the "cold war" began to overshadow our lives.   I have had hardly a day in office that has not been dominated by this all-embracing struggle—this conflict between those who love freedom and those would lead the world back into slavery and darkness.[8]

Recalling for the American people Soviet perfidy, Truman ticked off Greece and Turkey, the Marshall Plan, the various defense pacts, and Korea as instances of where the United States successfully confronted Soviet expansionism.

Truman's "course that can win" was also based partly on supernation rhetoric.   Arguing the historical analogies that he had mustered in his other important state speeches, Truman asked the American people to remember his policies:

These are great and historic achievements that we can all be proud of.   Think of the difference between our course now and our course thirty years ago.   After the First World War, we withdrew from world affairs—we failed to act in concert with other peoples against aggression—we helped to kill the League of Nations—and we built up tariffs and barriers which strangled world trade. This time we avoided those mistakes. We helped to found and to sustain the United Nations. We have welded alliances that include the greater part of the free world. And we have gone ahead with other free countries to help build their economies and link us all together in a healthy world trade.

Think back for a moment to the 1930's and you will see the difference. The Japanese moved into Manchuria and free men did not act. The Fascists moved into Ethiopia, and we did not act. The Nazis marched into the Rhineland, into Austria, into Czechoslovakia, and free men were paralyzed for lack of strength and unity of will.

Think about those years of weakness and indecision, and World War II which was their evil result. Then think about the speed and courage and decisiveness with which we have moved against the Communist threat since World War II.[9]

As for Korea, which appreciably accounted for Truman's rating of 23 percent in November, 1951, and 25 percent in February, 1952,[10] HST eschewed specificity for platitudes. Still, he based his reasoning on historical analogies that were hard to refute. Recalling the long plane ride from Independence to Washington in April 1950, HST rehearsed his basic reasoning for the Korean War, then and in 1953:

Flying back over the flatlands of the Middle West and over the Appalachians that summer afternoon I had a lot of time to think. I turned the problem over in my mind in many ways, but my thoughts kept coming back to the Nineteen Thirties—to Manchuria—Ethiopia—the Rhineland—Austria—and finally to Munich.

Here was history repeating itself. Here was another probing action, another testing action. If we let the republic of Korea go under, some other country would be next, and then another. And all the time, the courage and confidence of the free world would be ebbing away, just as it did in the Nineteen Thirties. And the United Nations would go the way of the League of Nations.

So a decision was reached—the decision I believe was the most important in my time as President.

Where free men had failed the test before, this time we met the test.[11]

And the "course that can win" was based partly on Truman's abiding faith in the American people and their democracy. It was also Truman's faith in the people's political instincts that innervated his Miracle of '48. Indeed, Truman's Manichaean faith in good versus evil, Democrats versus Republicans, and the United States versus Soviet communism was his abiding legacy:

> Then, some of you may ask, when and how will the "cold war" ever end? I think I can answer that simply. The Communist world has great resources, and it looks strong. But there is a fatal flaw in their society. Theirs is a godless system, a system of slavery; there is no freedom in it, no consent. The Iron Curtain, the secret police, the constant purges, all these are symptoms of a great basic weakness—the rulers' fear of their own people.
>
> In the long run, the strength of our free society, and our ideals will prevail over a system that has respect for neither God nor man.
>
> I have a deep and abiding faith in the destiny of free men.[12]

Has not Harry S. Truman's faith in the American people been vindicated?

Assuming an affirmation to that rhetorical question, I close with an excerpt from a person from San Francisco, California, who sadly responded to Truman's leave-taking: "It is always sad to say goodby to a good friend, and that is what I think you have been to the American people."[13]

NOTES

1. "Broadcast to the American People Announcing the Surrender of Germany," *HST: 1945*, p. 48.

2. President's secretary's files, speech file, box 51, pp. 1-18, HSTL.

3. Files of Charles S. Murphy, president's speech file, box 20, pp. 1-52, HSTL; papers of Richard Neustadt, subject file, box 8, second draft, 1-12-53, third draft, 1-13-53, fourth draft, 1-13-53, fifth draft, 1-13-53, sixth draft, 1-14-53, HSTL.

4. PPF-200, box 353, HSTL.

5. Quoted in Democratic National Committee clipping file, Harry S. Truman file, Farewell Address from the White House, January 15, 1953, box 47, HSTL.

6. Fifth draft, 1-13-53, president's secretary's files, box 51, p. 3, HSTL.

7. Cochran, *Harry Truman and the Crisis Presidency*, p. 399.

8. *HST: 1953*, p. 1199.

9. Ibid.

10. "Who Likes Ike?" *Time*, February 18, 1952, pp. 18-19.

11. *HST: 1953*, p. 1200.

12. Ibid., p. 1201.

13. PPF-200, box 353, HSTL.

II
COLLECTED SPEECHES

The Truman Doctrine

The gravity of the situation which confronts the world today necessitates my appearance before a joint session of the Congress. The foreign policy and the national security of this country are involved.

One aspect of the present situation, which I wish to present to you at this time for your consideration and decision, concerns Greece and Turkey.

The United States has received from the Greek Government an urgent appeal for financial and economic assistance. Preliminary reports from the American Economic Mission now in Greece and reports from the American Ambassador in Greece corroborate the statement of the Greek Government that assistance is imperative if Greece is to survive as a free nation.

I do not believe that the American people and the Congress wish to turn a deaf ear to the appeal of the Greek Government.

Greece is not a rich country. Lack of sufficient natural resources has always forced the Greek people to work hard to make both ends meet. Since 1940, this industrious and peace-loving country has suffered invasion, four years of cruel enemy occupation, and bitter internal strife.

When forces of liberation entered Greece they found that the retreating Germans had destroyed virtually all the railways, roads, port facilities, communications and merchant marine. More than a thousand villages had been burned. Eighty-five per cent of the children were tubercular. Livestock, poultry and draft animals had almost disappeared. Inflation had wiped out practically all savings.

As a result of these tragic conditions, a military minority, exploiting human want and misery, was able to create political chaos which, until now, has made economic recovery impossible.

Greece is today without funds to finance the importation of those goods which are essential to bare subsistence. Under these circumstances the people of Greece cannot make progress in solving their problems of reconstruction. Greece is in desperate need of financial and economic assistance to enable it to resume purchases of food, clothing, fuel and seeds. These are indispensable for the subsistence of its people and are obtainable only from abroad. Greece must have help to import the goods necessary to restore internal order and security so essential for economic and political recovery.

The Greek Government has also asked for the assistance of experienced American administrators, economists and technicians to insure that the financial and other aid given to Greece shall be used effectively in creating a stable and self-sustaining economy and in improving its public administration.

The very existence of the Greek state is today threatened by the terrorist activities of several thousand armed men, led by Communists, who defy the Government's authority at a number of points, particularly along the northern boundaries. A commission appointed by the United Nations Security Council is at present investigating disturbed conditions in northern Greece and alleged border violations along the frontier between Greece on the one hand and Albania, Bulgaria and Yugoslavia on the other.

Meanwhile, the Greek Government is unable to cope with the situation. The Greek Army is small and poorly equipped. It needs supplies and equipment if it is to restore the authority of the Government throughout Greek territory.

Greece must have assistance if it is to become a self-supporting and self-respecting democracy.

The United States must supply that assistance. We have already extended to Greece certain types of relief and economic aid but these are inadequate.

There is no other country to which democratic Greece can turn.

No other nation is willing and able to provide the necessary support for a democratic Greek Government.

The British Government, which has been helping Greece, can give no further financial or economic aid after March 31. Great Britain finds itself under the necessity of reducing or liquidating its commitments in several parts of the world, including Greece.

We have considered how the United Nations might assist in this crisis. But the situation is an urgent one requiring immediate action, and the United Nations and its related organizations are not in a position to extend help of the kind that is required.

It is important to note that the Greek Government has asked for our aid in utilizing effectively the financial and other assistance we may give to Greece, and in improving its public administration. It is of the utmost importance that we supervise the use of any funds made available to Greece, in such a manner that each dollar spent will count toward making Greece self-supporting, and will help to build an economy in which a healthy democracy can flourish.

No government is perfect.   One of the chief virtues of a democracy, however, is that its defects are always visible and under democratic processes can be pointed out and corrected. The Government of Greece is not perfect.   Nevertheless it represents 85 per cent of the members of the Greek Parliament who were chosen in an election last year. Foreign observers, including 692 Americans, considered this election to be a fair expression of the views of the Greek people.

The Greek Government has been operating in an atmosphere of chaos and extremism. It has made mistakes. The extension of aid by this country does not mean that the United States condones everything that the Greek Government has done or will do. We have condemned in the past, and we condemn now, extremist measure of the Right or the Left. We have in the past advised tolerance, and we advise tolerance now.

Greece's neighbor, Turkey, also deserves our attention.

The future of Turkey as an independent and economically sound State is clearly no less important to the freedom-loving peoples of the world than the future of Greece. The circumstances in which Turkey finds itself today are considerably different than those of Greece. Turkey has been spared the disasters that have beset Greece. And during the war, the United States and Great Britain furnished Turkey with material aid.

Nevertheless, Turkey now needs our support.

Since the war Turkey has sought financial assistance from Great Britain and the United States for the purpose of effecting that modernization necessary for the maintenance of its national integrity.

That integrity is essential to the preservation of order in the Middle East.

The British government has informed us that, owing to its own difficulties, it can no longer extend financial or economic aid to Turkey.

As in the case of Greece, if Turkey is to have the assistance it needs, the United States must supply it. We are the only country able to provide that help.

I am fully aware of the broad implications involved if the United States extends assistance to Greece and Turkey, and I shall discuss these implications with you at this time.

One of the primary objectives of the foreign policy of the United States is the creation of conditions in which we and other nations will be able to work out a way of life free from coercion. That was a fundamental issue in the war with Germany and Japan. Our victory was won over countries which sought to impose their will, and their way of life, upon other nations.

To ensure the peaceful development of nations, free from coercion, the United States has taken a leading part in establishing the United Nations. The United Nations is designed to make possible lasting freedom and independence for all its members. We shall not realize our objectives, however, unless we are willing to help free people to maintain their free institutions and their national integrity against aggressive movements that seek to impose upon them totalitarian regimes. This is no more than a frank recognition that totalitarian regimes imposed on free peoples, by direct or indirect aggression, undermine the foundations of international peace and hence the security of the United States.

The peoples of a number of countries of the world have recently had totalitarian regimes forced upon them against their will. The Government of the United States has made frequent protests against coercion and intimidation in violation of the Yalta agreement, in Poland, Rumania, and Bulgaria. I must also state that in a number of other countries there have been similar developments.

At the present moment in world history nearly every nation must choose between alternative ways of life. The choice is too often not a free one.

One way of life is based upon the will of the majority, and is distinguished by free institutions, representative government, free elections, guarantees of individual liberty, freedom of speech and religion, and freedom from political oppression.

The second way of life is based upon the will of a minority forcibly imposed upon the majority. It relies upon terror and oppression, a controlled press and radio, fixed elections, and the suppression of personal freedoms.

I believe that it must be the policy of the United States to support free peoples who are resisting attempted subjugation by armed minority or by outside pressures. I believe that we must assist free peoples to work out their own destinies in their own way. I believe that our help should be primarily through economic and financial aid which is essential to economic stability and orderly political processes.

The world is not static, and the status quo is not sacred. But we cannot allow changes in the status quo in violation of the Charter of the United Nations by such methods as coercion, or by such subterfuges as political infiltration. In helping free and independent nations to maintain their freedom, the United States will be giving effect to the principles of the Charter of the United Nations.

It is necessary only to glance at a map to realize that the survival and integrity of the Greek nation are of grave importance in a much wider situation. If Greece should fall under the control of an armed minority, the effect upon its neighbor, Turkey, would be immediate and serious. Confusion and disorder might well spread throughout the entire Middle East.

Moreover, the disappearance of Greece as an independent State would have a profound effect upon those countries in Europe whose peoples are struggling against great difficulties to maintain their freedoms and their independence while they repair the damages of war. It would be an unspeakable tragedy if these countries, which have struggled so long against overwhelming odds, should lose that victory for which they sacrificed so much. Collapse of free institutions and loss of independence would be disastrous not only for them but for the world. Discouragement and possibly failure would quickly be the lot of neighboring peoples striving to maintain their freedom and independence.

Should we fail to aid Greece and Turkey in this fateful hour, the effect will be far-reaching to the West as well as to the East. We must take immediate and resolute action.

I therefore ask the Congress to provide authority for assistance to Greece and Turkey in the amount of $400,000,000 for the period ending June 30, 1948. In requesting these funds, I have taken into consideration the maximum amount of relief assistance which would be furnished to Greece out of the $350,000,000 which I recently requested that the Congress authorize for the prevention of starvation and suffering in countries devastated by the war.

In addition to funds, I ask the Congress to authorize the detail of American civilian and military personnel to Greece and Turkey, at the request of those countries, to assist in the tasks of reconstruction, and for the purpose of supervising the use of such financial and material assistance as may be furnished. I recommend that authority also be provided for the instruction and training of selected Greek and Turkish personnel.

Finally, I ask that the Congress provide authority which will permit the speediest and most effective use, in terms of needed commodities, supplies and equipment, of such funds as may be authorized.

If further funds, or further authority, should be needed for purposes indicated in this message, I shall not hesitate to bring the situation before the Congress. On this subject the executive and legislative branches of the Government must work together.

This is a serious course upon which we embark. I would not recommend it except that the alternative is much more serious.

The United States contributed $341,000,000,000 toward winning World War II. This is an investment in world freedom and world peace. The assistance that I am recommending for Greece and Turkey amounts to little more than one-tenth of 1 percent of this investment. It is only common sense that we should safeguard this investment and make sure that it was not in vain.

The seeds of totalitarian regimes are nurtured by misery and want. They spread and grow in the evil soil of poverty and strife. They reach their full growth when the hope of people for a better life has died. We must keep that hope alive.

The free peoples of the world look to us for support in maintaining their freedoms. If we falter in our leadership, we may endanger the peace of the world—and we shall surely endanger the welfare of our own nation.

Great responsibilities have been placed upon us by the swift movement of events. I am confident that the Congress will face these responsibilities squarely.

Acceptance Speech

I am sorry that the microphones are in the way, but I must leave them the way they are because I have got to be able to see what I am doing—as I am always able to see what I am doing.

I can't tell you how very much I appreciate the honor which you have just conferred upon me. I shall continue to try to deserve it.

I accept the nomination.

And I want to thank this convention for its unanimous nomination of my good friend and colleague, Senator Barkley of Kentucky. He is a great man, and a great public servant. Senator Barkley and I will win this election and make these Republicans like it—don't you forget that!

We will do that because they are wrong and we are right, and I will prove it to you in just a few minutes.

This convention met to express the will and reaffirm the beliefs of the Democratic Party. There have been differences of opinion, and that is the democratic way. Those differences have been settled by a majority vote, as they should be.

Now it is time for us to get together and beat the common enemy. And that is up to you.

We have been working together for victory in a great cause. Victory has become a habit of our party. It has been elected four times in succession, and I am convinced it will be elected a fifth time next November.

The reason is that the people know that the Democratic Party is the people's party, and the Republican Party is the party of special interest, and it always has been and always will be.

The record of the Democratic Party is written in the

accomplishments of the last 16 years. I don't need to repeat them. They have been very ably placed before this convention by the keynote speaker, the candidate for Vice President, and by the permanent chairman.

Confidence and security have been brought to the people by the Democratic Party. Farm income has increased from less than $2 1/2 billion in 1932 to more than $18 billion in 1947. Never in the world were the farmers of any republic or any kingdom or any other country as prosperous as the farmers of the United States; and if they don't do their duty by the Democratic Party, they are the most ungrateful people in the world!

Wages and salaries in this country have increased from $29 billion in 1933 to more than $128 billion in 1947. That's labor, and labor never had but one friend in politics, and that is the Democratic Party and Franklin D. Roosevelt.

And I say to labor what I have said to the farmers: they are the most ungrateful people in the world if they pass the Democratic Party by this year.

The total national income has increased from less than $40 billion in 1933 to $203 billion in 1947, the greatest in all the history of the world. These benefits have been spread to all the people, because it is the business of the Democratic Party to see that the people get a fair share of these things.

This last, worst 80th Congress proved just the opposite for the Republicans.

The record on foreign policy of the Democratic Party is that the United States has been turned away permanently from isolationism, and we have converted the greatest and best of the Republicans to our viewpoint on that subject.

The United States has to accept its full responsibility for leadership in international affairs. We have been the backers and the people who organized and started the United Nations, first started under that great Democratic President, Woodrow Wilson, as the League of Nations. The League was sabotaged by the Republicans in 1920. And we must see that the United Nations continues as a strong and growing body, so we can have everlasting peace in the world.

We removed trade barriers in the world, which is the best asset we can have for peace. Those trade barriers must not be put back into operation again.

We have started the foreign aid program, which means the recovery of Europe and China, and the Far East. We instituted the program for Greece and Turkey, and I will say to you that all these things were done in a cooperative and bipartisan manner. The Foreign Relations

Committees of the Senate and House were taken into the full confidence of the President in every one of these moves, and don't let anybody tell you anything else.

As I have said time and time again, foreign policy should be the policy of the whole Nation and not the policy of one party or the other. Partisanship should stop at the water's edge; and I shall continue to preach that through this whole campaign.

I would like to say a word or two now on what I think the Republican philosophy is; and I will speak from actions and from history and from experience.

The situation in 1932 was due to the policies of the Republican Party control of the Government of the United States. The Republican Party, as I said a while ago, favors the privileged few and not the common everyday man. Ever since its inception, that party has been under the control of special privilege; and they have completely proved it in the 80th Congress. They proved it by the things they did *to* the people, and not for them. They proved it by the things they failed to do.

Now, let's look at some of them—just a few.

Time and time again I recommended extension of price control before it expired June 30, 1946. I asked for that extension in September 1945, in November 1945, in a Message on the State of the Union in 1946; and that price control legislation did not come to my desk until June 30, 1946, on the day on which it was supposed to expire. And it was such a rotten bill that I couldn't sign it. And 30 days after that they sent me one just as bad. I had to sign it, because they quit and went home.

They said, when OPA died, that prices would adjust themselves for the benefit of the country. They have been adjusting themselves all right! They have gone all the way off the chart in adjusting themselves, at the expense of the consumer and for the benefit of the people that hold the goods.

I called a special session of the Congress in November 1947 —November 17, 1947—and I set out a 10-point program for the welfare and benefit of this country, among other things standby controls. I got nothing. Congress has still done nothing.

Way back 4-1/2 years ago, while I was in the Senate, we passed a housing bill in the Senate known as the Wagner-Ellender-Taft bill. It was a bill to clear the slums in the big cities and to help to erect low-rent housing. That bill, as I said, passed the Senate 4 years ago. It died in the House. That bill was reintroduced in the 80th Congress as the Taft-Ellender-Wagner bill. The name was slightly changed, but it is practically the same bill. And it passed the Senate, but it was allowed to die in the House of Representatives; and they sat on that bill, and finally forced it out of the Banking and Currency Committee, and the Rules Committee took charge, and it still is in the Rules Committee.

But desperate pleas from Philadelphia in that convention that met here 3 weeks ago couldn't get that housing bill passed. They passed a bill they called a housing bill, which isn't worth the paper it's written on.

In the field of labor we needed moderate legislation to promote labor-management harmony, but Congress passed instead that so-called Taft-Hartley Act, which has disrupted labor-management relations and will cause strife and bitterness for years to come if it is not repealed, as the Democratic platform says it ought to be repealed.

On the Labor Department, the Republican platform of 1944 said, if they were in power, that they would build up a strong Labor Department. They have simply torn it up. Only one bureau is left that is functioning, and they cut the appropriation of that so it can hardly function.

I recommended an increase in the minimum wage. What did I get? Nothing. Absolutely nothing.

I suggested that the schools in this country are crowded, teachers underpaid, and that there is a shortage of teachers. One of our greatest national needs is more and better schools. I urged the Congress to provide $300 million to aid the States in the present educational crisis. Congress did nothing about it. Time and again I have recommended improvements in the social security law, including extending protection to those not now covered, and increasing the amount of benefits, to reduce the eligibility age of women from 65 to 60 years. Congress studied the matter for 2 years, but couldn't find the time to extend or increase the benefits. But they did find time to take social security benefits away from 750,000 people, and they passed that over my veto.

I have repeatedly asked the Congress to pass a health program. The Nation suffers from lack of medical care. That situation can be remedied any time the Congress wants to act upon it.

Everybody knows that I recommended to the Congress the civil rights program. I did that because I believed it to be my duty under the Constitution. Some of the members of my own party disagree with me violently on this matter. But they stand up and do it openly! People can tell where they stand. But the Republicans all professed to be for these measures. But Congress failed to act. They had enough men to do it, they could have had cloture, they didn't have to have a filibuster. They had enough people in that Congress that would vote for cloture.

Now everybody likes to have low taxes, but we must reduce the national debt in times of prosperity. And when tax relief can be given, it ought to go to those who need it most, and not those who need it least, as this Republican rich man's tax bill did when they passed it over my veto on the third try.

The first one of these was so rotten that they couldn't even stomach it themselves. They finally did send one that was somewhat improved, but it still helps the rich and sticks a knife into the back of the poor.

Now the Republicans came here a few weeks ago, and they wrote a platform. I hope you have all read that platform. They adopted the platform, and that platform had a lot of promises and statements of what the Republican Party is for, and what they would do if they were in power. They promised to do in that platform a lot of things I have been asking them to do that they have refused to do when they had the power.

The Republican platform cries about cruelly high prices. I have been trying to get them to do something about high prices ever since they met the first time.

Now listen! This is equally as bad, and as cynical. The Republican platform comes out for slum clearance and low-rental housing. I have been trying to get them to pass that housing bill ever since they met the first time, and it is still resting in the Rules Committee, that bill.

The Republican platform favors educational opportunity and promotion of education. I have been trying to get Congress to do something about that ever since they came there, and that bill is at rest in the House of Representatives.

The Republican platform is for extending and increasing social security benefits. Think of that! Increasing social security benefits! Yet when they had the opportunity, they took 750,000 off the social security rolls!

I wonder if they think they can fool the people of the United States with such poppy-cock as that!

There is a long list of these promises in that Republican platform. If it weren't so late, I would tell you all about them. I have discussed a number of these failures of the Republican 80th Congress. Every one of them is important. Two of them are of major concern to nearly every American family. They failed to do anything about high prices, they failed to do anything about housing.

My duty as President requires that I use every means within my power to get the laws the people need on matters of such importance and urgency.

I am therefore calling this Congress back into session July 26th.

On the 26th day of July, which out in Missouri we call "Turnip Day," I am going to call Congress back and ask them to pass laws to halt rising prices, to meet the housing crisis—which they are saying they are for in their platform.

At the same time I shall ask them to act upon other vitally needed measures such as aid to education, which they say they are for; a national health program; civil rights legislation, which they say they are for; an increase in minimum wage, which I doubt very much they are for; extension of the social security coverage and increased benefits, which they say they are for; funds for projects needed in our program to provide public power and cheap electricity. By indirection, this 80th Congress has tried to sabotage the power policies the United States has pursued for 14 years. That power lobby is as bad as the real estate lobby, which is sitting on the housing bill.

I shall ask for adequate and decent laws for displaced persons in place of this anti-Semitic, anti-Catholic law which this 80th Congress passed.

Now, my friends, if there is any reality behind that Republic platform, we ought to get some action from a short session of the 80th Congress. They can do this job in 15 days, if they want to do it. They will still have time to go out and run for office.

They are going to try to dodge their responsibility. They are going to drag all the red herrings they can across this campaign, but I am here to say that Senator Barkley and I are not going to let them get away with it.

Now, what the worst 80th Congress does in this special session will be the test. The American people will not decide by listening to mere words, or by reading a mere platform. They will decide on the record, the record as it has been written. And in the record is the stark truth, that the battle lines of 1948 are the same as they were in 1932, when the Nation lay prostrate and helpless as a result of Republican misrule and inaction.

In 1932 we were attacking the citadel of special privilege and greed. We were fighting to drive the money changers from the temple. Today, in 1948, we are now the defenders of the stronghold of democracy and of equal opportunity, the haven of the ordinary people of this land and not of the favored classes or the powerful few. The battle cry is just the same now as it was in 1932, and I paraphrase the words of Franklin D. Roosevelt as he issued the challenge, in accepting nomination in Chicago: "This is more than a political call to arms. Give me your help, not to win votes alone, but to win in this new crusade to keep America secure and safe for its own people."

Now my friends, with the help of God and the wholehearted push which you can put behind this campaign, we can save this country from a continuation of the 80th Congress, and from misrule from now on.

I must have your help. You must get in and push, and win this election. The country can't afford another Republican Congress.

Doctor Dewey and the Republican Record

Mr. Chairman, and fellow Democrats of Allegheny County:

I can't tell you how very much I appreciate this magnificent reception. I am always happy when I am with John Kane and Dave Lawrence, and Frank Myers and all the rest of the good Democrats of Pennsylvania.

I think a Presidential campaign is one of the most important elements in our democratic process. It's a chance to get things out in the open and discuss them and make decisions. I am an old campaigner, and I enjoy it.

This is about my 230th meeting, and I am still going strong, and I will be going strong at midnight of November the 1st.

You know, I would enjoy this campaign a lot more if my opponent had the courage to discuss the issues. The American people have the right to know where I stand and where my opponent stands on the issues that affect every person in this country.

Now, the people know where I stand. But the Republican candidate refuses to tell where he stands.

My opponent is conducting a very peculiar campaign. He has set himself up as some kind of doctor with a magic cure for all the ills of mankind.

Now, let's imagine that we, the American people, are going to see this doctor. It's just our usual routine checkup which we have every 4 years.

Now, we go into this doctor's office.

And, "Doctor," we say, "we're feeling fine."

"Is that so?" says the doctor. "I've been bothered much by issues lately. Have you been bothered much by issues, lately, too?"

"Not bothered, exactly," we say. "Of course, we've had a few. We've had the issues of high prices, and housing, and education, and social security, and a few others."

"That's too bad," says the doctor. "You shouldn't have so many issues."

"Is that right?" we say. "We thought that issues were a sign of political health."

"Not at all," says the doctor. "You shouldn't think about issues. What you need is my brand of soothing syrup—I call it 'unity.'"

Then the doctor edges up a little closer.

And he says, "Say, you don't look so good."

We say to him, "Well, that seems strange to me, Doc. I never felt stronger, never had more money, and never had a brighter future. What is wrong with me?"

Well, the doctor looks blank and he says, "I never discuss issues with a patient. But what you need is a major operation."

"Will it be serious, Doc?" we say.

"Not so very serious," he says. "It will just mean taking out the complete works and putting in a Republican administration."

Now, that's the kind of campaign you have been getting from the Republicans. They won't talk about the issues, but they insist that a major operation is necessary.

Take this vague talk of the Republican candidate about the "failures" of the present administration. That puzzled me for a little bit.

I thought of the fact that our national income is now running at the rate of over $220 billion a year—over five times as much as it was in 1932.

Is that what he calls a failure?

Or perhaps he was worried about the profits of the corporations. In 1932, corporations lost $3 billion—lost $3 billion. Now corporate profits are running at the rate of $19 billion a year, after taxes.

Is that what he calls a failure?

Perhaps he was thinking about our mighty undertakings to assist the free nations of the world to protect themselves against the inroads of communism. These efforts are proving successful.

Is that what he calls a failure?

In his speech here in Pittsburgh just a few days ago, the Republican candidate pretended to be upset about the way my administration has treated labor—about the terrible condition that labor was in in 1946. That's the excuse he gives for the passage of the Taft-Hartley law.

All right—all right, let's examine that.

In 1946, more people had jobs than ever before in the history of the country. Unions were healthier and had more members than ever before. And the workingmen and women of the United States produced more goods in 1946 than in any previous peacetime year.

The world wasn't perfect in 1946. But before any Republican begins complaining about that, he had better take a look at 1932—the last Republican year.

The Republican candidate talks about the workdays lost from strikes in 1946. Our industrial production in 1946 was three times as much as it was in 1932. And the days lost from strikes in 1946 were less than 1-1/2 percent of the total days worked this year.

Republicans don't like to talk about 1932—and I don't blame them. Do you? But it is a good year for you to remember when you start out to vote on election day.

When the Republican candidate finished telling you, here in Pittsburgh, how labor had suffered under my administration, he told you who had come to the rescue of labor.

Now, who do you think it was?

It was the Republicans, according to the Republican candidate.

Now, how do you suppose they did it?

They did it with the Taft-Hartley Act. That is how they came to the rescue of labor.

Yes, sir. The Republican candidate marched up proudly and embraced the Taft-Hartley law—lock, stock, and barrel. No workingman can have any doubt about that any more.

And in praising the Taft-Hartley law, he displayed his characteristic tendency of claiming credit where no credit is due. He tried to tell you that it is the Taft-Hartley Act that is driving the Communists out of labor unions.

Now, if you want to know how much truth there is in this claim, ask Bill Green—ask Phil Murray. They will tell you who got the Communists out.

It's being done in the good American way—the unions are doing it themselves.

Now in this speech the Republican candidate made here in Pittsburgh, he admitted, with characteristic modesty, that he is going to lead the country—and, indeed, the whole world—out of all its troubles. And he made a lot of promises.

He opened his mouth and he closed his eyes, and he swallowed the terrible record of that good-for-nothing Republican 80th Congress.

Now, 4 years ago this same Republican Presidential candidate went around the country saying that he was in favor of what the Democrats had done, but he could do it better. He said he was in favor of the National Labor Relations Act, the Wage and Hour Act, the Social Security Act, and "all the other Federal statutes designed to promote and protect the welfare of the American workingmen and women"—but he could do it better.

For some reason or other the American people did not believe him in 1944.

This year the same candidate is back with us, and he is saying much the same thing; that he likes the Democratic laws, but that he can run them better than we can.

It sounds to me like the same old phonograph record; but this year the record has a crack, and the needle gets stuck in that crack every once in a while.

Now the crack in the soothing syrup of that record was provided by the Republican 80th "do-nothing" Congress.

Now, in 1948, every time the Republican candidate says, "I can do it better," up comes an echo from the crack which says, "We're against it."

So the sounds coming out of the Republican Party this year are not very harmonious. And they are even less believable than they were in 1944.

The candidate said, and I quote: "The present minimum wage set by law is far too low and it will be raised."

Now, that's fine. I am glad he said that.

We're right with the candidate on that. In fact, we are 'way out ahead of him.

Time and time again in the last 2 years I urged the Republican "do-nothing" 80th Congress to raise the minimum wage from the present 40 cents an hour to at least 75 cents an hour.

But that Republican Congress—that crack in the record—said, "Nothing doing—we're against it."

And the minimum wage stayed where it was. Now, the Republicans like to say they are for a minimum wage, but it is perfectly clear that the smaller the minimum the better.

Now, let's look at another song on the record the candidate played for you here in Pittsburgh.

That Republican candidate for President said, and I quote: "We will overhaul the Social Security System for the unemployed and the aged, and go forward to extend its coverage and increase its benefits." That is a direct quote from his speech, made right here in Pittsburgh.

Now, that sounds good, although it's a little vague. But that's the candidate speaking. Where do the Republicans actually stand on social security?

As the President, I made every effort to get the Republican 80th Congress to extend social security coverage and increase social security benefits. What did that Congress do?

They took social security benefits *away* from nearly a million people.

What do you believe—campaign promises, or plain facts of Republican action?

Now, again that cracked record gives them away. It says, "We're against it."

In my recommendations to the special "do-nothing" session of Congress in July, I pointed out the desperate need to increase old-age insurance benefits at least 50 percent. At the present time the average insurance benefit payment for an old couple is less than $40 a month.

The Republican Congress did nothing about it—and neither did the Republican candidate for President.

He was silent as the tomb while the Congress was in session. Now, while he's campaigning, he suddenly takes quite an interest in increasing social security benefits. And I ask you: "Can you believe that kind of campaign promise?"

That Republican outfit went to Philadelphia and wrote a platform, and that platform was the most hypocritical document that ever was written; and I called them back to Washington to see whether they meant what they said in their platform. And they didn't.

Take another promise in that Pittsburgh speech. The Republican candidate said, and I quote: "We will make the Labor Department equal in actual Cabinet status to Commerce and Agriculture. It will make an important contribution to the national welfare." Doesn't that sound nice?

That promise is ridiculous in the face of what the Republicans in the 80th Congress did.

The Republican 80th Congress stripped the Mediation and Conciliation Service from the Labor Department.

The Republican 80th Congress cut the appropriations for the Bureau of Labor Statistics almost in half—apparently to prevent the Bureau from showing what's happening to the cost of living.

That's the plain factual record of what the Republicans have done to the Labor Department in the last 2 years.

Remember, the Republican candidate has said he is proud of the record of the 80th Congress.

But that crack in the record gives them away.

Here's another one of his promises. Here in Pittsburgh, the Republican candidate said, and I quote again: "We will bring a new and vigorous leadership to the Federal Conciliation and Mediation Service so that major disputes are settled before they become strikes."

Now that's a very, very peculiar promise. The present director of the Mediation Service is a well-known industrial leader named Cyrus Ching. Mr. Ching has been widely praised for his work in mediation. I think the Republican candidate is a bit confused here. And that is not the only thing he is confused on, either.

Let me take another campaign promise, here in Pittsburgh. The Republican candidate said right here: "We will encourage unions to grow in responsibility and strengthen the processes of collective bargaining."

I know it's hard to believe, but that's exactly what he said.

And he said it in the very same speech in which he went all out for the Taft-Hartley law.

Now, in this case, the candidate has fallen in the crack with the Republican Congress. He makes a promise, but the record says they're both against it.

Here's another promise by the Republican candidate; and I quote again: "We will vigorously and consistently enforce and strengthen our antitrust laws against business monopolies."

Now that's really fantastic. The Republican Party is notoriously favorable toward big business monopolies. The record of the Republican 80th Congress furnishes plenty of proof. They passed over my veto a bill to exempt railroads from antitrust laws. And at the same time they refused to pass, as I recommended, the O'Mahoney-Kefauver bill to plug loopholes in the antitrust laws.

In the fact of that record, the candidate now claims that the Republicans will strengthen the antitrust laws.

How can the Republican candidate say such things with a straight face?

But here's another—here's another! Here in Pittsburgh again, he said, and I quote: "We will break the log jam in housing so that decent houses may be provided at reasonable cost for the people."

For 2 solid years I tried in every way I knew to get the Republican 80th Congress to break the log jam in housing by passing the Taft-Ellender-Wagner bill.

The Republicans would not act.

In the face of pleading and urging from Governors and Mayors, from veterans and plain people all over the country, the Republican Congress refused to pass the housing bill. And I gave them four chances to do it.

But now—now in the middle of the campaign—the Republican candidate has the gall to promise that the Republican will take action on housing.

I certainly wouldn't have believed it if I hadn't seen it in print.

Let me quote just one more campaign promise from that incredible Pittsburgh speech.

"We will make sure," said the Republican candidate, I quote: "we will make sure that soaring prices do not steal food and clothing and other necessities from American families."

Now that one completely stops me.

Everybody in this country knows that the Republican 80th Congress refused, time and time again, to pass the laws we need to stop high prices. In November 1947, in January 1948, in July 1948, I asked that Republican Congress to act against inflation.

They didn't do a thing about it.

And neither did the Republican candidate. All through the time when the Congress was in session, stalling and blocking anti-inflation legislation, the Republican candidate was silent as the grave.

But now—now that he's trying to persuade the people to vote for him—the Republican candidate says the Republicans will do something about high prices. It looks to me as though it's a little late in the game for that promise, anyway.

Now, the candidate says—the Republican candidate says: "Me, too." But the Republican record still says, "We're against it." And if you return the Republicans to power, you will have the same clique in control of the Congress that is in control of it now.

These two phrases, "me, too," and "we're against it," sum up the whole Republican campaign.

My friends, it isn't funny at all. It's tragic, tragic for the everyday citizen.

This soft talk and double talk, this combination of crafty silence and resounding misrepresentation, is an insult to the intelligence of the American voter. It proceeds upon the assumption that you can fool all the people—or enough of them—all the time.

In this campaign you don't have to rely on promises. This time, you have the record. You don't have to play just the Republican side of that record. Turn it over.

Our side—the Democratic side—doesn't say, "We're against it." It says, "We can do it." And we will do it—if you will give us a chance.

Our side is the Victory March—a victory on November 2d for all the people and for the people's party—the Democratic Party.

Inaugural Address

Mr. Vice President, Mr. Chief Justice, fellow citizens:

I accept with humility the honor which the American people have conferred upon me. I accept it with a resolve to do all that I can for the welfare of this Nation and for the peace of the world.

In performing the duties of my office, I need the help and the prayers of every one of you. I ask for your encouragement and for your support. The tasks we face are difficult. We can accomplish them only if we work together.

Each period of our national history has had its special challenges. Those that confront us now are as momentous as any in the past. Today marks the beginning not only of a new administration, but of a period that will be eventful, perhaps decisive, for us and for the world.

It may be our lot to experience, and in a large measure bring about, a major turning point in the long history of the human race. The first half of this century has been marked by unprecedented and brutal attacks on the rights of man, and by the two most frightful wars in history. The supreme need of our time is for men to learn to live together in peace and harmony.

The peoples of the earth face the future with grave uncertainty, composed almost equally of great hopes and great fears. In this time of doubt, they look to the United States as never before for good will, strength, and wise leadership.

It is fitting, therefore, that we take this occasion to proclaim to the world the essential principles of the faith by which we live, and to declare our aims to all peoples.

The American people stand firm in the faith which has inspired this

Nation from the beginning. We believe that all men have a right to equal justice under law and equal opportunity to share in the common good. We believe that all men have a right to freedom of thought and expression. We believe that all men are created equal because they are created in the image of God.

From this faith we will not be moved.

The American people desire, and are determined to work for, a world in which all nations and all peoples are free to govern themselves as they see fit, and to achieve a decent and satisfying life. Above all else, our people desire, and are determined to work for, peace on earth—a just and lasting peace—based on genuine agreement freely arrived at by equals.

In the pursuit of these aims, the United States and other like-minded nations find themselves directly opposed by a regime with contrary aims and a totally different concept of life.

That regime adheres to a false philosophy which purports to offer freedom, security, and greater opportunity to mankind. Misled by that philosophy, many peoples have sacrificed their liberties only to learn to their sorrow that deceit and mockery, poverty and tyranny, are their reward.

That false philosophy is communism.

Communism is based on the belief that man is so weak and inadequate that he is unable to govern himself, and therefore requires the rule of strong masters.

Democracy is based on the conviction that man has the moral and intellectual capacity, as well as the inalienable right, to govern himself with reason and justice.

Communism subjects the individual to arrest without lawful cause, punishment without trial, and forced labor as the chattel of the state. It decrees what information he shall receive, what art he shall produce, what leaders he shall follow, and what thoughts he shall think.

Democracy maintains that government is established for the benefit of the individual, and is charged with the responsibility of protecting the rights of the individual and his freedom in the exercise of those abilities of his.

Communism maintains that social wrongs can be corrected only by violence.

Democracy has proved that social justice can be achieved through peaceful change.

Communism holds that the world is so widely divided into opposing classes that war is inevitable.

Democracy holds that free nations can settle differences justly and maintain a lasting peace.

These differences between communism and democracy do not concern the United States alone. People everywhere are coming to realize that what is involved is material well-being, human dignity, and the right to believe in and worship God.

I state these differences, not to draw issues of belief as such, but because the actions resulting from the Communist philosophy are a threat to the efforts of free nations to bring about world recovery and lasting peace.

Since the end of hostilities, the United States has invested its substance and its energy in a great constructive effort to restore peace, stability, and freedom to the world.

We have sought no territory. We have imposed our will on none. We have asked for no privileges we would not extend to others.

We have constantly and vigorously supported the United Nations and related agencies as a means of applying democratic principles to international relations. We have consistently advocated and relied upon peaceful settlement of disputes among nations.

We have made every effort to secure agreement on effective international control of our most powerful weapon, and we have worked steadily for the limitation and control of all armaments.

We have encouraged, by precept and example, the expansion of world trade on a sound and fair basis.

Almost a year ago, in company with 16 free nations of Europe, we launched the greatest cooperative economic program in history. The purpose of that unprecedented effort is to invigorate and strengthen democracy in Europe, so that the free people of that continent can resume their rightful place in the forefront of civilization and can contribute once more to the security and welfare of the world.

Our efforts have brought new hope to all mankind. We have beaten back despair and defeatism. We have saved a number of countries from losing their liberty. Hundreds of millions of people all over the world now agree with us, that we need not have war—that we can have peace.

The initiative is ours.

We are moving on with other nations to build an even stronger structure of international order and justice. We shall have as our partners countries which, no longer solely concerned with the problem of national survival, are now working to improve the standards of living of all their people. We are ready to undertake new projects to strengthen a free world.

In the coming years, our program for peace and freedom will emphasize four major courses of action.

First, we will continue to give unfaltering support to the United Nations and related agencies, and we will continue to search for ways to strengthen their authority and increase their effectiveness. We believe that the United Nations will be strengthened by the new nations which are being formed in lands now advancing toward self-government under democratic principles.

Second, we will continue our programs for world economic recovery.

This means, first of all, that we must keep our full weight behind the European recovery program. We are confident of the success of this major venture in world recovery. We believe that our partners in this effort will achieve the status of self-supporting nations once again.

In addition, we must carry out our plans for reducing the barriers to world trade and increasing its volume. Economic recovery and peace itself depend on increased world trade.

Third, we will strengthen freedom-loving nations against the dangers of aggression.

We are now working out with a number of countries a joint agreement designed to strengthen the security of the North Atlantic area. Such an agreement would take the form of a collective defense arrangement within the terms of the United Nations Charter.

We have already established such a defense pact for the Western Hemisphere by the treaty of Rio de Janeiro.

The primary purpose of these agreements is to provide unmistakable proof of the joint determination of the free countries to resist armed attack from any quarter. Every country participating in these arrangements must contribute all it can to the common defense.

If we can make it sufficiently clear, in advance, that any armed attack affecting our national security would be met with overwhelming force, the armed attack might never occur.

I hope soon to send to the Senate a treaty respecting the North Atlantic security plan.

In addition, we will provide military advice and equipment to free nations which will cooperate with us in the maintenance of peace and security.

Fourth, we must embark on a bold new program for making the benefits of our scientific advances and industrial progress available for the improvement and growth of underdeveloped areas.

More than half the people of the world are living in conditions approaching misery. Their food is inadequate. They are victims of disease. Their poverty is a handicap and a threat both to them and to more prosperous areas.

For the first time in history, humanity possesses the knowledge and skill to relieve the suffering of these people.

The United States is pre-eminent among nations in the development of industrial and scientific techniques. The material resources which we can afford to use for assistance of other peoples are limited. But our imponderable resources in technical knowledge are constantly growing and are inexhaustible.

I believe that we should make available to peace-loving peoples the benefits of our store of technical knowledge in order to help them realize their aspirations for a better life. And, in cooperation with other nations, we should foster capital investment in areas needing development.

Our aim should be to help the free peoples of the world, through their own efforts, to produce more food, more clothing, more materials for housing, and more mechanical power to lighten their burdens.

We invite other countries to pool their technological resources in this undertaking. Their contributions will be warmly welcomed. This should be a cooperative enterprise in which all nations work together through the United Nations and its specialized agencies whenever practicable. It must be a worldwide effort for the achievement of peace, plenty, and freedom.

With the cooperation of business, private capital, agriculture, and labor in this country, this program can greatly increase the industrial activity in other nations and can raise substantially their standards of living.

Such new economic developments must be devised and controlled to the benefit of the peoples of the areas in which they are established. Guarantees to the investor must be balanced by guarantees in the interest of the people whose resources and whose labor go into these developments.

The old imperialism—exploitation for foreign profit—has no place in our plans. What we envisage is a program of development based on the concepts of democratic fair-dealing.

All countries, including our own, will greatly benefit from a constructive program for the better use of the world's human and natural resources. Experience shows that our commerce with other countries expands as they progress industrially and economically.

Greater production is the key to prosperity and peace. And the key to greater production is a wider and more vigorous application of modern scientific and technical knowledge.

Only by helping the least fortunate of its members to help themselves can the human family achieve the decent, satisfying life that is the right of all people.

Democracy alone can supply the vitalizing force to stir the peoples of the world into triumphant action, not only against their human oppressors, but also against their ancient enemies—hunger, misery, and despair.

On the basis of these four major courses of action we hope to help create the conditions that will lead eventually to personal freedom and happiness for all mankind.

If we are to be successful in carrying out these policies, it is clear that we must have continued prosperity in this country and we must keep ourselves strong.

Slowly but surely we are weaving a world fabric of international security and growing prosperity.

We are aided by all who wish to live in freedom from fear—even by those who live today in fear under their own governments.

We are aided by all who want relief from lies and propaganda—those who desire truth and sincerity.

We are aided by all who desire self-government and a voice in deciding their own affairs.

We are aided by all who long for economic security—for the security and abundance that men in free societies can enjoy.

We are aided by all who desire freedom of speech, freedom of religion, and freedom to live their own lives for useful ends.

Our allies are the millions who hunger and thirst after righteousness.

In due time, as our stability becomes manifest, as more and more nations come to know the benefits of democracy and to participate in growing abundance, I believe that those countries which now oppose us will abandon their delusions and join with the free nations of the world in a just settlement of international differences.

Events have brought our American democracy to new influence and new responsibilities. They will test our courage, our devotion of duty, and our concept of liberty.

But I say to all men, what we have achieved in liberty, we will surpass in greater liberty.

Steadfast in our faith in the Almighty, we will advance toward a world where man's freedom is secure.

To that end we will devote our strength, our resources, and our firmness of resolve. With God's help, the future of mankind will be assured in a world of justice, harmony, and peace.

On Korea I

I conferred Sunday evening with the Secretaries of State and Defense, their senior advisers, and the Joint Chiefs of Staff about the situation in the Far East created by unprovoked aggression against the Republic of Korea.

The Government of the United States is pleased with the speed and determination with which the United Nations Security Council acted to order a withdrawal of the invading forces to positions north of the 38th parallel. In accordance with the resolution of the Security Council, the United States will vigorously support the effort of the Council to terminate this serious breach of the peace.

Our concern over the lawless action taken by the forces from North Korea, and our sympathy and support for the people of Korea in this situation, are being demonstrated by the cooperative action of American personnel in Korea, as well as by steps taken to expedite and augment assistance of the type being furnished under the Mutual Defense Assistance Program. Those responsible for this act of aggression must realize how seriously the Government of the United States views such threats to the peace of the world. Willful disregard of the obligation to keep the peace cannot be tolerated by nations that support the United Nations Charter.

On Korea II

In Korea the Government forces, which were armed to prevent border raids and to preserve internal security, were attacked by invading forces from North Korea. The Security Council of the United Nations called upon the invading troops to cease hostilities and to withdraw to the 38th parallel. This they have not done, but on the contrary have pressed the attack. The Security Council called upon all members of the United Nations to render every assistance to the United Nations in the execution of this resolution. In these circumstances I have ordered United States air and sea forces to give the Korean Government troops cover and support.

The attack upon Korea makes it plain beyond all doubt that communism has passed beyond the use of subversion to conquer independent nations and will now use armed invasion and war. It has defied the order of the Security Council of the United Nations issued to preserve international peace and security. In these circumstances the occupation of Formosa by Communist forces would be a direct threat to the security of the Pacific area and to the United States forces performing their lawful and necessary functions in that area.

Accordingly, I have ordered the Seventh Fleet to prevent any attack on Formosa. As a corollary of this action I am calling upon the Chinese Government on Formosa to cease all air and sea operations against the mainland. The Seventh Fleet will see that this is done. The determination of Formosa must await the restoration of security in the Pacific, a peace settlement with Japan, or consideration by the United Nations.

I have also directed that United States Forces in the Philippines be strengthened and that military assistance to the Philippine Government be accelerated.

I have similarly directed acceleration in the furnishing of military assistance to the forces of France and the Associate States of Indochina and the dispatch of a military mission to provide close working relations with those forces.

I know that all members of the United Nations will consider carefully the consequences of this latest aggression in Korea in defiance of the Charter of the United Nations.   A return to the rule of force in international affairs would have far-reaching effects.   The United States will continue to uphold the rule of law.

I have instructed Ambassador Austin, as the representative of the United States to the Security Council, to report these steps to the Council.

Far Eastern Policy

I want to talk to you tonight about what we are doing in Korea and about our policy in the Far East. In the simplest terms what we are doing in Korea is this: We are trying to prevent a third world war.

I think most people in this country recognized that fact last June. And they warmly supported the decision of the Government to help the Republic of Korea against the Communist aggressors. Now, many persons, even some who applauded our decision to defend Korea, have forgotten the basic reasons for our action.

It is right for us to be in Korea now. It was right last June. It is right today.

I want to remind you why this is true.

The Communists in the Kremlin are engaged in a monstrous conspiracy to stamp out freedom all over the world. If they were to succeed, the United States would be numbered among their principal victims. It must be clear to everyone that the United States cannot—and will not—sit idly by and await foreign conquest. The only question is: When is the best time to meet the threat and how?

The best time to meet the threat is in the beginning. It is easier to put out a fire in the beginning when it is small than after it has become a roaring blaze.

And the best way to meet the threat of aggression is for the peace-loving nations to act together. If they don't act together, they are likely to be picked off, one by one.

If they had followed the right policies in the 1930's—if the free countries had acted together, to crush the aggression of the dictators, and if they had acted in the beginning, when the aggression was small—there probably would have been no World War II.

If history has taught us anything, it is that aggression anywhere in the world is a threat to the peace everywhere in the world. When that aggression is supported by the cruel and selfish rulers of a powerful nation who are bent on conquest, it becomes a clear and present danger to the security and independence of every free nation.

This is a lesson that most people in this country have learned thoroughly. This is the basic reason why we have joined in creating the United Nations. And, since the end of World War II, we have been putting that lesson into practice—we're working with other free nations to check the aggressive designs of the Soviet Union before they can result in a third world war.

This is what we did in Greece, when that nation was threatened by the aggression of international Communists.

The attack against Greece could have led to a general war. But this country came to the aid of Greece. The United Nations supported Greek resistance. With our help, the determination and efforts of the Greek people defeated the attack on the spot.

Another big Communist threat to peace was the Berlin blockade. That, too, could have led to war. But again it was settled because free men would not back down in an emergency.

The aggression against Korea is the boldest and most dangerous move the Communists have yet made.

The attack on Korea was part of a greater plan for conquering all of Asia.

I would like to read to you from a secret intelligence report which came to us after the attack. I have that report right here. It is a report of a speech a Communist Army officer in North Korea gave to a group of spies and saboteurs last May, one month before South Korea was invaded. The report shows in great detail how this invasion was a part of a carefully prepared plot. Here is part of what the Communist officer, who had been trained in Moscow, told his men:

"Our forces," he said, "are scheduled to attack South Korean forces about the middle of June. . . The coming attack on South Korea marks the first step toward the liberation of Asia."

Notice that he used the word "liberation." This is Communist double-talk meaning "conquest."

I have another secret intelligence report here. This one tells what another Communist officer in the Far East told his men several months before the invasion of Korea. And here's what he said: "In order to successfully undertake the long awaited world revolution, we must first unify Asia. . . . Java, Indo-China, Malaya, India, Tibet, Thailand,

Philippines, and Japan are our ultimate targets. . . . The United States is the only obstacle on our road for the liberation of all countries in Southeast Asia. In other words we must unify the people of Asia and crush the United States." Again, liberation in Commie language means conquest.

That's what the Communist leaders are telling their people, and that is what they've been trying to do.

They want to control all Asia from the Kremlin.

This plan of conquest is in flat contradiction to what we believe. We believe that Korea belongs to the Koreans. We believe that India belongs to the Indians. We believe all the nations of Asia should be free to work out their affairs in their own way. This is the basis of peace in the Far East and it is the basis of peace everywhere else.

The whole Communist imperialism is back of the attack on peace in the Far East. It was the Soviet Union that trained and equipped the North Koreans for aggression. The Chinese Communists massed forty-four well-trained and well-equipped divisions on the Korean frontier. These were the troops they threw into battle when the North Korean Communists were beaten.

The question we have had to face is whether the Communist plan of conquest can be stopped without a general war. Our Government and other countries associated with us in the United Nations believe that the best chance of stopping it without a general war is to meet the attack in Korea and defeat it there.

That is what we have been doing. It is a difficult and bitter task.

But so far it has been successful.

So far, we have prevented World War III.

So far, by fighting a limited war in Korea, we have prevented aggression from succeeding, and bringing on a general war. And the ability of the whole free world to resist Communist aggression has been greatly improved.

We have taught the enemy a lesson. He has found out that aggression is not cheap or easy. Moreover, men all over the world who want to remain free have been given new courage and new hope. They know now that the champions of freedom can stand up and fight and that they will stand up and fight.

Our resolute stand in Korea is helping the forces of freedom now fighting in Indo-China and other countries in that part of the world. It has already slowed down the time-table of conquest.

In Korea itself, there are signs that the enemy is building up his ground forces for a new mass offensive. We also know that there have been large increases in the enemy's available air forces.

If a new attack comes, I feel confident it will be turned back. The

United Nations fighting forces are tough and able and well equipped. They are fighting for a just cause. They are proving to all the world that the principle of collective security will work. We are proud of all these forces for the magnificent job they have done against heavy odds. We pray that their efforts may succeed, for upon their success may hinge the peace of the world.

The Communist side must now choose its course of action. The Communists rulers may press the attack against us. They may take further action which will spread the conflict. They have that choice, and with it the awful responsibility for what may follow. The Communists also have the choice of a peaceful settlement which could lead to general relaxation of the tensions in the Far East. The decision is theirs, because the forces of the United Nations will strive to limit the conflict if possible.

We do not want to see the conflict in Korea extended. We are trying to prevent a world war—not to start one. And the best way to do that is to make it plain that we and the other free countries will continue to resist the attack.

But you may ask why can't we take other steps to punish the aggressor. Why don't we bomb Manchuria and China itself? Why don't we assist the Chinese Nationalist troops to land on the mainland of China?

If we were to do these things we would be running a very grave risk of starting a general war. If that were to happen, we would have brought about the exact situation we are trying to prevent.

If we were to do these things we would become entangled in a vast conflict on the Continent of Asia and our task would become immeasurably more difficult all over the world.

What would suit the ambitions of the Kremlin better than for our military forces to be committed to a full scale war with Red China?

It may well be that, in spite of our best efforts, the Communists may spread the war. But it would be wrong—tragically wrong—for us to take the initiative in extending the war.

The dangers are great. Make no mistake about it. Behind the North Koreans and Chinese Communists in the front lines stand additional millions of Chinese soldiers. And behind the Chinese stand the tanks, the planes, the submarines, the soldiers, and the scheming rulers of the Soviet Union.

Our aim is to avoid the spread of the conflict.

The course we have been following is the one best calculated to avoid an all out war. It is the course consistent with our obligation to do all we can to maintain international peace and security. Our experience in Greece and Berlin shows that it is the most effective course of action we can follow.

First of all, it is clear that our efforts in Korea can blunt the will of the Chinese Communists to continue the struggle. The United Nations forces have put up a tremendous fight in Korea and have inflicted very heavy casualties on the enemy. Our forces are stronger now than they have been before. These are plain facts which may discourage the Chinese Communists from continuing their attack.

Second, the free world as a whole is growing in military strength every day. In the United States, in Western Europe, and throughout the world, free men are alert to the Soviet threat and are building their defenses. This may discourage the Communists rulers from continuing the war in Korea—and from undertaking new acts of aggression elsewhere.

If the Communist authorities realize they cannot defeat us in Korea, if they realize it would be foolhardy to widen the hostilities beyond Korea, then they may recognize the folly of continuing their aggression. A peaceful settlement may then be possible. The door is always open.

Then we may achieve a settlement in Korea which will not compromise the principles and purposes of the United Nations.

I have thought long and hard about this question of extending the war in Asia. I have discussed it many times with the ablest military advisers in the country. I believe with all my heart that the course we are following is the best course.

I believe that we must try to limit the war to Korea for these vital reasons: To make sure that the precious lives of our fighting men are not wasted; to see that the security of our country and the free world is not needlessly jeopardized; and to prevent a third world war.

A number of events have made it evident that General MacArthur did not agree with that policy. I have therefore considered it essential to relieve General MacArthur so that there would be no doubt or confusion as to the real purpose and aim of our policy.

It was with the deepest personal regret that I found myself compelled to take this action. General MacArthur is one of our greatest military commanders. But the cause of world peace is more important than any individual.

The change in commands in the Far East means no change whatever in the policy of the United States. We will carry on the fight in Korea with vigor and determination in an effort to bring the war to a speedy and successful conclusion. The new commander, Lieut. Gen. Matthew Ridgway has already demonstrated that he has the good qualities of military leadership needed for the task.

We are ready, at any time, to negotiate for a restoration of peace in the area. But we will not engage in appeasement. We are only interested in real peace.

Real peace can be achieved through a settlement based on the following factors:

1. The fighting must stop.
2. Concrete steps must be taken to insure that the fighting will not break out again.
3. There must be an end of the aggression.

A settlement founded upon these elements would open the way for the unification of Korea and the withdrawal of all foreign forces.

In the meantime, I want to be clear about our military objective. We are fighting to resist an outrageous aggression in Korea. We are trying to keep the Korean conflict from spreading to other areas. But at the same time we must conduct our military activities so as to insure the security of our forces. This is essential if they are to continue the fight until the enemy abandons its ruthless attempts to destroy the Republic of Korea.

That is our military objective—to repel attack and to restore peace.

In the hard fighting in Korea, we are proving that collective action among nations is not only a high principle but a workable means of resisting aggression. Defeat of aggression in Korea may be the turning point in the world's search for a practical way of achieving peace and security.

The struggle of the United Nations in Korea is a struggle for peace.

The free nations have united their strength in an effort to prevent a third world war.

That war can come if the Communist rulers want it to come. But this nation and its allies will not be responsible for its coming.

We do not want to widen the conflict. We will use every effort to prevent that disaster. And in so doing, we know that we are following the great principles of peace, freedom, and justice.

Chronology of Speeches

1945

Address Before Joint Session of Congress, Washington, D.C., April 16, 1945.

Address to United Nations Conference in San Francisco, broadcast from White House, Washington, D.C., April 25, 1945.

Broadcast to the American People Announcing Surrender of Germany, Washington, D.C., May 8, 1945.

Remarks Before Congress on Presenting the Medal of Honor to Sergeant Jake W. Lindsey, Washington, D.C., May 21, 1945.

Address, Closing Session of the United Nations Conference, San Francisco, California, June 26, 1945.

Remarks Upon Receiving Honorary Degree, University of Kansas, Kansas City, Missouri, June 28, 1945.

Address Before the Senate Urging Ratification of the Charter of the United Nations, Washington, D.C., July 2, 1945.

Remarks, Raising the Flag Over the U.S. Group Control Council Headquarters, Berlin, Germany, July 20, 1945.

Radio Report to the American People on the Potsdam Conference, Washington, D.C., August 9, 1945.

Radio Address to the American People After the Signing of the Terms of Unconditional Surrender by Japan, Washington, D.C., September 1, 1945.

Radio Address to Members of the Armed Forces, Washington, D.C., September 2, 1945.

Radio Address, Opening the 1945 National War Fund Campaign,

Washington, D.C., October 2, 1945.

Remarks, Pemiscot County Fair, Caruthersville, Missouri, October 7, 1945.

Address, Dedication of the Kentucky Dam, Gilbertsville, Kentucky, October 10, 1945.

Address to Joint Session of Congress on Universal Military Training, Washington, D.C., October 23, 1945.

Address, Commissioning of the *U.S.S. Franklin D. Roosevelt*, New York City, October 27, 1945.

Address on Foreign Policy, Navy Day Celebration, New York City, October 27, 1945.

Radio Address on Wages and Prices in the Reconversion Period, Washington, D.C., October 30, 1945.

Address, Opening Session of the Labor-Management Conference, Washington, D.C., November 5, 1945.

Address, Lighting of the National Community Christmas Tree, Washington, D.C., December 24, 1945.

1946

Radio Report to the American People on the Status of the Reconversion Program, Washington, D.C., January 3, 1946.

State of the Union, Washington, D.C., January 21, 1946.

Radio Remarks, March of Dimes Campaign, Washington, D.C., January 30, 1946.

Remarks, Heads of Agencies and Personnel Directors on Reconversion of the Civil Service, Washington, D.C., February 9, 1946.

Remarks to Jewish Delegation From the United Jewish Appeal, Washington, D.C., February 25, 1946.

Remarks, Conference Called to Develop a Food Conservation Program, Washington, D.C., March 1, 1946.

Radio Remarks, Opening the Red Cross War Fund Drive, Washington D.C., March 1, 1946.

Address, Conference of Federal Council of Churches, Columbus, Ohio, March 6, 1946.

Address, Jackson Day Dinner, Washington, D.C., March 23, 1946.

Address, Army Day, Chicago, Illinois, April 6, 1946.

Address, Dedication of the Home of Franklin D. Roosevelt as a National Shrine, Hyde Park, New York, April 12, 1946.

Address, Governing Board of the Pan American Union, Washington, D.C. April 15, 1946.

Radio Address, Food Conservation to Relieve Hunger Abroad,

Washington, D.C., April 19, 1946.

Address, President's Highway Safety Conference, Washington, D.C., May 8, 1946.

Address, Fordham University, New York City, May 11, 1946.

Radio Address, the Railroad Strike Emergency, Washington, D.C., May 24, 1946.

Radio Address, Price Controls, Washington, D.C., June 29, 1946.

Remarks, Conference on Emergency Problems in Higher Education, Washington, D.C., July 11, 1946.

Remarks, Youth Conference on Famine Relief, Washington, D.C., July 15, 1946.

Remarks, Editors and Executives of McGraw-Hill Publishing Company, Washington, D.C., July 17, 1946.

Remarks, Delegates of Boys Nation, Washington, D.C., August 9, 1946.

Remarks, National Conference of Business Paper Editors, Washington, D.C., September 13, 1946.

Remarks, Group of Democratic Congressional Candidates, Washington, D.C., September 24, 1946.

Remarks, U.S. Nation Commission for UNESCO, Washington, D.C., September 25, 1946.

Remarks, Cadet Corps, West Point, New York, September 28, 1946.

Radio Address, Opening Campaigns for Community Chest and United Service Organizations, Washington, D.C., October 1, 1946.

Radio Address, Lifting of Major Price Controls, Washington, D.C., October 14, 1946.

Address, Opening Session of the United Nations General Assembly, New York City, October 23, 1946.

Remarks, President's Advisory Commission on Universal Training, Washington, D.C., December 20, 1946.

Address, Lighting of the National Community Christmas Tree, Washington, D.C., December 24, 1946.

1947

State of the Union, Washington, D.C., January 6, 1947.

Remarks, President's Committee on Civil Rights, Washington, D.C., January 15, 1947.

Radio Remarks, March of Dimes Campaign, January 30, 1947.

Remarks, American Council of Voluntary Agencies for Foreign Service, Washington, D.C., February 27, 1947.

Remarks, Presentation of the Wendell Willkie Awards for Journalism, Washington, D.C., February 28, 1947.

Radio Remarks, Opening the Red Cross Campaign, Washington, D.C., February 28, 1947.

Address, Mexico City, Mexico, March 3, 1947.

Address, Foreign Economic Policy, Baylor University, Waco, Texas, March 6, 1947.

Special Message to the Congress on Greece and Turkey, "The Truman Doctrine," Washington, D.C., March 12, 1947.

Address, Jefferson Day Dinner, Washington, D.C., April 5, 1947.

Broadcast Remarks, Franklin D. Roosevelt Memorial Program, Washington, D.C., April 12, 1947.

Remarks, American Society of Newspaper Editors, Washington, D.C., April 17, 1947.

Address, Annual Luncheon of the Associated Press, New York City, April 21, 1947.

Remarks, Role of the Press in Traffic Safety, Washington, D.C., May 1, 1947.

Address, Opening of the Conference on Fire Prevention, Washington, D.C., May 5, 1947.

Address, 35th Division Reunion Memorial Service, Kansas City, Missouri, June 7, 1947.

Address, Canadian Parliament, Ottawa, Canada, June 11, 1947.

Commencement Address, Princeton, University, Princeton, New Jersey, June 17, 1947.

Address, Opening the President' Second Highway Safety Conference, Washington, D.C., June 18, 1947.

Radio Address, Veto of the Taft-Hartley Bill, Washington, D.C., June 20, 1947.

Radio Broadcast, Second Anniversary of the United Nations, Washington, D.C., June 26, 1947.

Address, National Association for the Advancement of Colored People, Washington, D.C., June 29, 1947.

Independence Day Address, Home of Thomas Jefferson, Charlottesville, Virginia, July 4, 1947.

Remarks to Reporters Following the Death of the President's Mother, Washington, D.C., August 1, 1947.

Address, Inter-American Conference for the Maintenance of Continental Peace and Security, Rio De Janeiro, Brazil, September 2, 1947.

Address, Joint Session of Congress of Brazil, Rio de Janeiro, Brazil, September 5, 1947.

Radio Address, Opening the Community Chest Campaign, Washington, D.C., September 26, 1947.

Remarks, Citizen's Food Committee, Washington, D.C., October 1, 1947.

Radio and Television Address, Citizens Food Committee, Washington, D.C., October 5, 1947.

Broadcast Address to the Women of the United States, Washington, D.C., October 8, 1947.

Remarks, National Conference of Editorial Writers, Washington, D.C., October 17, 1947.

Radio Address on the Special Session of Congress, Washington, D.C., October 24, 1947.

Special Message to the Congress on the First Day of the Special Session, Washington, D.C., November 17, 1947.

Address, Dedication of Everglades National Park, Everglades City, Florida, December 6, 1947.

Address, Lighting of the National Community Christmas Tree, Washington, D.C., December 24, 1947.

1948

State of the Union, Washington, D.C., January 7, 1948.

Jefferson-Jackson Day Dinner Address, Washington, D.C., February 19, 1948.

Address, San Juan, Puerto Rico, February 21, 1948.

Remarks, St. Thomas, Virgin Islands, February 22, 1948.

Remarks, St. Croix, Virgin Islands, February 23, 1948.

Remarks, Red Cross Fund, Key West, Florida, February 29, 1948.

Threat to the Freedom of Europe, Joint Session of Congress, Washington, D.C., March 17, 1948.

St. Patrick's Day Address, New York City, March 17, 1948.

Radio Address Opening the Savings Bond Campaign, Washington,D.C., April 14, 1948.

Address, American Society of Newspaper Editors, Washington, D.C., April 17, 1948.

Address, Observance of the Fiftieth Anniversary of Cuban Independence, Joint Session of Congress, Washington, D.C., April 19, 1948.

Remarks, National Health Assembly Dinner, Washington, D.C., May 1, 1948.

Remarks, National Conference on Family Life, Washington, D.C., May 6, 1948.

Remarks, Young Democrats Dinner, Washington, D.C., May 14, 1948.

Remarks, Girard College Chapel, Philadelphia, Pennsylvania, May 20, 1948.

Rear Platform Remarks in Crestline, Ohio; Fort Wayne and Gary, Indiana, June 4, 1948.

Address, Swedish Pioneer Centennial Association, Chicago, Illinois, June 4, 1948.

Remarks in Omaha and Boys Town, Nebraska, June 5, 1948.

Address, Reunion of the 35th Division Association, Omaha, Nebraska, June 5, 1948.

Rear Platform Remarks, Grand Island, Kearney, North Platte, and Sidney, Nebraska; Cheyenne, Laramie, and Rawlings, Wyoming, June 6, 1948.

Rear Platform Remarks, Pocatello, Idaho, June 7, 1948.

Rear Platform Remarks, Arco, Blackfoot, and Idaho Falls, Idaho; Dillon, Montana, June 8, 1948.

Address, Butte, Montana, June 8, 1948.

Rear Platform Remarks, Spokane, Ephrata, Wenatchee, Skyomish, and Everett, Washington, June 9, 1948.

Remarks, Bremerton, Seattle, Tacoma, and Olympia, Washington, June 10, 1948.

Address, Washington State Press Club, Seattle, Washington, June 10, 1948.

Rear Platform Remarks, Portland, Salem, Albany, Oakridge, and Klamath Falls, Oregon, June 11, 1948.

Rear Platform Remarks, Roseville, Davis, and Berkley, California, June 12, 1948.

Commencement Address, University of California, Berkeley, California, June 12, 1948.

Remarks, San Francisco, and Golden Gate Park, California, June 13, 1948.

Rear Platform Remarks, Santa Barbara and San Bernadino, California, June 14, 1948.

Address, Greater Los Angeles Press Club, Los Angeles, California, June 14, 1948.

Rear Platform Remarks, Winslow, Arizona; Gallup, Albuquerque, Las Vegas, and Raton, New Mexico, June 15, 1948.

Rear Platform Remarks, Dodge City, Hutchinson, Newton, and Emporia, Kansas, June 16, 1948.

Rear Platform Remarks, Warrensburg, Sedalia, and Jefferson City, Missouri; East St. Louis, Illinois; Terre Haute, Indianapolis, and Richmond, Indiana; Columbus, Ohio, June 17, 1948.

Rear Platform Remarks, Altoona, Harrisburg, and York, Pennsylvania; Baltimore, Maryland, June 18, 1948.

Address, Dedication of Simon Bolivar Memorial Statue, Bolivar, Missouri, July 5, 1948.

Convention Address, Accepting Democratic Nomination, Philadelphia, July

15, 1948.

Speech to Joint Session of Congress, Washington, D.C., July 27, 1948.

Remarks, Dedication of Idlewild Airport, New York City, July 31, 1948.

Rear Platform Remarks (opening of the 1948 campaign), Grand Rapids, Lansing, Detroit, Pontiac, and Flint, Michigan; Toledo, Ohio, September 6, 1948.

Labor Day Address, Detroit, Michigan, September 6, 1948.

Address, American Association for the Advancement of Science, Washington, D.C., September 13, 1948.

Rear Platform Remarks, Pittsburgh, Pennsylvania; Crestline, Ohio, September 17, 1948.

Rear Platform Remarks, Rock Island, Illinois; Davenport, Iowa City, Oxford, Grinnell, Des Moines, Dexter, Des Moines, Melcher, and Chariton, Iowa; Trenton and Polo, Missouri, September 18, 1948.

Rear Platform Remarks, Junction City, Kansas; Denver, Colorado Springs, Pueblo, Canon City, and Salida, Colorado, September 20, 1948.

Rear Platform Remarks, Grand Junction, Colorado; Price, Helper, Springville, Provo, American Fork, Salt Lake City, and Ogden, Utah, September 21, 1948.

Rear Platform Remarks, Sparks and Reno, Nevada; Truckee, Roseville, San Francisco, and Lakeside, California, September 22, 1948.

Rear Platform Remarks, Merced, Fresno, Tulare, Bakersfield, Tehachapi, Mojave, and Burbank, California, September 23, 1948.

Address, Gilmore Stadium, Los Angeles, California, September 23, 1948.

Rear Platform Remarks, San Diego, Oceanside, and Colton, California; Yuma, Arizona, September 24, 1948.

Address, Phoenix, Arizona, September 24, 1948.

Rear Platform Remarks, Lordsburg and Deming, New Mexico; El Paso, Valentine, Marfa, Alpine, and Sanderson, Texas, September 25, 1948.

Address, El Paso, Texas, September 25, 1948.

Speech, San Antonio, Texas, September 26, 1948.

Remarks Recorded for Broadcast, Democratic Women's Day, September 27, 1948 (recorded in Los Angeles on September 23).

Rear Platform Remarks, San Marcos, Austin, Georgetown, Temple, Waco, Hillsboro, Fort Worth, Grand Prairie, Dallas, Greenville, and Bells, Texas, September 27, 1948.

Address, Bonham, Texas, September 27, 1948.

Rear Platform Remarks, Sherman, Whitesboro, and Gainesville, Texas; Marietta, Ardmore, Davis, Pauls Valley, Purcell, and Norman, Oklahoma, September 28, 1948.

Address, Oklahoma City, September 28, 1948.

Rear Platform Remarks, Shawnee, Seminole, Wewoka, Holdenville, McAlester, Eufaula, Muskogee, Tulsa, Claremore, Chelsea, Vinita, and Afton, Oklahoma; Neosho, Monett, Springfield, and Marshfield, Missouri, September 29, 1948.

Address, Tulsa, Oklahoma, September 29, 1948.

Rear Platform Remarks, Mount Vernon, West Frankport, Herrin, Carbondale, Marion, Eldorado, and Carmi, Illinois; Mount Vernon and Evansville, Indiana; Henderson, Owsensboro, Hawesville, and Irvington, Kentucky, September 30, 1948.

Address, University of Southern Illinois, Carbondale, Illinois, September 30, 1948.

Address, Louisville, Kentucky, September 30, 1948.

Radio Address, opening the Nationwide Community Chest Campaign, Louisville, Kentucky, September 30, 1948.

Rear Platform Remarks, Shelbeyville, Frankfort, Lexington, Winchester, Mt. Sterling, Morehead, Olive Hill, and Ashland, Kentucky; Huntington and Montgomery, West Virginia, October 1, 1948.

Address, Charleston, West Virginia, October 1, 1948.

Rear Platform Remarks, Wilmington, Delaware; Philadelphia, Pennsylvania; Camden, New Jersey, October 6, 1948.

Address, Convention Hall, Philadelphia, Pennsylvania, October 6, 1948.

Rear Platform Remarks, Bridgeport, Reading, Allentown, Bethlehem, and Easton, Pennsylvania; Elizabeth, Newark, and Jersey City, New Jersey, October 7, 1948.

Rear Platform Remarks, Albany, Schenectady, Amsterdam, Little Falls, Utica, Rome, Oneida, Syracuse, Auburn, Seneca Falls, Geneva, Rochester, and Batavia, New York, October 8, 1948.

Address, Buffalo, New York, October 8, 1948.

Rear Platform Remarks, Cincinnati, Hamilton, Dayton, Sidney, Lima, Ottawa, Deshler, Fostoria, Willard, and Rittman, Ohio, October 11, 1948.

Address, Akron, Ohio, October 11, 1948.

Rear Platform Remarks, Richmond, Greenfield, and Crawfordsville, Indiana; Danville, Tolono, and Decatur, Illinois, October 12, 1948.

Address, Springfield, Illinois, October 12, 1948.

Rear Platform Remarks, Adams, Altoona, Spooner, and Superior, Wisconsin; Duluth, Minnesota, October 13, 1948.

Address, St. Paul, Minnesota, October 13, 1948.

Rear Platform Remarks, Mankato, Waseca, Rochester, and Winona, Minnesota; Sparta, Elroy, and Waukesha, Wisconsin, October 14, 1948.

Address, University of Wisconsin, Madison, Wisconsin, October 14, 1948.

Address, Milwaukee, Wisconsin, October 14, 1948.

Rear Platform Remarks, Hammond, North Judson, Logansport, Kokomo, Tipton, and Noblesville, Indiana, October 15, 1948.

Address, Indianapolis, Indiana, October 15, 1948.

Rear Platform Remarks, Clarksburg, Grafton, and Keyser, West Virginia, October 16, 1948.

Address, American Legion Convention, Miami, Florida, October 18, 1948.

Address, Raleigh, North Carolina, October 19, 1948.

Address, State Fair Grounds, Raleigh, North Carolina, October 19, 1948.

Radio Address, International Ladies Garment Workers Union Campaign Committee, Washington, D.C., October 21, 1948.

Address, Scranton, Pennsylvania, October 23, 1948.

Address, Wilkes-Barre, Pennsylvania, October 23, 1948.

Rear Platform Remarks, Lock Haven, Pennsylvania, October 23, 1948.

Address, Johnstown, Pennsylvania, October 23, 1948.

Address, Pittsburgh, Pennsylvania, October 23, 1948.

Rear Platform Remarks, Garrett, Indiana, October 25, 1948.

Address, Memorial Auditorium, Gary, Indiana, October 25, 1948.

Address, Chicago Stadium, Chicago, Illinois, October 25, 1948.

Rear Platform Remarks, South Bend and Elkhart, Indiana; Toledo, Sandusky, and Elyria, Ohio, October 26, 1948.

Address, Cleveland Municipal Auditorium, Cleveland, Ohio, October 26, 1948.

Rear Platform Remarks, Pittsfield, Massachusetts; Thompsonville and Hartford, Connecticut; Springfield, Worchester, and Framingham, Massachusetts, October 27, 1948.

Address, Mechanics Hall, Boston, Massachusetts, October 27, 1948.

Rear Platform Remarks, Quincy, Brockton, Taunton, and Fall River, Massachusetts; Providence, Rhode Island; New London, New Haven, Bridgeport, and South Norwalk, Connecticut; New York City (six separate appearances), October 28, 1948.

Address, Madison Square Garden, New York City, October 28, 1948.

Informal Remarks, Yonkers (2 separate talks), Bronx, Harlem, and Queens, New York, October 29, 1948.

Address, Harlem, New York, October 29, 1948.

Address, Brooklyn Academy of Music, Brooklyn, New York, October 29, 1948.

Rear Platform Remarks, Bellefontaine, Ohio; Terre Haute, Indiana; Mattoon, Illinois; St. Louis, Missouri, October 30, 1948.

Address, Kiel Auditorium, St. Louis, Missouri, October 30, 1948.

Radio Remarks, Election Eve, Independence, Missouri, November 1, 1948.

Remarks, Victory Celebration, Independence, Missouri, November 3, 1948.

Remarks, Enroute to Washington, D.C., through St. Louis, Missouri; Vincennes, Indiana; Cincinnati, Ohio, November 4, 1948.

Remarks on Arrival at White House, Washington, D.C., November 5, 1948.

Address, Food and Agriculture Organization of the United Nations, New York City, November 24, 1948.

Radio Remarks, Lighting of the National Community Christmas Tree, Washington, D.C., December 24, 1948.

1949

State of the Union, Washington, D.C., January 5, 1949.

Remarks, Truman-Barkley Dinner, Washington, D.C., January 18, 1949.

Remarks, Luncheon of Finance Committee, Democratic National Committee, Washington, D.C., January 19, 1949.

Remarks, Dinner of Presidential Electors Association, Washington, D.C., January 19, 1949.

Remarks, Battery D. Breakfast, Washington, D.C., January 20, 1949.

Inaugural Address, Washington, D.C., January 20, 1949.

Remarks, Women's Division of the Democratic National Committee, Washington, D.C., January 21, 1949.

Remarks, National Planning Association, Washington, D.C., February 1, 1949.

Remarks, Young Representatives from Marshall Plan Countries, Washington, D.C., February 3, 1949.

Remarks, Officers of the Veterans of Foreign Wars, Washington, D.C., February 18, 1949.

Remarks, Dinner in Honor of General Vaughn, Reserve Officers Association, Arlington, Virginia, February 22, 1949.

Remarks, Savings Bond Dinner, Washington, D.C., February 23, 1949.

Remarks, Jefferson-Jackson Day Dinner, Washington, D.C., February 24, 1949.

Address, Jefferson-Jackson Day Dinner, Washington, D.C., February 24, 1949.

Radio Address, Opening the Red Cross Campaign, Washington, D.C., February 28, 1949.

Remarks, Eighth Annual Science Talent Search, Washington, D.C., March 3, 1949.

Remarks, American Legion, Washington, D.C., March 4, 1949.

Address, Rollins College, Winter Park, Florida, March 8, 1949.

Remarks, Graduation Exercises, Fleet Sonar School, U.S. Naval Base, Key West, Florida, March 18, 1949.

Address, United States Conference of Mayors, Washington, D.C., March 21, 1949.

Address, President's Conference on Industrial Safety, Washington, D.C., March 23, 1949.

Radio Address, "One Great Hour," Interdenominational Program, Washington, D.C., March 26, 1949.

Address, Signing of the North Atlantic Treaty, Washington, D.C., April 4, 1949.

Remarks, New Democratic Senators and Representatives, Washington, D.C., April 6, 1949.

Remarks, Supper for Jefferson-Jackson Day Executive Committee, April 8, 1949.

Remarks, Floor of Senate on Fourth Anniversary of Death of President Roosevelt, Washington, D.C., April 12, 1949.

Remarks, Members of National Conference of Business Paper Editors, Washington, D.C., April 15, 1949.

Address, Dinner Honoring Volunteers in the Savings Bond Campaign, Washington, D.C., April 19, 1949.

Remarks, American Society of Newspaper Editors, Washington, D.C., April 22, 1949.

Remarks, National Association of Radio Farm Directors, Washington, D.C., May 2, 1949.

Remarks, Members of Agricultural Editors Association, Washington, D.C., May 3, 1949.

Radio Remarks, Opening the Opportunity Savings Bond Drive, Washington, D.C., May 16, 1949.

Remarks, Members of the Brazilian Press, Washington, D.C., May 19, 1949.

Remarks, President's Conference on Community Responsibility to Our Peacetime Servicemen and Women, Washington, D.C., May 25, 1949.

Address, President's Conference on Highway Safety, Washington, D.C., June 2, 1949.

Remarks, Foreign Delegates of the Inter-American Bar Association, Washington, D.C., June 2, 1949.

Address, Dinner in Honor of General George C. Marshall, Washington, D.C., June 5, 1949.

Informal Remarks, Reunion of the 35th Division Association, Little Rock,

Arkansas, June 10-11, 1949.

Address, Dedication of the World War Memorial, Little Rock, Arkansas, June 11, 1949.

Remarks, Delegates to the National 4-H Club Camp, Washington, D.C., June 16, 1949.

Radio and Television Report to the American People on the State of the National Economy, Washington, D.C., July 13, 1949.

Address, Imperial Council Session of the Shrine of North America, Chicago, Illinois, July 19, 1949.

Remarks, Shriners Diamond Jubilee Banquet, Chicago, Illinois, July 19, 1949.

Address, Golden Jubilee Convention of the Veterans of Foreign Wars, Miami, Florida, August 22, 1949.

Remarks, Dinner Honoring William Boyle, New Chairman of the Democratic National Committee, Washington, D.C., August 24, 1949.

Remarks, American Legion Convention Luncheon, Philadelphia, Pennsylvania, August 29, 1949.

Address, American Legion Convention, Philadelphia, Pennsylvania, August 29, 1949.

Labor Day Address, Allegheny County Free Fair, Pittsburgh, Pennsylvania, September 5, 1949.

Labor Day Address, Convention of the American Veterans of World War II, Des Moines, Iowa, September 5, 1949.

Remarks, National Citizens Committee for United Nations Day, Washington, D.C., September 15, 1949.

Radio Address, Democratic Women's Day, Washington, D.C., September 27, 1949.

Address, Dinner Honoring Democratic National Chairman William M. Boyle, Jr., Kansas City, Missouri, September 29, 1949.

Radio Remarks, Opening the Community Chest Campaign, Washington, D.C., September 30, 1949.

Remarks, Officers Luncheon, Fort Bragg, North Carolina, October 4, 1949.

Remarks, Ambassadors to the Council of the Organization of American States, October 12, 1949.

Address, Laying of Cornerstone of United Nations Building, New York City, October 24, 1949.

Remarks, United Nations Day Luncheon, New York City, October 24, 1949.

Radio Address, "Religion in American Life," Washington, D.C., October 30, 1949.

Remarks, American Society of Civil Engineers, Washington, D.C., November 2, 1949.

Remarks and Address, Minnesota's Truman Day Celebration, St. Paul, Minnesota, November 3, 1949.

Radio Address, Independent Citizens Committee of Lehman for Senator, Washington, D.C., November 5, 1949.

Remarks, Women's National Democratic Club Dinner, Washington, D.C., November 8, 1949.

Address, Luncheon, National Conference of Christians and Jews, Washington, D.C., November 11, 1949.

Address, Annual Meeting of the National Council of Negro Women, Inc., Washington, D.C., November 15, 1949.

Address, Unveiling of Memorial Carillon, Arlington National Cemetery, Arlington, Virginia, December 21, 1949.

Address, Lighting of National Community Christmas Tree, Washington, D.C., December 24, 1949.

1950

State of the Union, Washington, D.C., January 4, 1950.

Remarks, American Federation of Labor's Samuel Gompers Centennial Dinner, Washington, D.C., January 5, 1950.

Remarks, Supper for Democratic Senators and Representatives, Washington, D.C., January 12, 1950.

Remarks, Dinner by the Chairmen and Directors of Federal Reserve Banks, Washington, D.C., January 16, 1950.

Remarks, Delegation from the National Emergency Civil Rights Mobilization Conference, Washington, D.C., January 17, 1950.

Remarks, Women's Patriotic Conference on National Defense, Washington, D.C., January 26, 1950.

Remarks, Baptist Missionaries, Washington, D.C., February 3, 1950.

Address, Attorney General's Conference on Law Enforcement Problems, Washington, D.C., February 15, 1950.

Address, Jefferson-Jackson Day Dinner, Washington, D.C., February 16, 1950.

Remarks, Masonic Breakfast on Washington's Birthday, Washington, D.C., February 22, 1950.

Address on Foreign Policy, George Washington National Masonic Memorial, Alexandria, Virginia, February 22, 1950.

Radio Remarks, Opening the Red Cross Campaign, Washington, D.C., February 28, 1950.

Remarks, Ninth Annual Science Talent Search, Washington, D.C., March

2, 1950.

Remarks, U.S. National Commission for UNESCO, Washington, D.C.,
April 13, 1950.

Address on Foreign Policy, Luncheon of the American Society of
Newspaper Editors, Washington, D.C., April 20, 1950.

Address, Dinner of the Federal Bar Association, Washington, D.C., April
24, 1950.

Rear Platform Remarks, Galesburg, Illinois; Burlington, Ottumwa,
Creston, and Pacific Junction, Iowa; Grand Island, Ravenna,
Broken Bow, and Seneca, Nebraska, May 8, 1950.

Address, Lincoln, Nebraska, May 8, 1950.

Address, Casper, Wyoming, May 9, 1950.

Rear Platform Remarks, Wendover and Rawlins, Wyoming, May 9, 1950.

Address, Cheyenne, Wyoming, May 9, 1950.

Address, Laramie, Wyoming, May 9, 1950.

Rear Platform Remarks, Pocatello, Shoshone, Glenns Ferry, Boise, and
Nampa, Idaho; Ontario, Huntington, Baker, La Grande, and
Umatilla, Oregon; Wallula, Washington, May 10, 1950.

Address, Pendleton, Oregon, May 10, 1950.

Rear Platform Remarks, Coulee City, Grand Coulee Dam, Wilbur, and
Spokane, Washington; Sandpoint, Idaho; Paradise, Montana, May
11, 1950.

Address, Dedication of Grand Coulee Dam, Grand Coulee, Washington,
May 11, 1950.

Address, Gonzaga University, Spokane, Washington, May 11, 1950.

Rear Platform Remarks, Missoula, Garrison, Helena, Great Falls, Big
Sandy, and Havre, Montana, May 12, 1950.

Address, Butte, Montana, May 12, 1950.

Rear Platform Remarks, Fort Peck Dam and Glasgow, Montana;
Williston, Minot, New Rockford, and Breckenridge, North
Dakota, May 13, 1950.

Address, Fargo, North Dakota, May 13, 1950.

Rear Platform Remarks, Altoona, Elroy, and Madison, Wisconsin, May
14, 1950.

Address, Dedication of the Credit Union National Association's Filene
House, Madison, Wisconsin, May 14, 1950.

Radio Remarks, Opening the Savings Bond Drive, Chicago, Illinois, May
15, 1950.

Address, National Democratic Conference and Jefferson Jubilee, Chicago,
Illinois, May 15, 1950.

Rear Platform Remarks, Cumberland, Maryland, May 16, 1950.

Address, Dedication of the Publication of the First Volume of the Jefferson

Papers, Washington, D.C., May 17, 1950.

Remarks, Armed Forces Dinner, May 19, 1950.

Remarks, Democratic Women's National Council Dinner, Washington, D.C., May 20, 1950.

Remarks, Delegates to the Fifth Annual Conference on Citizenship, Washington, D.C., May 23, 1950.

Remarks, Ohio Farm Bureau, Washington, D.C., May 24, 1950.

Address, President's Conference on Industrial Safety, Washington, D.C., June 5, 1950.

Address, Dinner of the Better Business Bureau, Washington, D.C., June 16, 1950.

Remarks, Ninety-first Annual National Convention of the Augustana Lutheran Church, Washington, D.C., June 7, 1950.

Commencement Address, University of Missouri, Columbia, Missouri, June 9, 1950.

Rear Platform Remarks, Columbia, and Mexico, Missouri, June 9, 1950.

Remarks, Thirtieth Reunion of the 35th Division Association, St. Louis, Missouri, June 10, 1950.

Address, Jefferson National Expansion Memorial, St. Louis, Missouri, June 10, 1950.

Remarks, National Association of Radio Farm Directors, Washington, D.C., June 12, 1950.

Remarks, U.S. Marine Corps Base, Quantico, Virginia, June 12, 1950.

Address, Dedication of Friendship International Airport, Baltimore, Maryland, June 24, 1950.

Remarks, Members of Reserve Officers Association, Washington, D.C., June 28, 1950.

Address, Annual Convention of the American Newspaper Guild, Washington, D.C., June 28, 1950.

Remarks, Washington Student Citizenship Seminar, Washington, D.C., June 28, 1950.

Address, Boy Scout Jamboree, Valley Forge, Pennsylvania, June 30, 1950.

Radio and Television Address to the American People on the Situation in Korea, Washington, D.C., July 19, 1950.

Remarks, President's Committee on National Employ the Physically Handicapped Week, Washington, D.C., August 9, 1950.

Radio and Television Report to the American People on the Situation in Korea, Washington, D.C., September 1, 1950.

Remarks, Marine Corps League, Washington, D.C., September 7, 1950.

Remarks, National Citizens' Committee for United Nations Day, Washington, D.C., September 7, 1950.

Radio and Television Address to the American People Following the

Singing of the Defense Production Act, Washington, D.C., September 9, 1950.

Remarks, National Association of Postal Supervisors, Washington, D.C., September 13, 1950.

Recorded Broadcast Address, Democratic Women's Day, September 27, 1950.

Radio Remarks, Opening the Community Chest Campaign, Washington, D.C., September 29, 1950.

Remarks, Installation of Mary Jane Truman as Worthy Grand Matron, Order of the Eastern Star, St. Louis, Missouri, October 11, 1950.

Remarks, Commissioned Officers Mess, Pearl Harbor, Hawaii, October 13, 1950.

Address, War Memorial Opera House, San Francisco, California, October 17, 1950.

Address, United Nations General Assembly, New York City, October 24, 1950.

Remarks, National Guard Association, Washington, D.C., October 25, 1950.

Remarks, Arlington Cemetery, Arlington, Virginia, November 1, 1950.

Address, Kiel Auditorium, St. Louis, Missouri, November 4, 1950.

Remarks, Liberty Bell Luncheon, Independence, Missouri, November 6, 1950.

Address, Dedication of the Liberty Bell, Independence, Missouri, November 6, 1950.

Address, Midcentury White House Conference on Children and Youth, Washington, D.C., December 5, 1950.

Radio and Television Report to the American People on the National Emergency, Washington, D.C., December 15, 1950.

Remarks, Dinner of the Knights of the Red Cross of Constantine, Kansas City, Missouri, December 22, 1950.

Remarks, Luncheon for the Press, Kansas City, Missouri, December 23, 1950.

Remarks, Order of the Eastern Star, Grandview, Missouri, September 23, 1950.

Remarks, Dedication Services of the Grandview Baptist Church, Grandview, Missouri, December 24, 1950.

Recorded Message for Broadcast on World Day of Prayer, Washington, D.C., December 24, 1950.

Recorded Address, Lighting of the National Community Christmas Tree, Washington, D.C., December 24, 1950.

1951

State of the Union, Washington, D.C., January 8, 1951.

Remarks, Woodrow Wilson Foundation Award Ceremonies, Washington, D.C., January 10, 1951.

Remarks, Buffet Supper for Democratic Members of Congress, January 11, 1951.

Remarks, Members of the National Advisory Committee on the Selection of Physicians, Dentists, and Allied Specialists, Washington, D.C., January 12, 1951.

Remarks, Dinner of the Society of Business Magazine Editors, Washington, D.C., January 19, 1951.

Remarks, Special Ceremony for Sam Rayburn, Washington, D.C., January 30, 1951.

Remarks, Democratic National Congressional Committee Dinner, Washington, D.C., January 31, 1951.

Address, Dedication of the Chapel of the Four Chaplains, Philadelphia, Pennsylvania, February 3, 1951.

Remarks, Group of Methodist Ministers, February 7, 1951.

Remarks, Swearing In of the President's Commission on Internal Security and Individual Rights, Washington, D.C., February 12, 1951.

Remarks, Group of Trainees from NATO Countries, Washington, D.C., February 13, 1951.

Remarks, Enlisted Men's Mess Hall, Aberdeen, Maryland, Proving Ground, Aberdeen, Maryland, February 17, 1951.

Remarks, Voice of Democracy Contest Winners, Washington, D.C., February 20, 1951.

Remarks, Masonic Breakfast, Washington, D.C., February 21, 1951.

Remarks, White House Photographer's Association Awards Ceremonies, Washington, D.C., February 24, 1951.

Remarks, 82d Airborne Division, Washington, D.C., February 27, 1951.

Radio and Television Remarks, Opening the Red Cross Campaign, Washington, D.C., February 27, 1951.

Remarks, Winner of the Tenth Annual Science Talent Search, Washington, D.C., March 1, 1951.

Remarks, Floor of the Senate at a Gavel Presentation Ceremony for Vice President Barkley, Washington, D.C., March 1, 1951.

Address, Opening the Meeting of the Foreign Ministers of the American Republics, Washington, D.C., March 26, 1951.

Remarks, Members of the Associated Church Press, March 28, 1951.

Address, Cornerstone Laying of the New York Avenue Presbyterian Church, Washington, D.C., April 3, 1951.

Radio Report to the American People on Korea and U.S. Policy in the Far East, Washington, D.C., April 11, 1951.

Address, Jefferson-Jackson Day Dinner, Washington, D.C., April 14, 1951.

Remarks, British Publishers and Editors, Washington, D.C., April 20, 1951.

Remarks, Group of Foreign Journalists, Washington, D.C., May 3, 1951.

Address, Dinner of the Civil Defense Conference, Washington, D.C., May 7, 1951.

Remarks, Conference of the Industry Advisory Councils of the Department of the Interior, Washington, D.C., May 9, 1951.

Remarks, Ceremony in Observance of National Music Week, Washington, D.C., May 9, 1951.

Address, National Conference on Citizenship, Washington, D.C., May 17, 1951.

Remarks, Armed Forces Day Dinner, Washington, D.C., May 18, 1951.

Remarks, Conference of United States Attorneys, Washington, D.C., May 24, 1951.

Remarks, Dedication of the Carter Barron Amphitheater, Washington, D.C., May 25, 1951.

Remarks, Highway Safety Conference, Washington, D.C., June 13, 1951.

Remarks, Delegates to the Twenty-first National 4-H Club Camp, Washington, D.C., June 14, 1951.

Radio and Television Report to the American People on the Need for Extending Inflation Controls, Washington, D.C., June 14, 1951.

Remarks, Newsboy Bond Salesman, Washington, D.C., June 21, 1951.

Address, Dedication of the National Institutes of Health Clinical Center, Washington, D.C., June 22, 1951.

Address, Dedication of the Arnold Engineering Development Center, Tullahoma, Tennessee, June 25, 1951.

Remarks, Members of the Student Citizenship Seminar, Washington, D.C., June 27, 1951.

Address, Ceremonies Commemorating the 175th Anniversary of the Declaration of Independence, Washington, D.C., July 4, 1951.

Remarks, Presentation of Congressional Medals of Honor, Washington, D.C., July 5, 1951.

Remarks, Members of the 25th Infantry Division Association, July 7, 1951.

Remarks, Accepting a Piece of the Rock of Corregidor from the People of the Philippines, Washington, D.C., July 10, 1951.

Remarks, After Viewing Flood Disaster Area, Grandview, Missouri, July 17, 1951.

Remarks, French Provincial Press, Washington, D.C., July 18, 1951.

Remarks, Danish Boys from the International Boys Camp, Inc., Washington, D.C., July 19, 1951.

Remarks, Delegates to the Sixth Annual American Legion Boys Nation, Washington, D.C., July 25, 1951.

Address, Celebration of Detroit's 250th Anniversary, Detroit, Michigan, July 28, 1951.

Remarks, Delegates of Girls Nation, Washington, D.C., August 1, 1951.

Remarks, United Defense Fund, Washington, D.C., August 2, 1951.

Address, Dedication of the Presidential Lounge at Union Station for the Use of Servicemen and Servicewomen, Washington, D.C., August 8, 1951.

Address, Dedication of the New Washington Headquarters of the American Legion, Washington, D.C., August 14, 1951.

Remarks, Exchange Teachers from Great Britain, France, and Canada, Washington, D.C., August 16, 1951.

Remarks, Annual Meeting of the President's Committee on National Employ the Physically Handicapped Week, Washington, D.C., August 17, 1951.

Remarks, High School Students from Kansas, Washington, D.C., August 24, 1951.

Remarks, Presentation of a Floral Replica of a Defense Bond, Washington, D.C., August 31, 1951.

Radio Address, Opening the Defense Bond Drive, Washington, D.C., September 3, 1951.

Remarks, Luncheon for Democrats from Western States, San Francisco, California, September 4, 1951.

Address, Opening of the Conference on the Japanese Peace Treaty, San Francisco, California, September 4, 1951.

Remarks, Delegates to the Japanese Peace Conference, San Francisco, California, September 4, 1951.

Remarks, Dedication of the Organized Reserve Corps Armory, Kansas City, Missouri, September 6, 1951.

Address, Joint Meeting of the International Bank for Reconstruction and Development and the International Monetary Fund, Washington, D.C., September 10, 1951.

Remarks, International Council of the Independent Order of Odd Fellows, Washington, D.C., September 10, 1951.

Address, Cornerstone Laying of the New General Accounting Office Building, Washington, D.C., September 11, 1951.

Remarks, National Citizens' Committee for United Nations Day, September 12, 1951.

Address, Constitution Day Ceremonies at the Library of Congress, Washington, D.C., September 17, 1951.

Address, National Association of Postmasters, Washington, D.C., September 17, 1951.

Remarks, Delegates to the First National Conference on Israel, Washington, D.C., September 21, 1951.

Address, Dedication of Equestrian Statues, a Gift of the People of Italy, Washington, D.C., September 26, 1951.

Remarks, Group of Korean Soldiers, Washington, D.C., September 26, 1951.

Remarks Recorded for Broadcast, Democratic Women's Day, Washington, D.C., September 27, 1951.

Address, Washington Pilgrimage of American Churchmen, Washington, D.C., September 28, 1951.

Radio Remarks, Opening the Nation's Community Chest Campaign, Washington, D.C., September 30, 1951.

Remarks, Members of the Directing Council of the Pan American Sanitary Organization, Washington, D.C., October 1, 1951.

Remarks, Golden Jubilee of the American Motion Picture Theater, Washington, D.C., October 8, 1951.

Remarks, Delegation from the American Hungarian Federation, Washington, D.C., October 12, 1951.

Remarks, Luncheon in Winston-Salem, North Carolina, October 15, 1951.

Address, Groundbreaking Ceremonies, Wake Forest College, Winston-Salem, North Carolina, October 15, 1951.

Remarks, Officers and Members of the Board of Trustees, American Dental Association, Washington, D.C., October 16, 1951.

Remarks, Members of the Supreme Council, Ancient and Accepted Scottish Rite, Washington, D.C., October 17, 1951.

Remarks, Industrialists from Colombia, Washington, D.C., October 22, 1951.

Remarks, Seventy-third General Conference of the National Guard Association, Washington, D.C., October 24, 1951.

Address, Cornerstone Laying of the District of Columbia Red Cross Building, Washington, D.C., October 24, 1951.

Remarks, Group of United Nations Veterans from the Fighting Front in Korea, Washington, D.C., October 24, 1951.

Address, Dedication of a Square in Washington to the Memory of Samuel Gompers, Washington, D.C., October 27, 1951.

Remarks, Members of the Defense Advisory Committee on Women in the Services, Washington, D.C., November 5, 1951.

Remarks, Breakfast of the National Cartoonist Association, Washington,

D.C., November 6, 1951.

Remarks, Executive Committee of the Polish Legion of American Veterans, Washington, D.C., November 6, 1951.

Radio and Television Report to the American People on International Arms Reduction, November 7, 1951.

Radio Address to the American People on Armistice Day, Washington, D.C., November 11, 1951.

Address, Woman's National Democratic Club, Washington, D.C., November 20, 1951.

Remarks, Presenting the Collier Award Trophy for 1950, Washington, D.C., December 17, 1951.

Address, Lighting of the National Community Christmas Tree, Washington, D.C., December 24, 1951.

1952

State of the Union, Washington, D.C., January 9, 1952

Remarks, Veterans of Foreign Wars Dinner, Washington, D.C., February 5, 1952.

Remarks, Methodist Ministers from Illinois, Washington, D.C., February 20, 1952.

Remarks, Winners of the Fifth Annual Voice of America Democracy Contest, Washington, D.C., February 20, 1952.

Remarks, Masonic Breakfast, Washington, D.C., February 21, 1952.

Remarks, Group from the Navajo Tribal Council, Washington, D.C., February 21, 1952.

Remarks, Recorded for Broadcast, Opening of the Red Cross Campaign, Washington, D.C., February 28, 1952.

Remarks, Winners of the Eleventh Annual Science Talent Search, Washington, D.C., February 29, 1952.

Address Broadcast from the Voice of America Floating Radio Transmitter *Courier*, Washington, D.C., March 4, 1952.

Remarks, Members of a Catholic University Dramatic Group Leaving for Korea, Washington, D.C., March 6, 1952.

Radio and Television Address to the American People on the Mutual Security Program, Washington, D.C., March 6, 1952.

Address, Convention of the Columbia Scholastic Press Association, New York City, March 15, 1952.

Address, Jefferson-Jackson Day Dinner, Washington, D.C., March 29, 1952.

Remarks, Reception by the Democratic National Committee, Washington, D.C., March 30, 1952.

Remarks, Ceremony Commemorating the Third Anniversary of the Signing of the North Atlantic Treaty, Washington, D.C., April 4, 1952.

Address, National Conference on International Economic and Social Development, Washington, D.C., April 8, 1952.

Radio and Television Address to the American People on the Need for Government Operation of the Steel Mills, Washington, D.C., April 8, 1952.

Remarks, Floods in the Upper Missouri and Mississippi Valleys, Omaha, Nebraska, April 16, 1952.

Remarks, Members of the Associated Church Press, Washington, D.C., April 18, 1952.

Address, Dedication of the New AMVETS Headquarters, Washington, D.C., April 18, 1952.

Address, Seventieth Anniversary Meeting of the National Civil Service League, Washington, D.C., May 2, 1952.

Remarks, Meeting with Steel Industry and Labor Leaders, Washington, D.C., May 3, 1952.

Address, Sixth Annual Honor Awards Program of the Department of Agriculture, Washington, D.C., May 15, 1952.

Remarks, Luncheon in the Cadet Dining Hall, West Point, New York, May 20, 1952.

Address, Sesquicentennial Convocation of the United States Military Academy, West Point, New York, May 20, 1952.

Remarks, Winner of the Teacher of the Year Award, Washington, D.C., May 21, 1952.

Remarks, Members of the National Advisory Committee of the Veterans Administration Voluntary Services, Washington, D.C., May 21, 1952.

Remarks, Luncheon in the Midshipmen's Mess Hall, Annapolis, Maryland, May 24, 1952.

Address, Electric Consumers Conference, Washington, D.C., May 26, 1952.

Address, Dinner of the Jewish National Fund, Washington, D.C., May 26, 1952.

Address, President's Conference on Industrial Safety, Washington, D.C., June 2, 1952.

Remarks, Breakfast of the 35th Division Association, Springfield, Missouri, June 7, 1952.

Address, Thirty-second Reunion of the 35th Division Association, Springfield, Missouri, June 7, 1952.

Special Message to Joint Session of Congress on the Steel Strike,

Washington, D.C., June 10, 1952.

Commencement Address, Howard University, Washington, D.C., June 13, 1952.

Address, Keel Laying of the First Atomic Energy Submarine, Groton, Connecticut, June 14, 1952.

Remarks, Luncheon, Officers' Club, U.S. Submarine Base, New London, Connecticut, June 14, 1952.

Remarks, "Task Force Smith," Washington, D.C., June 16, 1952.

Remarks Upon Receiving Medal from Students from William Chrisman High School, Independence, Missouri, June 17, 1952.

Remarks, Delegates to the Twenty-second Annual National 4-H Club Camp, Washington, D.C., June 19, 1952.

Remarks, Washington Student Citizenship Seminar, Washington, D.C., June 25, 1952.

Rear Platform Remarks, Newport, Arkansas, July 1, 1952.

Address, Dedication of the Norfork and Bull Shoals Dams, Bull Shoals, Arkansas, July 2, 1952.

Rear Platform Remarks, Bull Shoals, Batesville, and Newport, Arkansas, July 2, 1952.

Address, Democratic National Convention, Chicago, Illinois, July 26, 1952.

Remarks, Delegates of Girls Nation, Washington, D.C., August 6, 1952.

Remarks, Delegates to a CIO-PAC Rally, Washington, D.C., August 15, 1952.

Rear Platform Remarks, Pittsburgh, Pennsylvania, and Crestline, Ohio, September 1, 1952.

Labor Day Address, Milwaukee, Wisconsin, September 1, 1952.

Rear Platform Remarks, Cincinnati, Ohio; Parkersburg, Keyser, and Martinsburg, West Virginia, September 2, 1952.

Remarks, President's Committee on National Employ the Physically Handicapped Week, September 4, 1952.

Remarks, Ceremony Marking the Issuance of the "Women in the Armed Services" Commemorative Stamp, Washington, D.C., September 1, 1952.

Address, American Hospital Association Convention, Philadelphia, Pennsylvania, September 16, 1952.

Remarks, Delegates to the Theaters Owners Convention, Washington, D.C., September 17, 1952.

Address, National Conference on Citizenship, Washington, D.C., September 17, 1952.

Remarks, U.S. Coast Guard Academy, New London, Connecticut, September 20, 1952.

Remarks, National Citizen's Committee on United Nations Day, Washington, D.C., September 26, 1952.

Remarks, Representatives of the National Council of Churches, Washington, D.C., September 26, 1952.

Remarks, Luncheon with Members of the National Symphony Orchestra, Washington, D.C., September 26, 1952.

Radio and Television Remarks, Opening Community Chest Campaign, Washington, D.C., September 27, 1952.

Rear Platform Remarks, Breckenridge, Minnesota; Fargo, Grand Forks, Larimore, Lakota, Devil's Lake, Minot, Berthhold, Stanley, Tioga, and Williston, North Dakota; Wolf Point, Montana, September 29, 1952.

Rear Platform Remarks, Wolf Point, Glasgow, Malta, Chinook, Havre, Shelby, Cut Bank, and Belton, Montana, September 30, 1952.

Address, Tiber Dam, Montana, September 30, 1952.

Rear Platform Remarks, Columbia Falls, Hungry Horse, Kalispell, Whitefish, Eureka, Libby, and Troy, Montana; Bonners Ferry, and Sandpoint, Idaho, October 1, 1952.

Address, Hungry Horse Dam, Hungry Horse, Montana, October 1, 1952.

Address, Auditorium of the Eagles Lodge, Spokane, Washington, October 1, 1952.

Recorded Radio Address, Sponsored by the International Ladies Garment Workers Union Campaign Committee, broadcast from Washington, D.C., October 1, 1952.

Rear Platform Remarks, Ephrata, Wenatchee, Skyomish, Snohomish, Everett, and Kent, Washington, October 2, 1952.

Address, Auditorium of the Fraternal Order of the Eagles, Seattle, Washington, October 2, 1952.

Address, Rally in the Armory, Tacoma, Washington, October 2, 1952.

Rear Platform Remarks, Klamath Falls, Oregon; Dunsmuir, Redding, Red Bluff, Gerber, and Davis, California, October 3, 1952.

Address, Palace Hotel, San Francisco, California, October 4, 1952.

Address, Oakland Auditorium, Oakland, California, October 4, 1952.

Rear Platform Remarks, Salt Lake City and Helper, Utah; Grand Junction and Rifle, Colorado, October 6, 1952.

Address, Brigham Young University, Salt Lake City, Utah, October 6, 1952.

Rear Platform Remarks, Malta, Canon City, Pueblo, Colorado Springs, Limon, Denver, and Akron, Colorado, October 7, 1952.

Rear Platform Remarks, Pacific Junction, Hamburg, and Shenandoah, Iowa; St. Joseph, Sedalia, and Jefferson City, Missouri, October 8, 1952.

Rear Platform Remarks, Indianapolis, Anderson, and Muncie, Indiana; Bellefontainne, and Galion, Ohio; Erie, Pennsylvania, October 9, 1952.

Address, Cleveland, Ohio, October 9, 1952.

Address, Memorial Hall, Buffalo, New York, October 9, 1952.

Rear Platform Remarks, Batavia, Rochester, Syracuse, Oneida, Rome, Utica, Amsterdam, Schenectady, Albany, Hudson, Yonkers, and Grand Central Station, New York, October 10, 1952.

Address, Receiving Franklin Roosevelt Award, Harlem, New York, October 11, 1952.

Address, Columbus Day Dinner, New York City, October 11, 1952.

Rear Platform Remarks, North Haven, Wallingford, Meriden, Middletown, New Britain, Windsor Locks, and Thompsonville, Connecticut; Springfield, Worcester, Clinton, and Lowell, Massachusetts; Nashua and Manchester, New Hampshire, October 16, 1952.

Address, Hartford, Connecticut, October 16, 1952.

Address, Armory, Manchester, New Hampshire, October 16, 1952.

Rear Platform Remarks, Portsmouth, Somersworth, Dover, Rockingham, Exeter, and Plaistow, New Hampshire; Haverhill, Lawrence, and Malden, Massachusetts, October 17, 1952.

Address, Boston, Massachusetts, October 17, 1952.

Rear Platform Remarks, Brockton, Taunton, and Fall River, Massachusetts; Westerly, Rhode Island; New London, Old Saybrook, New Haven, Bridgeport, Norwalk, and Stamford, Connecticut; New Rochelle and New York City (2), New York, October 18, 1952.

Address, Providence, Rhode Island, October 18, 1952.

Address, Brooklyn, New York, October 18, 1952.

Rear Platform Remarks, Wilmington, Delaware; Jersey City, Newark, Elizabeth, New Brunswick, Trenton, and Camden, New Jersey; Bridgeport, and Reading, Pennsylvania, October 21, 1952.

Address, Pottsville, Pennsylvania, October 21, 1952.

Address, Philadelphia, Pennsylvania, October 21, 1952.

Rear Platform Remarks, Scranton, Wilkes-Barre, Bloomsburg, Northumberland, Williamsport, Altoona, Johnstown, and Pittsburgh, Pennsylvania, October 22, 1952.

Address, Syria Mosque, Pittsburgh, Pennsylvania, October 22, 1952.

Rear Platform Remarks, Wheeling, West Virginia; Braddock, McKeesport, Connellsville, Rockwood, and Myersdale, Pennsylvania; Cumberland, Maryland; Harpers Ferry, West Virginia; Washington, D.C., October 23, 1952.

Rear Platform Remarks, Willard and Deshler, Ohio; Garrett, Indiana, October 27, 1952.

Address, Gary, Indiana, October 27, 1952.

Rear Platform Remarks, Winona, Red Wing, Hastings, St. Paul, Minneapolis, and Duluth, Minnesota, October 28, 1952.

Address, Hibbing, Minnesota, October 28, 1952.

Rear Platform Remarks, Waterloo, Cedar Rapids, West Liberty, and Davenport, Iowa; Moline, Negro War Memorial in Chicago, Illinois, October 29, 1952.

Address, Chicago, Illinois, October 29, 1952.

Rear Platform Remarks, Muskegon, Grand Rapids, Lansing, Durand, Flint, Pontiac, Hamtramack, and Detroit, Michigan, October 30, 1952.

Address, State Fair Coliseum, Detroit, Michigan, October 30, 1952.

Rear Platform Remarks, Toledo, Ottawa, Sidney, Troy, Dayton, and Hamilton, Ohio, October 31, 1952.

Address, Cincinnati, Ohio, October 31, 1952.

Rear Platform Remarks, Vincennes and Terre Haute, Indiana; Danville, Decautur, Taylorville, Litchfield, and Granite City, Illinois, November 1, 1952.

Address, Kiel Auditorium, St. Louis, Missouri, November 1, 1952.

Radio and Television Remarks, Election Eve, Kansas City, Missouri, November 3, 1952.

Remarks, Directors of the National Newspaper Publishers Association, Washington, D.C., November 14, 1952.

Remarks, Laying the Cornerstone of the New Temple of the Washington Hebrew Congregation, Washington, D.C., November 16, 1952.

Address, Association of Military Surgeons, Washington, D.C., November 19, 1952.

Remarks, Cornerstone Laying of the Westminster Presbyterian Church, Alexandria, Virginia, November 23, 1952.

Remarks, Business Paper Editors, Washington, D.C., November 25, 1952.

Address, National Archives Dedicating the New Shrine for the Declaration of Independence, the Constitution, and the Bill of Rights, Washington, D.C., December 15, 1952.

Address, Alumni Association of the Industrial College of the ARmed Forces, Washington, D.C., December 16, 1952.

Remarks, Wright Memorial Dinner of the Aero Club of Washington, Washington, D.C., December 17, 1952.

Address, National War College, Washington, D.C., December 19, 1952.

Remarks, Lighting of the National Community Christmas Tree, Washington, D.C., December 24, 1952.

1953

State of the Union, Washington, D.C., January 7, 1953.
Farewell Address to the People, Washington, D.C., January 15, 1953.

Bibliography

This bibliography is divided into three sections: (1) speech sources in the Harry S. Truman Library, (2) Harry S. Truman's primary written sources, and (3) secondary sources.

THE HARRY S. TRUMAN LIBRARY

The most important sources for the study of Harry S. Truman's presidential rhetoric are in the Harry S. Truman Library, Independence, Missouri. The library contains finding aides for all materials, and the staff is helpful and knowledgeable in the arcane art of conducting research in a presidential library.

The papers of Harry S. Truman, speech files, contain preliminary drafts as well as the final reading copy for all of his speeches and addresses. Unfortunately, the drafts are not always numbered or dated, nor do they always indicate who wrote and/or emended them. Although Truman did make last minute changes on the final reading copy, one may most often encounter Truman's underlining words and phrases for vocal emphasis.

The president's secretary's files, speech files, also contain important drafts and pertinent memorandum for the process of inventing and editing the speech. On the drafts, one may expect to find Truman's emendations, although these are not, as a rule, copious.

One must also consult the papers of Truman's principal speech advisers. These include the papers of David Bell, Clark Clifford, George Elsey, Joseph Jones, David Lloyd, Charles Murphy, Richard Neustadt, and

Samuel Rosenman. In these individual's papers, one may usually find speech drafts (which are sometimes duplicated in other folders), positions papers, suggested drafts that were never used, and other miscellaneous information.

In truth, one may expect to find pieces of the rhetorical puzzle scattered among the papers of Truman's speech staff as well as in Truman's and the secretary's speech files. In order to help the researcher sort all of this out, the Library has samples of handwriting from the major figures in the Truman administration. Truman's bold, large handwriting is easily spotted, although one is often unsure as to the penmanship of others who contributed emendations to the drafts.

From an oratorical perspective, certain oral history interviews are invaluable. The oral histories of David Bell, Clark Clifford, Matthew Connelly, George Elsey, Charles Murphy, Leonard Reinsch, and Samuel I. Rosenman are particularly insightful concerning Truman's rhetorical practices and his interactions with the speech staff. The oral histories are conveniently indexed.

With respect to the president's delivery, the library maintains an invaluable collection of audiovisual materials. These include clips from newreels, voice recordings, and television tapes. The library also has an extensive photographic collection. All of the audiovisual materials are indexed from a variety of entries.

The president's personal file, PPF-200, contains the letters and telegrams that were sent to the president with regard to his speeches and addresses.

The library also has indexes to dissertations and scholarly articles on all aspects of Truman's presidency. One may view the dissertations on microfilm, and the articles are usually offprints. Additionally, the library maintains its own collection of books on the Truman presidency and era.

HARRY S. TRUMAN'S PRIMARY WRITTEN SOURCES

President Truman wrote his memoirs in two volumes, *Memoirs by Harry S. Truman*. Volume I, *Year of Decision*, and volume II, *Years of Hope and Trial*, were published by Doubleday in 1955 and 1956.

The Public Papers of the Presidents: Harry S. Truman, 1945 to 1952-1953, contain HST's speeches, addresses, statements, and press conferences. The texts of the speeches are accurate, although Truman did ad lib. Definitive texts may be obtained by comparing the texts with actual voice recordings.

SECONDARY SOURCES

Anderson, Terry H. *The United States, Great Britain, and the Cold War 1944-1947*. Columbia: University of Missouri Press, 1981.

Andrews, James R. *The Practice of Rhetorical Criticism*. New York: Macmillan, 1983.

"Bold New Program." *Time*, January 31, 1949, p. 16.

Bullock, Alan. *Hitler: A Study in Tyranny*. New York: Bantam Books, 1961.

Burke, Kenneth. *Permanence and Change*. 2d ed. Indianapolis: Bobbs-Merrill, 1965.

Burns, Richard Dean. *Harry S. Truman: A Bibliography of His Times and Presidency*. Wilmington: Scholarly Resources, 1984.

"But What Comes Next?" *Life*, October 9, 1950, p. 38.

Ceaser, James W., Glen E. Thurow, Jeffrey Tulis, and Joseph Bessette, "The Rise of the Rhetorical Presidency." *Presidential Studies Quarterly* 11 (1981): 158-71.

Clifford, Clark. *Counsel to the President*. New York: Random House, 1991.

Cochran, Bert. *Harry Truman and the Crisis Presidency*. New York: Funk and Wagnalls, 1973.

Cumings, Bruce. "Korean War." In *The Harry S. Truman Encyclopedia*. Edited by Richard S. Kirkendall. Boston: G. K. Hall, 1989.

"The Days Ahead." *Time*, September 11, 1950, p. 22.

"Dismissal Angers South California." *New York Times*, April 12, 1951, p. 7.

Donovan, Robert J. *Conflict and Crisis: The Presidency of Harry S. Truman, 1945-1948*. New York: W. W. Norton, 1977.

_____. *Nemesis: Truman and Johnson in the Coils of War in Asia*. New York: St. Martin's-Marek, 1984.

Duffy, Bernard K. "President Harry S. Truman and General Douglas MacArthur: A Study of Rhetorical Confrontation." In *Oratorical Encounters: Selected Studies and Sources of Twentieth-Century Political Accusations and Apologies*. Edited by Halford Ross Ryan. Westport, Conn.: Greenwood Press, 1988.

"Excerpts from Editorials on the President's Nomination." *New York Times*, July 16, 1948, p. 2.

"The Fabric of Peace." *Time*, July 31, 1950, p. 10.

Fenton, John M. *In Your Opinion*. Boston: Little, Brown, 1960.

Freeland, Richard M. *The Truman Doctrine and the Origins of McCarthyism*. New York: Schocken Books, 1974.

Germino, Dante. *The Inaugural Addresses of American Presidents: The*

Public Philosophy and Rhetoric. Preface and foreword by Kenneth W. Thompson. Lanham: University Press of America, 1984.

Gosnell, Harold F. *A Political Biography of Harry S. Truman*. Westport, Conn.: Greenwood Press, 1980.

Gould, Jack. "10,000,000 Viewers See the Ceremony." *New York Times*, January 21, 1949, p. 6.

Graebner, Norman A. "NSC 68." In *The Harry S. Truman Encyclopedia*. Edited by Richard S. Kirkendall. Boston: G. K. Hall, 1989.

"Hail to the Chief." *New York Times*, January 21, 1949, p. 55.

Hamby, Alonzo L. *Beyond the New Deal: Harry S. Truman and American Liberalism*. New York: Columbia University Press, 1973.

Harriman, W. Averell. "Mr. Truman's Way with Crisis." In *The Korean War: A 25-Year Perspective*. Edited by Francis H. Heller. Lawrence: The Regents Press of Kansas, 1977.

Harris, Merne Arthur. "The MacArthur Dismissal—A Study of Political Mail." Diss: University of Iowa, 1966.

"Harry Truman on His Own Now." *New Republic*, January 24, 1949, p. 5.

"Headwinds." *New Republic*, March 31, 1947, pp. 5-6.

Hinds, Lynn Boyd, and Theodore Otto Windt, Jr. *The Cold War as Rhetoric: The Beginnings, 1945-1950*. New York: Praeger, 1991.

Hinton, Harold B. "Legislators Hail Action by Truman." *New York Times*, June 28, 1950, p. 1.

"Instituting a War." *Time*, September 4, 1950, pp. 11-12.

Jones, Joseph. *The Fifteen Weeks*. New York: Viking Press, 1955.

Kaufman, Burton I. *The Korean War: Challenges in Crisis, Credibility, and Command*. Philadelphia: Temple University Press, 1986.

Kennan, George F. *Memoirs: 1925-1950*. Boston: Little, Brown, 1967.

Kirchwey, Freda. "Manifest Destiny, 1947." *Nation*, March 22, 1947, pp. 317-19.

Kirkendall, Richard S. *The Harry S. Truman Encyclopedia*. Boston: G. K. Hall, 1989.

"Let the Nations Be Glad." *Newsweek*, March 24, 1947, p. 24.

Lindley, Ernest K. "The President's Fourth Course." *Newsweek*, January 31, 1949, p. 19.

Lippmann, Walter. "The Inaugural." *Washington Post*, January 24, 1949, p. 3.

Mazuzan, George T. "United Nations." In *The Harry S. Truman Encyclopedia*. Edited by Richard S. Kirkendall. Boston: G. K. Hall, 1989.

McClellan, David S. *Dean Acheson: The State Department Years*. New York: Dodd, Mead, 1976.

McCoy, Donald R. *The Presidency of Harry S. Truman.* Lawrence: University Press of Kansas, 1984.

McKerrow, Ray E. "Truman and Korea: Rhetoric in the Pursuit of Victory." *Central States Speech Journal* 28 (1977): 1-12.

"Message Praised by British Papers." *New York Times*, January 21, 1949, p. 6.

Miller, Merle. *Plain Speaking: An Oral Biography of Harry S Truman.* New York: G. P. Putnam's Sons, 1973.

"Missouri's 'Turnip Day' Is Explained by Truman." *New York Times*, July 16, 1948, p. 2.

"The National Pendulum Swings." *Life*, November 20, 1950, p. 44.

Packenham, Robert. *Liberal America and The Third World.* Princeton: Princeton University Press, 1973.

Patterson, Thomas G. *Meeting the Communist Threat: Truman to Reagan.* New York: Oxford University Press, 1988.

"Peace Aims for Korea." *New Republic*, September 25, 1950, pp. 5-7.

Pemberton, William E. *Harry S. Truman: Fair Dealer and Cold Warrior.* Boston: Twayne, 1989.

Perlmeter, Irving. Oral history interview, May 23 and 24, 1964, HSTL.

"Policy: 'Containment' of Communism." *Newsweek*, March 17, 1947, p. 27.

"The Presidency." *Time*, March 24, 1947, pp. 17-20.

"President on Radio." *New York Times*, April 12, 1951, p. 7.

"President Truman's Global Plans." *New Republic*, January 31, 1949, pp. 5-6.

Rees, David. *Korea: The Limited War.* New York: St. Martin's Press, 1964.

"Relief Felt in U.N. on the Dismissal." *New York Times*, April 12, 1951, p. 1.

Reston, James. "Speech Seen as Aid to Western World." *New York Times*, January 21, 1949, p. 1.

Ridgway, Matthew B. *The Korean War.* Garden City: Doubleday, 1967.

Rovere, Richard H. "Truman after Seven Years." *Harpers*, May 1952, p. 29.

Ryan, Halford R. "Harry Truman." In *American Orators of the Twentieth Century: Critical Studies and Sources.* Edited by Bernard K. Duffy and Halford R. Ryan. Westport, Conn.: Greenwood Press, 1987.

Ryan, Halford R. *Franklin D. Roosevelt's Rhetorical Presidency.* Westport, Conn.: Greenwood Press, 1988.

Ryan, Halford R. "Harry S Truman (1884-1972), Thirty-Third President of the United States." In *Methods of Rhetorical Criticism: A*

Twentieth-Century Perspective. 3d ed. Edited by Bernard L. Brock, Robert L. Scott, and James W. Chesebro. Detroit: Wayne State University Press, 1989.

Ryan, Herman Butterfield, Jr. "The American Intellectual Tradition Reflected in the Truman Doctrine." *American Scholar* 42 (1973): 294-307.

"The Shape of Things." *Nation*, September 23, 1950, p. 257.

Smith, Craig Allen, and Kathy B. Smith. *The President and the Public: Rhetoric and National Leadership.* Lanham: University Press of America, 1985.

Smith, Howard K. "Thou Art Soldier Only." *Nation*, April 21, 1951, p. 363.

Stokesbury, James L. *A Short History of the Korean War.* New York: William Morrow, 1988.

Strictly Personal and Confidential: The Letters Harry Truman Never Mailed. Edited by Monte M. Poen. Boston: Little, Brown and Company, 1982.

The Truman Administration. Edited by Barton J. Bernstein and Allen J. Matusow. New York: Harper Colophon Books, 1966.

"Truman Calls Dewey's Labor Plan 'Me Too.'" *New York Herald Tribune*, October 24, 1948, p. 1.

Truman, Margaret. *Harry S. Truman.* New York: William Morrow, 1973.

The Truman Period as a Research Field. Edited by Richard S. Kirkendall. Columbia: University of Missouri Press, 1967.

"Truman Sworn in, the 32d President." *New York Times*, January 21, 1949, p. 2.

Tulis, Jeffrey K. *The Rhetorical Presidency.* Princeton: Princeton University Press, 1987.

"Two Voices." *Time*, September 4, 1950, pp. 9-10.

Underhill, Robert. *The Truman Persuasions.* Ames: The Iowa State University Press, 1981.

_____. "Speeches and Speech Writing." In *The Harry S. Truman Encyclopedia.* Edited by Richard S. Kirkendall. Boston: G. K. Hall, 1989.

"Wallace Calls Talk of Truman Warlike." *New York Times*, January 21, 1949, p. 5.

White, Eugene E., and Clair R. Henderlider. "What Harry S. Truman Told Us About His Speaking." *Quarterly Journal of Speech* 40 (1954): 37-42.

"Who Likes Ike?" *Time*, February 18, 1952, pp. 18-19.

Windt, Theodore. "The Presidency and Speeches on International Crises:

Repeating the Rhetorical Past." In *Essays in Presidential Rhetoric*. Edited by Theodore Windt, with Beth Ingold. Dubuque: Kendall/Hunt, 1983.

_____. *Presidential Rhetoric (1961-1980)*. Dubuque: Kendall/Hunt, 1983.

Wittner, Lawrence S. "The Truman Doctrine and the Defense of Freedom." *Diplomatic History* 4 (1980): 161-187.

Wolfarth, Donald L. "John F. Kennedy in the Tradition of Inaugural Speeches." *Quarterly Journal of Speech* 47 (1961): 124-132.

Woods, Randall B., and Howard Jones. *Dawning of the Cold War: The United States' Quest for Order*. Athens: University of Georgia Press, 1991.

"World Fair Deal." *Newsweek*, January 31, 1949, p. 18.

Index

About the Author

HALFORD R. RYAN is professor of English and public speaking, Washington and Lee University, Lexington, Virginia. He teaches courses in public speaking, argumentation and debate, the history and criticism of American public address, feminist rhetoric, and presidential rhetoric.

He edited *American Rhetoric from Roosevelt to Reagan*, which, in its third edition, is now entitled *Contemporary American Public Discourse*; *Oratorical Encounters: Selected Studies and Sources of Twentieth-Century Political Accusations and Apologies*; and *The Inaugural Addresses of Twentieth-Century American Presidents*. He co-edited with Bernard K. Duffy *American Orators Before 1900* and *Twentieth-Century American Orators*. He wrote *Persuasive Advocacy*; *Franklin D. Roosevelt's Rhetorical Presidency*; *Harry Emerson Fosdick: Persuasive Preacher*; *Henry Ward Beecher: Peripatetic Preacher*; and *Classical Communication for the Contemporary Communicator*.

Great American Orators

Edward Everett: Unionist Orator
Ronald F. Reid

Theodore Roosevelt and the Rhetoric of Militant Decency
Robert V. Friedenberg

Patrick Henry, The Orator
David A. McCants

Anna Howard Shaw: Suffrage Orator and Social Reformer
Wil A. Linkugel and Martha Solomon

William Jennings Bryan: Orator of Small-Town America
Donald K. Springen

Robert M. La Follette, Sr.: The Voice of Conscience
Carl R. Burgchardt

Ronald Reagan: The Great Communicator
Kurt Ritter and David Henry

Clarence Darrow: The Creation of an American Myth
Richard J. Jensen

"Do Everything" Reform: The Oratory of Frances E. Willard
Richard W. Leeman

Abraham Lincoln the Orator: Penetrating the Lincoln Legend
Lois J. Einhorn

Mark Twain: Protagonist for the Popular Culture
Marlene Boyd Vallin

Delightful Conviction: Jonathan Edwards and the Rhetoric of Conversion
Stephen R. Yarbrough and John C. Adams

DATE DUE